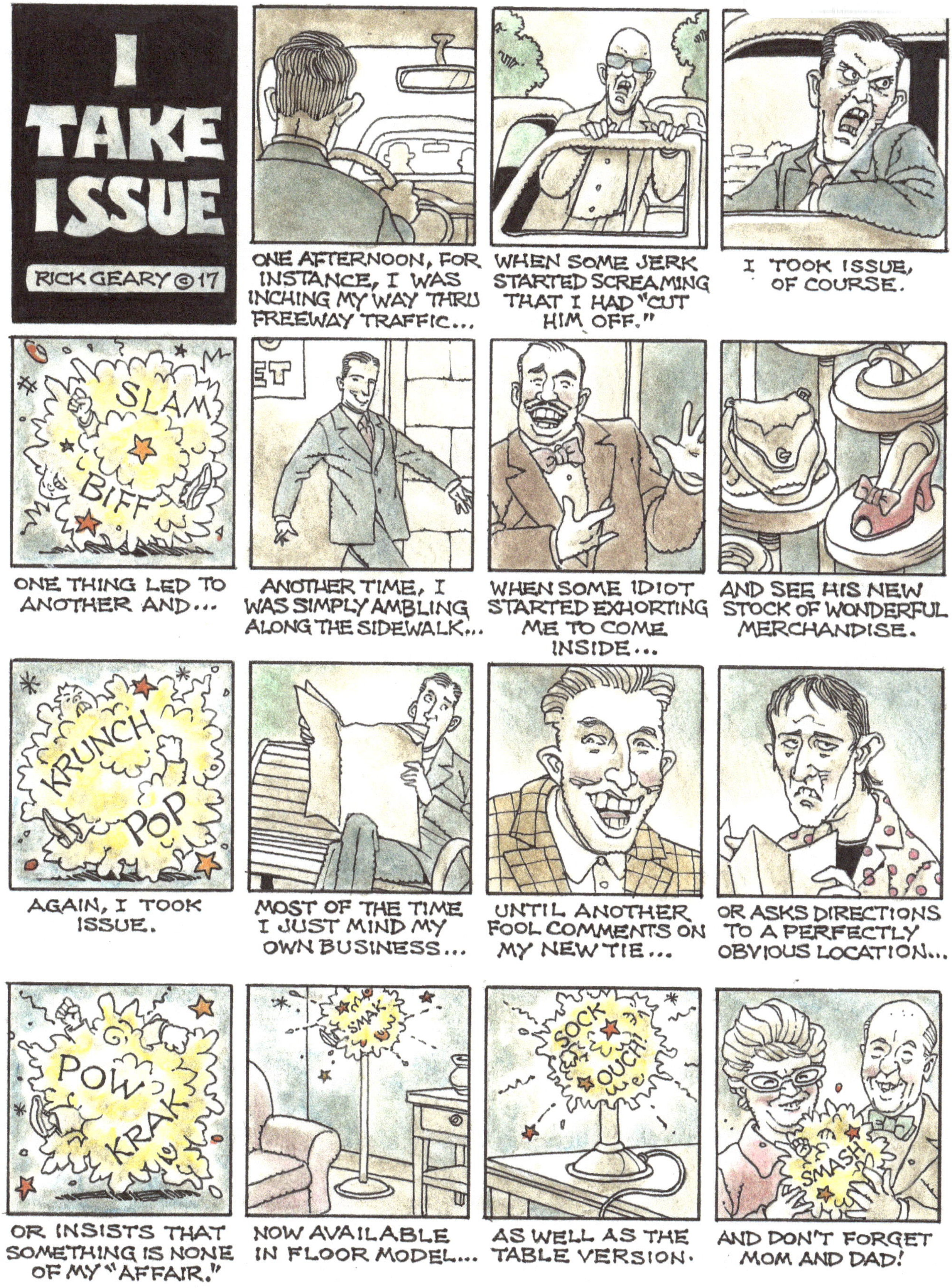
I TAKE ISSUE
RICK GEARY © 17
ONE AFTERNOON, FOR INSTANCE, I WAS INCHING MY WAY THRU FREEWAY TRAFFIC...
WHEN SOME JERK STARTED SCREAMING THAT I HAD "CUT HIM OFF."
I TOOK ISSUE, OF COURSE.
SLAM
BIFF
ONE THING LED TO ANOTHER AND...
ANOTHER TIME, I WAS SIMPLY AMBLING ALONG THE SIDEWALK...
WHEN SOME IDIOT STARTED EXHORTING ME TO COME INSIDE...
AND SEE HIS NEW STOCK OF WONDERFUL MERCHANDISE.
KRUNCH
POP
AGAIN, I TOOK ISSUE.
MOST OF THE TIME I JUST MIND MY OWN BUSINESS...
UNTIL ANOTHER FOOL COMMENTS ON MY NEW TIE...
OR ASKS DIRECTIONS TO A PERFECTLY OBVIOUS LOCATION...
POW
KRAK
OR INSISTS THAT SOMETHING IS NONE OF MY "AFFAIR."
SMAK
NOW AVAILABLE IN FLOOR MODEL...
SOCK
OUCH!
AS WELL AS THE TABLE VERSION.
SMASH!
AND DON'T FORGET MOM AND DAD!

B

PUBLISHER'S LETTER
BY MICHAEL GERBER

JEFFERSON CITY HALLOWEEN 1977
A scary tale.

The rot emerged at a different time and place for everybody, but for me it started in 1977. It was Halloween night, and we'd just moved from St. Louis to Jefferson City. Jefferson City is the capital of Missouri, but don't let that fool you; it was — and I suspect still is — a sleepy little burg wheezing along on the miniscule pleasures and manufactured excitements of small-town life. Trips to the pizza parlor. Church socials. High school football.

Some people love this life, but even at age 8, Jeff City was not for me. Our old neighborhood in the Central West End was like Paris in the '20's compared, and my mother the painter had gotten off on the wrong foot when she asked the gingham-clad mother of my school chum, "Are there any good bars in town?"

Mrs. Smith (we'll call her that) certainly didn't wear pearls, but whatever she did wear, she clutched. In small-town America, it's not polite to discuss one's pleasures. Those are things to be feared, then given into in secret — at home with the lights off, or in the woods, or at a truck stop men's room six miles out on Highway 50.

Tragically, all this shame turns the natural and inevitable search for a little fun into something that might ruin your life. Back then the scourges were pregnancy and paraquat, but the Jeff City I knew was an opioid crisis waiting to happen. People there didn't worship God, as much as hide behind Him — praying He'd protect them from themselves.

And that brings me back to the rot.

Halloween had always been a favorite holiday of mine. First, my mom made awesome costumes. Second, people seemed to be more themselves on Halloween, and I've always found that reassuring. Back in the CWE, on Halloween gay people got a little gayer; blacks and whites got along a little better; bartenders would give you an extra cherry in your Shirley Temple.

I was going as a bum, and between Mom's expert styling and Dad's overcoat, I looked great. My best friend, Ross, had an awesome Chewbacca costume which, in that Year of *Star Wars*, promised to be a crowd-pleaser. The two of us were poised to extract so much candy that High and McCarty Streets would require a full twelve months to recover.

Ross and I planned it like a military campaign. We'd start out on his block, where the homes were a little bigger; big houses give out big candy, especially in the early evening when stocks are plentiful. We'd work five blocks of McCarty, then turn and go down High, toward my house, where we'd finish the night. This, too, was part of the plan; Ross's father was ex-Navy and could be strict. My dad was young and artsy, a professional photographer, and likely to turn a blind eye to anything we did, as long as we didn't actually throw up.

Plus, my parents loved Ross. In that inauthentic town, he was always 100% himself. This didn't always serve him in school — he did well in the classes he liked, and nodded off in the ones he didn't — but he was the best kind of friend. He was kind and imaginative and funny, and when he told you something, you knew it was the truth…if only to him.

The night started out perfectly, and soon we were holding so much candy that the black handles on our little plastic pumpkins were beginning to give. "Let's go to my house and dump," I said when we finished McCarty. "Then we do High."

Ross looked dubious. I had a crazy dog named Gus, half black Lab, half devil. "Gus eats books and bras," Ross said. "Just think what he'd do to candy."

Straining, I raised my plastic pumpkin. "Your dad sees all this, he's going to end our mission. And your mom is going to throw most of yours away."

Ross had a problem with sugar. His problem was, he loved it; loved it like a foot fetishist loves stilettos. Once, when he was spending the night, my parents made the huge error of letting us go to Whaley's Drugstore and buy Hostess cupcakes. Mom, Dad and I watched in amazement as Ross basically reverse-engineered the thing. First he removed its cap of black, slightly rubbery icing; then he peeled off the white strip of squiggles. After breaking the icing into 20, roughly equal pieces, Ross then split the cake in half. He licked out the center filling, expertly, then began to eat the cake. Each bite of the spongy, bitter pastry was paired with a piece of icing. As Ross finished, we all resisted the urge to clap, so intense was his commitment to this harmless pleasure. (Harmless until about an hour later, when the sugar hit. Bedtime came late that night.)

Back under the streetlights, Ross knew I was right. "Okay," he said, "we'll go to your place."

Walking into my house, we fought Gus off and went into my bedroom. Helping

MICHAEL GERBER (@mgerber937) is Editor & Publisher of *The American Bystander*.

each other raise our buckets, we dumped our massive haul onto the dresser. “Can I have your Butterfinger?”

“Sure.” I didn't like them anyway. “But wait to eat it. I need you sharp.”

Dad stuck his head in. “Done already?”

“Please don't let Gus in here!” I said as we pushed past. “You can have some candy.”

Ross was appalled. “Why did you say that?” he hissed as we galumphed down the rotting wooden stairs of our rotting wooden house. “Because, Ross, Dad will eat less than Gus will.”

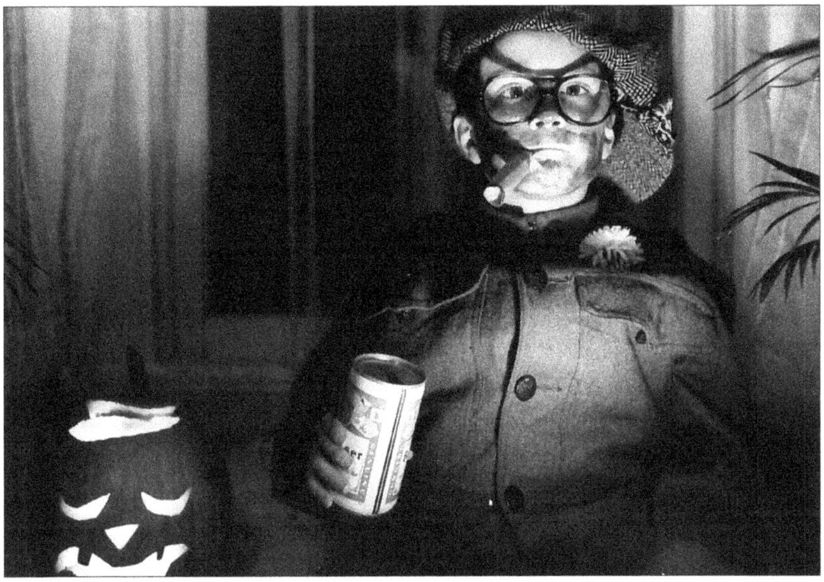

Your author on the night in question. Dad snapped this before the hunt began.

GREGORY GERBER

High Street was, if anything, better than McCarty. A lot of parents were impressed by my costume — I had a cork 5 o'clock shadow, and smoked a carrot wrapped in brown construction paper. “Are you a gorilla?” the clueless ones asked Ross, and after a while, we started saying “yes” just to save time.

Halfway down the block, I looked over at Ross. His mask was slid up on his head; and his mouth was covered in Butterfinger crumbs. “I couldn't help it,” he said.

From that moment, I was racing against time — could we finish our rounds, get home and divvy up the loot, before all that high-fructose corn syrup hit Ross's bloodstream? The smart thing would've been to stop right then, but I couldn't stop. We were on a roll.

By the time we got to the last house, Ross's movements were sudden and erratic, and his skin was coated in a fine layer of sweat. When he spoke, it came out in a rush, and invariably had to do with more candy. Ross had decided that I was walking too slowly, and sprinted ahead. As I walked up to the porch, he was doing ragged cartwheels in the lawn, candy wrappers falling from his pockets.

“Couldn't help it!” he said as he bounded up onto the porch. I was glad this was it; the only other house between this one and mine was owned by an obese ex-merchant marine named Charlie with no front teeth who (it was said) gave out beers for Halloween. I didn't want beer, though I thought Ross could probably use one.

This house, though, was where our friends Ben and Luke lived. “Have you seen the twins tonight?”

“No,” Ross said. “Maybe they're sick?”

“We'll give 'em some of our candy.” The lights were on inside, we could see that, but nothing happened after the first press of the doorbell. I got an ominous feeling. “We should go,” I said, and had turned when Ross, mad with candy-lust, gave the bell a vicious stab-and-hold. He was still pressing it when Mrs. Smith came to the door. As usual, she was dressed like Holly Hobbie.

“Trick or treat!” Ross yelled. He was pogoing.

“Hello, boys,” she said. “I'm sorry to see you.”

“Oh, Ross just ate some candy,” I said. “He'll be fine in the morning.”

“Are Ben and Luke sick?” Ross said.

“They're not the sick ones,” Mrs. Smith said. Behind her shoulder I saw our friends. They were sitting at the dining room table, with their father, holding hands. The three of them were praying hard; they looked...scared. Mrs. Smith looked scared, too. Hands trembling, she gave us each a couple of small paper booklets. “Read these, while there's still time.” Then she closed the door.

When the divvying came, Ross was in no condition to do business, so I just let him take whatever candy he wanted, and took his discards without protest. (That was the year I learned to like Mary Janes.) Then, we made a small pile for Ben and Luke, and hid it in the heating register next to my bed. (Unfortunately, the weather changed the next day, fusing it into a giant glob of sucrose and wrappers. Gus discovered it, licked it, then vomited.)

I ended up with all the pamphlets. I knew what my mom would say: “This guy can't draw.” But if the pictures sucked, the stories were even worse: Everyone I knew and liked, including myself, was going to hell. One pamphlet was about Catholics, that was us. Another talked about men like those nice friends of my parents, the couple who made beautiful Christmas ornaments. Jews like my friend Rolf. African-Americans like my friend Stanley.

This was the rot. Sure, the Smiths were nice — to our faces. But if this was the God they loved, some part of them must hate us. And fear us, too. If they feared us, what might they do to us, if they ever got the chance? That was a scary thought.

But I also felt bad for them. To look at two 8-year-olds dressed for Halloween and see Satan — the manifestation of pure evil — that sounds awful. It sounds like hell. What do you do for people that scared, that crazy? I still don't know, but I'm proud of what the 8-year-old me decided: I would be so good and kind to the Smiths that they'd have to realize I wasn't Satan. And once they saw that, maybe they'd see that Jews, homosexuals and blacks weren't either. I knew that whatever they were calling Satan, it was the thing that made people hate and fear one another, and themselves. So I resolved to be kind.

...and to get the hell out of Jefferson City. B

TABLE OF CONTENTS

JOHN CUNEO

DEPARTMENTS
Frontispiece: "I Take Issue" *by Rick Geary* 1
Publisher's Letter *by Michael Gerber* 2
News and Notes 9
Classifieds 87
Index to This Issue *by Dirk Voetberg* 91
Crossword: "Actor Natalie's Castles" *by Matera & Goldberg* .. 92

GALLIMAUFRY
Ron Hauge, Steve Young, Alan Goldberg, Dylan Brody, Andrew Barlow, Paul Guay, Sarah Booth, James Finn Garner, Jeff Albers, Luke Burns, Lance Hansen, Laura Galaviz, Dirk Voetberg, Osman Siddique, Jonathan Zeller, Lee Sachs, Zack Bornstein, Liza Donnelly.

SHORT STUFF
A Poem *by M.K. Brown* 5
American Bystanders #3 *by Drew Friedman* 7
Dark Carnival *by Nick Downes* 12
Young George Washington *by Ed Subitzky* 27
The Details of My Escape *by Lars Kenseth* 28
Tips for Staying Hydrated *by Steve Young* 30
Introducing Your New MTA! *by Joe Keohane* 32
Human Society Defensively Explained
  to Aliens *by Evan Waite & River Clegg* 34

FEATURES
Comedy of Manners *by Dylan Brody* 37
The Twisted Cross *by Sam Gross* 42

The AMERICAN BYSTANDER
#6 • Vol. 2, No. 2 • Fall 2017

EDITOR & PUBLISHER
Michael Gerber
HEAD WRITER Brian McConnachie
SENIOR EDITOR Alan Goldberg
DEPUTY EDITORS
Michael Thornton, Ben Orlin
CONTACTEE Scott Marshall
ORACLE Steve Young
STAFF LIAR P.S. Mueller
LIAISON James Folta (*New York*)

CONTRIBUTORS
Luke Adams, Jeff Albers, Andrew Barlow, Ron Barrett, Charles Barsotti, R.O. Blechman, George Booth, Sarah Booth, Zack Bornstein, Steve Brodner, Dylan Brody, M.K. Brown, Luke Burns, Roz Chast, David Chelsea, River Clegg, John Cuneo, Etienne Delessert, Nate Dern, Liza Donnelly, Nick Downes, Curtis Edwards, Randall Enos, Liana Finck, Drew Friedman, Laura Galaviz, Tom Gammill, James Finn Gardner, Rick Geary, Gregory Gerber, Alan Goldberg, Sam Gross, Paul Guay, Tom Hachtman, Lance Hansen, Ron Hauge, Noah Jones, Farley Katz, Lars Kenseth, Joe Keohane, Adam Koford, Ken Krimstein, Stephen Kroninger, Peter Kuper, Sara Lautman, Stan Mack, Merrill Markoe, Matt Matera, Hana Michels, Tom Motley, Joe Oesterle, Jonathan Plotkin, Mimi Pond, Andy Prieboy, Simon Rich, Arnold Roth, Lee Sachs, Cris Shapan, Mike Shiell, Osman Siddique, Jim Siergey, Rich Sparks, Nick Spooner, Ed Subitzky, Tom Toro, Dirk Voetberg, Evan Waite, D. Watson, Jonathan Zeller and Alan Zweibel.
COPYEDITING
Cheryl Levenbrown, God bless 'er
THANKS TO
Kate Powers, Rae Barsotti, Lanky Bareikis, Jon Schwarz, Alleen Schultz, Molly Bernstein, Joe Lopez, Eliot Ivanhoe, Neil Gumenick, Thomas Simon, Greg and Patricia Gerber and many, many others.
NAMEPLATES BY
Mark Simonson
ISSUE CREATED BY
Michael Gerber

BOOTH

Vol. 2, No.2. ©2017 Good Cheer LLC, all rights reserved. Proudly produced in California, USA.

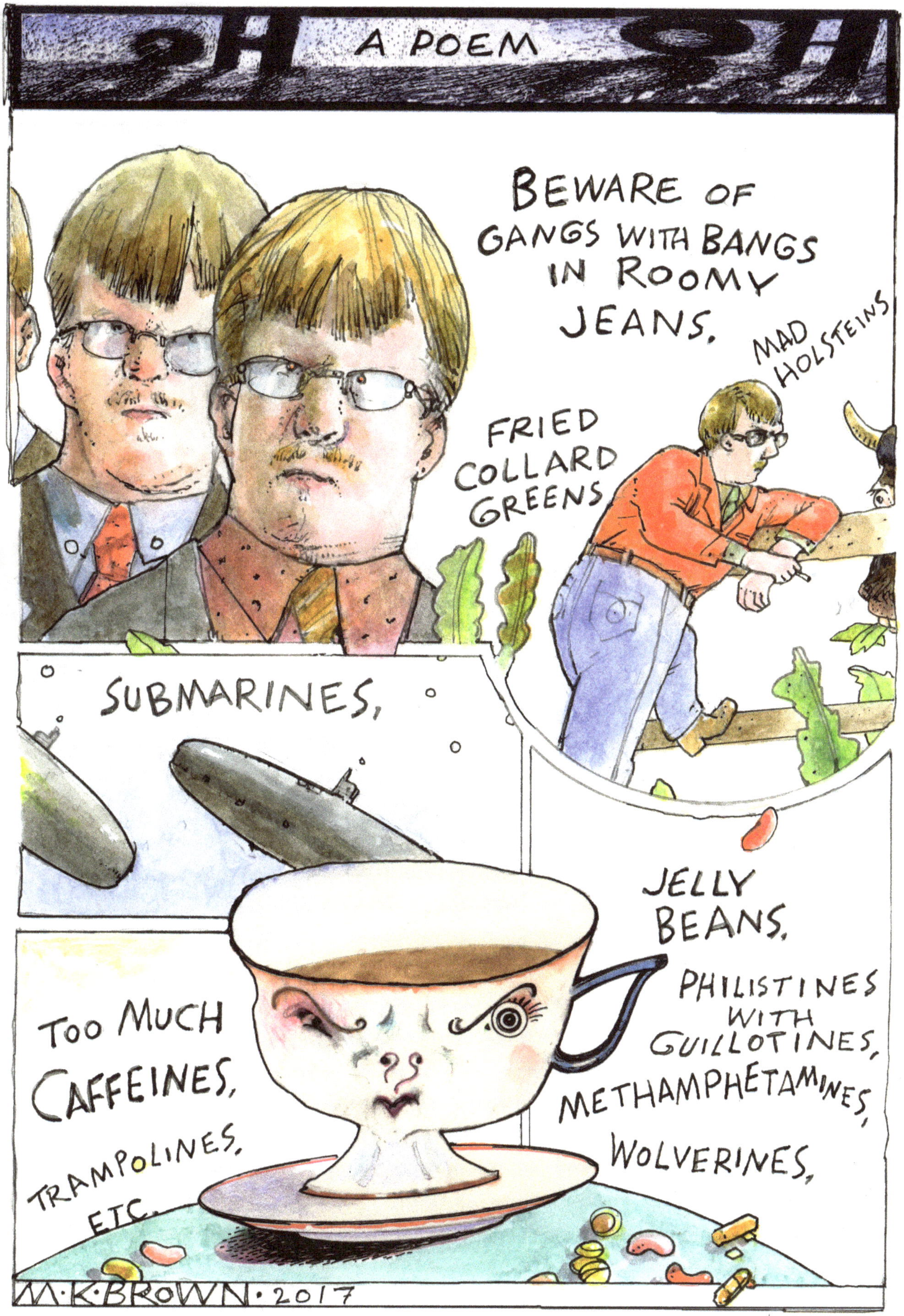
A POEM
BEWARE OF GANGS WITH BANGS IN ROOMY JEANS.
MAD HOLSTEINS
FRIED COLLARD GREENS
SUBMARINES,
JELLY BEANS,
PHILISTINES WITH GUILLOTINES,
TOO MUCH CAFFEINES,
METHAMPHETAMINES,
TRAMPOLINES,
WOLVERINES,
ETC.
M·K·BROWN·2017

The Secret Life of Walter Mitty,
  Firearms Enthusiast *by Joe Keohane*..................45
Donald the Menace *by Peter Kuper*........................47
No Coffee *by Simon Rich & Farley Katz*..................55
Pricks Up Front *song by Andy Prieboy*...................56
A Man Called Grumpy *by Merrill Markoe*................59
I Saw Your Mother's Ass *by Alan Zweibel*................61

MARVY
Cover: "Witches' Brew" *by Tom Toro*.....................63
Comic Page *by Adam Koford*..................................64
Hector *by T. Motley*...65
Wacko Panic Attack! *by Mimi Pond*.......................66
Gorilla, You're a Desperado! *by Jim Siergey*..........70
A Week in Gold Panning With
  Pyrite Jack, Local Prospector *by Lucas Adams*...73
An Old Story *by R.O. Blechman*............................74
Many Unhappy Returns *by Ron Barrett*..............75
Chicken Gutz *by Randall Enos*.............................76
The Doozies *by Tom Gammill*..............................76
Gertrude's Follies: "Heil Hitler and Coco Chanel!"
  by Tom Hachtman & Sam Gross........................77

OUR BACK PAGES
Joan's Other Kitchen *by Brian McConnachie*.......79
P.S. Mueller Thinks Like This *by P.S. Mueller*......81
Chunk-Style Nuggets *by Steve Young*..................83
Know Your Bystanders *by Hana Michels*.............85

CARTOONS & ILLUSTRATIONS BY
C. Barsotti, G. Booth, S. Brodner, M.K. Brown, R. Chast, D. Chelsea, J. Cuneo, J. C. Duffy, C. Edwards, R. Enos, L. Finck, D. Friedman, G. Gerber, S. Gross, T. Hachtman, C. Hankin, N. Jones, F. Katz, K. Krimstein, S. Kroninger, P. Kuper, S. Lautman, S. Mack, P.S. Mueller, J. Oesterle, C. Shapan, M. Simonson, T. Toro and D. Watson.

"We don't need men. We can lick our own vaginas."

COVER

This issue's offering is courtesy of the awe-inspiring **Arnold Roth**, who bears distant responsibility for this whole magazine. Arnie first met your intrepid editor over 25 years ago, and illustrated the cover of Mike's ill-fated *Puck*, a humor magazine inserted inside college newspapers that was sort of a proto-*Bystander*. If not for Arnie and Caroline's friendship and encouragement all those years ago, Mike might well have dropped his peculiar obsession in favor of a more sensible line of work. So thanks you two — for everything.

ACKNOWLEDGMENTS

All material is ©2017 its creators, all rights reserved; please do not reproduce or distribute it without written consent of the creators and *The American Bystander*. The following material has previously appeared, and is reprinted here with permission of the author(s): Stan Mack's "Father Knows Best" first appeared in *The Village Voice*. The illustration on page 29 is from Etienne Delessert's book, *The Seven Dwarfs*. The Steve Brodner illustration on page 67 first appeared in *The Nation*.

THE AMERICAN BYSTANDER, *Vol. 2, No. 2*, (978-0-692-98307-2). Publishes ~4x/year. ©2017 by Good Cheer LLC. No part of this magazine can be reproduced, in whole or in part, by any means, without the written permission of the Publisher. For this and other queries, email *Publisher@americanbystander.org*, or write: Michael Gerber, Publisher, *The American Bystander*, 1122 Sixth St., #403, Santa Monica, CA 90403. Subscribe at www.patreon.com/bystander. Other info can be found at www.americanbystander.org.

DREW FRIEDMAN

American Bystanders #3
Newton Hooten

THE HOT LIST *Plantar warts?* **HOT!** *Adult-onset Type I Diabetes?* **NOT.** *The left side of your body?* **HOT!** *The right side of your body?* **NOT.** *Cats?* **HOT!** *Slightly bigger cats?* **NOT.** *Danny Kaye?* **HOT!** *Donald O'Connor?* **NOT.** *Post-Its?* **HOT!** *Little scraps of paper?* **NOT.** *Zoroastrianism?* **HOT!** *Ancient Roman mystery religions?* **NOT.** *Sardinia?* **HOT!** *Nebraska?* **NOT.** *Ant farms?* **HOT!** *Philately?* **NOT.** *Polka dots?* **HOT!** *Sort of wavy lines?* **NOT.** *Serge Gainbourg's demo of "Crazy Train"?* **HOT!** *The Thai national anthem?* **NOT.** *The Aztecs?* **HOT!** *The Olmecs?* **NOT.** **ON OUR RADAR:** *Big shoulder pads…Barry Manilow…Going outside without a coat…Umlauts…Georgian cinema…Nervous giggling.*

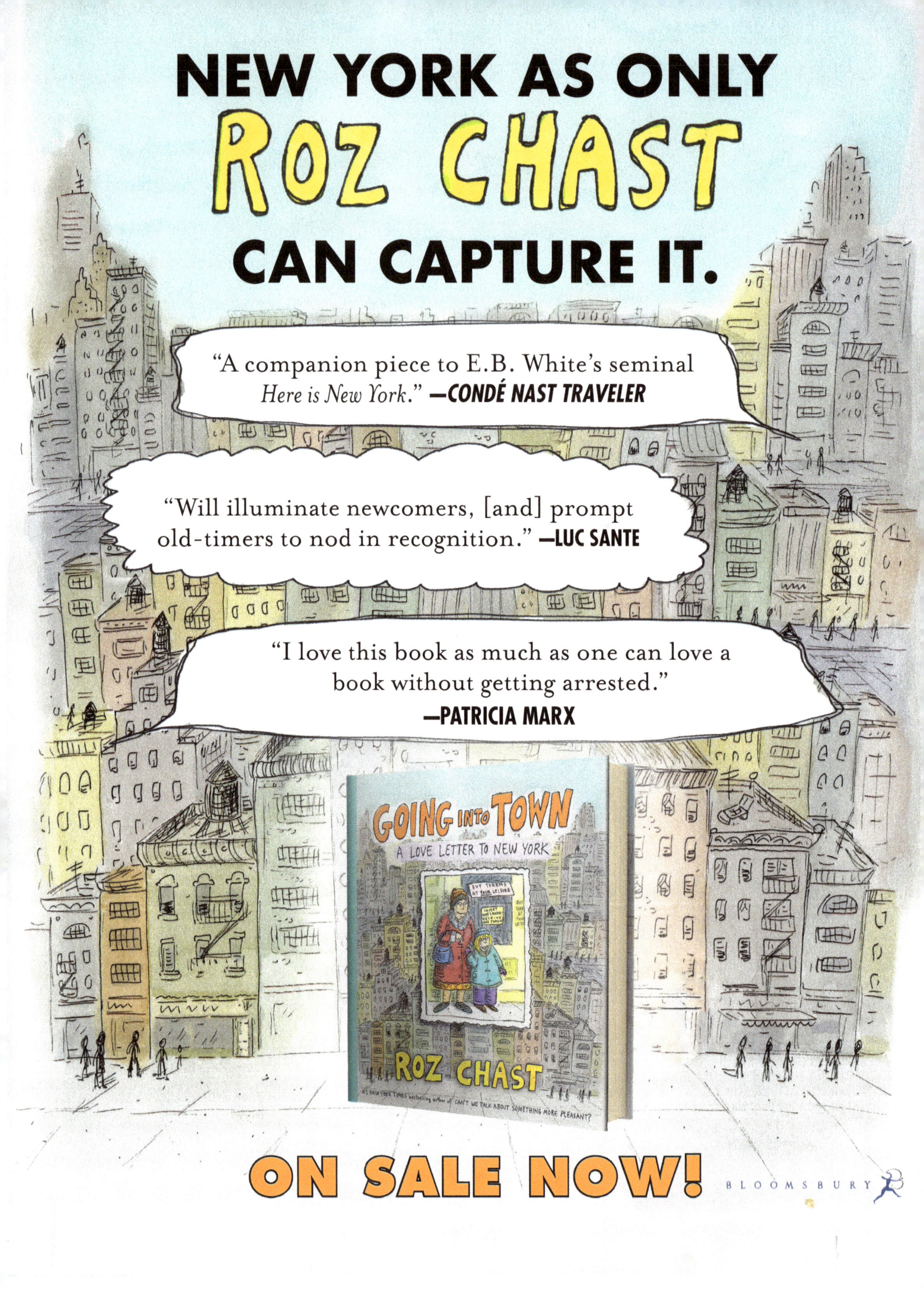
NEW YORK AS ONLY
ROZ CHAST
CAN CAPTURE IT.
“A companion piece to E.B. White’s seminal *Here is New York*.” —CONDÉ NAST TRAVELER
“Will illuminate newcomers, [and] prompt old-timers to nod in recognition.” —LUC SANTE
“I love this book as much as one can love a book without getting arrested.” —PATRICIA MARX
GOING INTO TOWN
A LOVE LETTER TO NEW YORK
ROZ CHAST
#1 NEW YORK TIMES bestselling author of CAN'T WE TALK ABOUT SOMETHING MORE PLEASANT?
ON SALE NOW!
BLOOMSBURY

NEWS & NOTES

It's prime time to see Bystanders in the flesh. If, y'know, that's your thing.

If you lurrve this mag, meeting our contributors is the natural next step. Our writers and artists are vastly charming — certainly much more so than the dorks at any other magazine — and with the holiday season, many of *Bystander*'s Finest are brightly trotting from place to place, flogging various projects. All of you within striking distance are heartily encouraged to show your face, and tell them you totally dig their stuff, man.

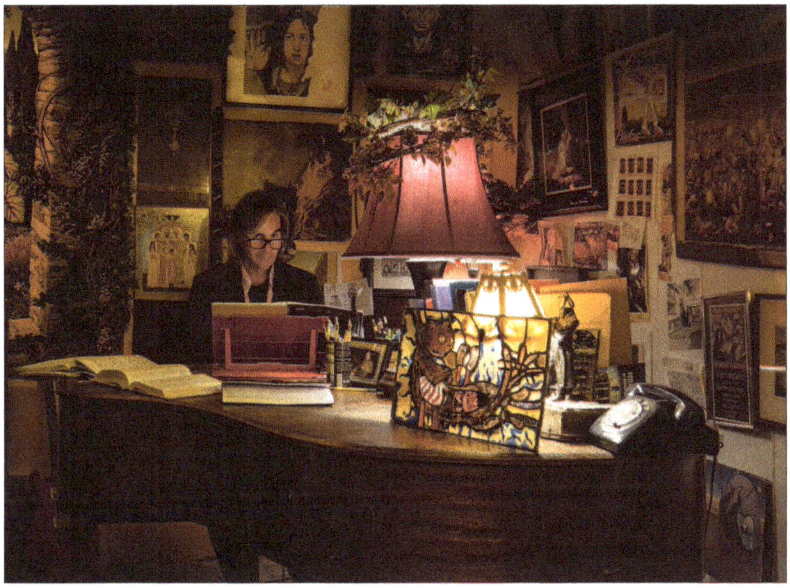

After I put out a call for "photos of your desk" (see the next page), Andy Prieboy sent me this. Goddammit, you guys, I should've been a musician.

The preponderance of these events are in New York City, but as we continue to provide these listings, those of you in other towns will get your opportunity. Because we're a quarterly, these are only a few of the events; the best way to keep abreast is to subscribe at *www.patreon.com/bystander*. We'll post events to our beloved Patrons as soon as we learn of them.

............◆............

OUT AND ABOUT: Illustrator **RON BARRETT** has a couple of book signings coming up. On December 8, he'll be at the Barnes & Noble in Yonkers, NY, signing books from 6:00-8:00 PM. The following day, Ron will be at the Galapagos Bookstore Fair, in the Community Centre of Hastings-on-Hudson, NY, from noon to 6:00 PM.... Now this is an intersting venue: a retrospective of **R.O. BLECHMAN'S** work will be on display from December 16 to June 16 in the lobby of 157 Columbus Avenue in NYC. Tbere's a reception on December 15, from 6:00-8:00 PM. Anyone interested in attending the reception should RSVP to either the Brodsky Organization (212-315-5555), or Landmark West (212-496-8110). Bob says it's a very innovative display, and since it's a lobby, it's open evenings as well as the daytime.... We're right in the middle of the big **GEORGE BOOTH** exhibition at the Society of Illustrators, 128 East 63rd Street in New York City. The space is great — I was there in June for the **JACK ZIEGLER** memorial — and if you like *Bystander*, you'll love this brownstone crammed with framed illustrations. The retrospective is curated by J.J.. Sedelmaier, a cherished subscriber whose name you might remember from a little show called *SNL*....Those of you in Milan, Italy, are heartily encouraged to darken the door of Galleria Nuages and check out **ETIENNE DELESSERT'S** new collection of drawings, *Sbalzi d'Amore* ("Mood Swings," for those of you whose college Italian is as time-murked as mine). Etienne's work will be on display until December 9, 2017. If you go, send a picture.... **DREW FRIEDMAN'S** book *Chosen People* is getting him in front of crowds all over. As our Patreon backers know, Drew appeared at one of my happy places, the Strand bookstore, on Wednesday, November 15, interviewed by Friend of *Bystander* Frank Santopadre. But if you live in Los Angeles, you're still in luck: Saturday, December 2 at Book Soup in West Hollywood, Drew will be appearing with fellow Bystander **MERRILL MARKOE** (I'll be there, too, cowering in the crowd and pilfering small items). Since LA's an early town, the event starts at 3:00 PM. Come, buy Drew's book, and meet a bunch of us at once....Back in New York, **PETER KUPER** will be discussing two projects, one old and one new. *World War 3 Illustrated* has been fighting the good fight for 38 years — Peter has co-edited that magazine since 1979. His new baby, Opp Art, is a joint-venture with *The Nation*; Peter's part of a ruling troika that also includes *Bystander* stalwart Steve Brodner and Andrea Arroyo. Peter's talk will be at the SVA Amphitheater, Tuesday, December 5, from 7:00-10:00 PM; it's at 209 East 23rd Street, Room 311. If you're alarmed about what's going on today (and how could you not be?), Peter's talk is the place for you.

............◆............

THE HOME FRONT: Those of us working from home tend to bond especially strongly with our pets. Case in point: Sir Corwin the Beautiful Dog-Faced Dog, Brindled Beast of Sylmar, unable to climb stairs because of aging hips, requires **DYLAN BRODY** and his wife (whose name escapes him at the moment) to take alternate nights sleeping downstairs. This is no great sacrifice as their marriage has reached the point at which one suggests sex and other says what time it is... In lieu of humanizing her exes by using their Christian names, **MEGAN KOESTER** has begun referring to them as her "loathesome conquests," *e.g.*, "My loathesome conquest is still dating the girl from Orange County he cheated on me with while we were married."...**JAMES FINN GARNER** had his first short play, *Locavores*, about a trendy cannibalistic restaurant, produced in the Chicago area in August. To celebrate, he decamped north to Wisconsin, where he promptly caught eight of the fattest bluegills Prong Lake has ever seen. But you'll have to take his word for it; because he was fishing with a bunch of whiners, he didn't keep and clean them, and was forced to eat hot dogs for dinner....You want a glimpse behind the curtain? **P.S. MUELLER** is happy to oblige. "As the voice of *Onion Radio News* anchor/savant Doyle Redland for over 20 years, I still put on a brown suit and hat before recording him." Imagining this delights me. "I draw more cartoons than I should," Pete says, "for probably the same reason that bees make more honey than they need."...**RON BARRETT** cheerily shares the following: "*Home Is a Sewer* is the title of a book I'm designing and illustrating. Written as a humorous memoir and how-to by immortal copywriter David Altschiller, it recalls every game you played as a kid that kids don't play any more, from stickball to Johnny-on-the-Pony." I'd buy that book, Ron. Also, random fact I just learned from *Gilbert Gottfried's Amazing Colossal Podcast*: Know who is really good at stickball? Comedian Richard Lewis.... Tucked underneath Robert Moses' roaring BQE, **JAMES FOLTA** is celebrating the release of his latest satirical project about the weasel from Wisconsin, *Paul Ryan Magazine*. Looking forward to seeing it, James.... **ANDREW BARLOW** reports that he went into the city, got back to Brooklyn, then bought three "Buy Two, Get One Free" Payday bars at the Rite Aid, before remembering he had moved from Brooklyn to Manhattan. "I'm joking," he writes, "I live in Queens." For those of our readers who didn't go to college, Payday is the peanuts, nougat and caramel candy bar, and it's mentioned in a "Cheech and Chong" skit. Here's what we think Andrew did next: he ate one Payday, slept from about 6:30 P.M. to 3:30 A.M., then ate the other two Paydays. We're just teasing. Andrew did not submit a blurb. "Yes, I *did*," he adds. "*This* is *it*; you're just taking *credit* for other people's *work*!" Am I right? Classic. "I thought it was Buy *One*, Get *Two* Free," he adds, italics ours. "No, I *didn't*!", he then continues, clearly a joke to flaunt his mega-bucks....Since the last time he checked in with us, **PAUL LANDER** has been retweeted three more times by Judd Apatow. He now has over 41K Twitter followers, which, Paul reports, impressed everyone he told while waiting on line at the local Costco. **B**

WHERE THE MAGIC HAPPENS.

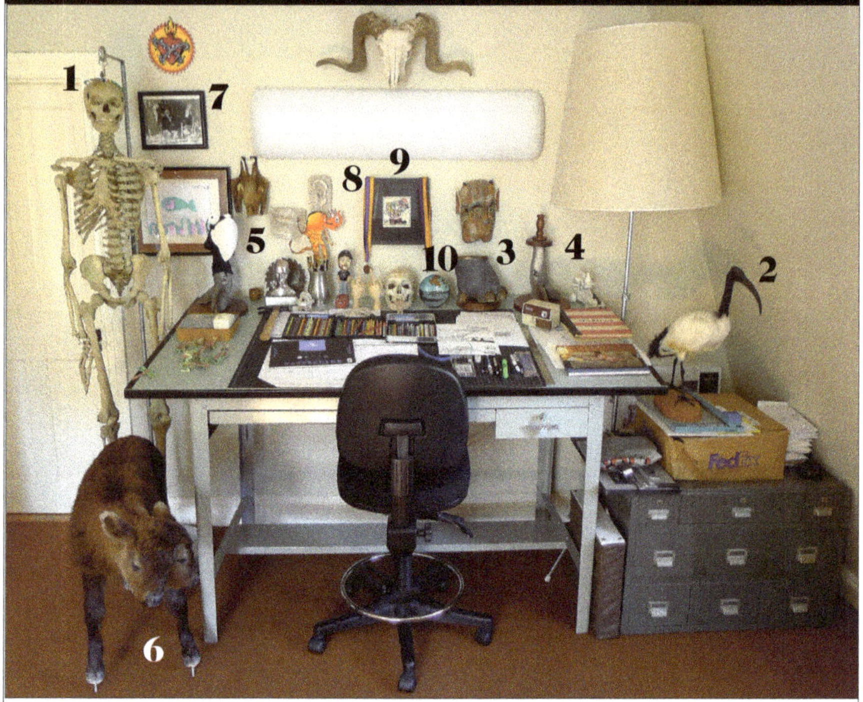

1
2
3
4
5
6
7
8
9
10

This issue's Magic comes from cartoonist **NICK SPOONER**, *who provided the following key. "The skeleton (***1***) has an interesting history. It's over 100 years old and is remarkably well-assembled. There are felt cushions wherever cartilage once was (between the vertebrae, phalanges, knees, etc.) and the lower mandible is hinged, with a string attached so you can puppeteer the jaw to 'speak.' It came from an Odd Fellows hall, and apparently was part of some sort of initiation ritual. The teeth are uncannily perfect, which indicates an individual of great wealth and health. Oh yeah...it also has all of the desiccated ribcage cartilage still attached from rib to sternum. It's a really odd specimen.*

*"The Ibis (***2***) is a totem of the* Harvard Lampoon; *it represents the Egyptian god Thoth, god of wisdom, knowledge and writing. I took it as partial payment for an advertising job I shot in Australia once.*

*The taxidermed hippo foot/ashtray (***3***) is from the collection of Teddy Roosevelt (don't ask how I obtained it). I also have ostrich feet candlesticks (***4***), and a South American vampire bat (***5***). The two-headed calf (***6***) on the floor is real — not a 'gaffe.'*

*The B&W photo on the wall (***7***) shows me with Malcolm Forbes at the party celebrating our* Forbes 400 *parody at the* Lampoon Castle *in '90. He "Weinsteined" me all night long. There are two* Lampoon *medals (***8***) hanging from an original 'Pizz' piece of art (***9***) in the center. Stephen Pizzuro was an amazing underground/cartoon artist from LA, who passed away a few years ago. When we were in a show together with Big Daddy Roth and Robert Williams, I traded him a sculpture of mine for the piece.*

*My favorite thing of all in this photo is the ceramic bowl (***10***) next to the skull on the table. It's a rare piece of 'Pollutoware' by American ceramic master Kenneth Price, who was a family friend. I'm terrified one of my kids will break it."*

FROM FANTAGRAPHICS BOOKS "FU" COLLECTION

NOT WAVING BUT DRAWING

JOHN CUNEO

IN STORES NOW

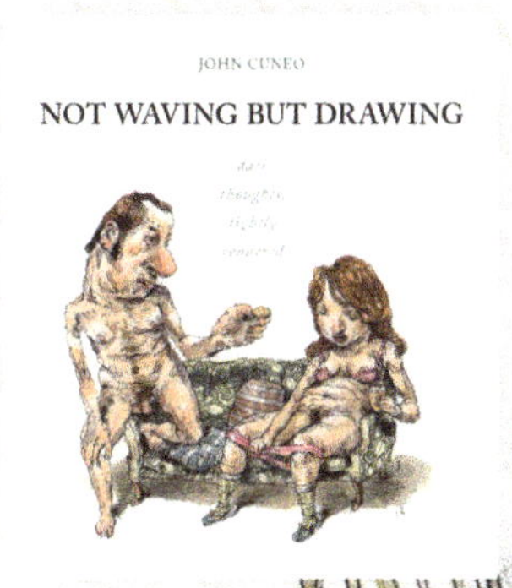
JOHN CUNEO
NOT WAVING BUT DRAWING

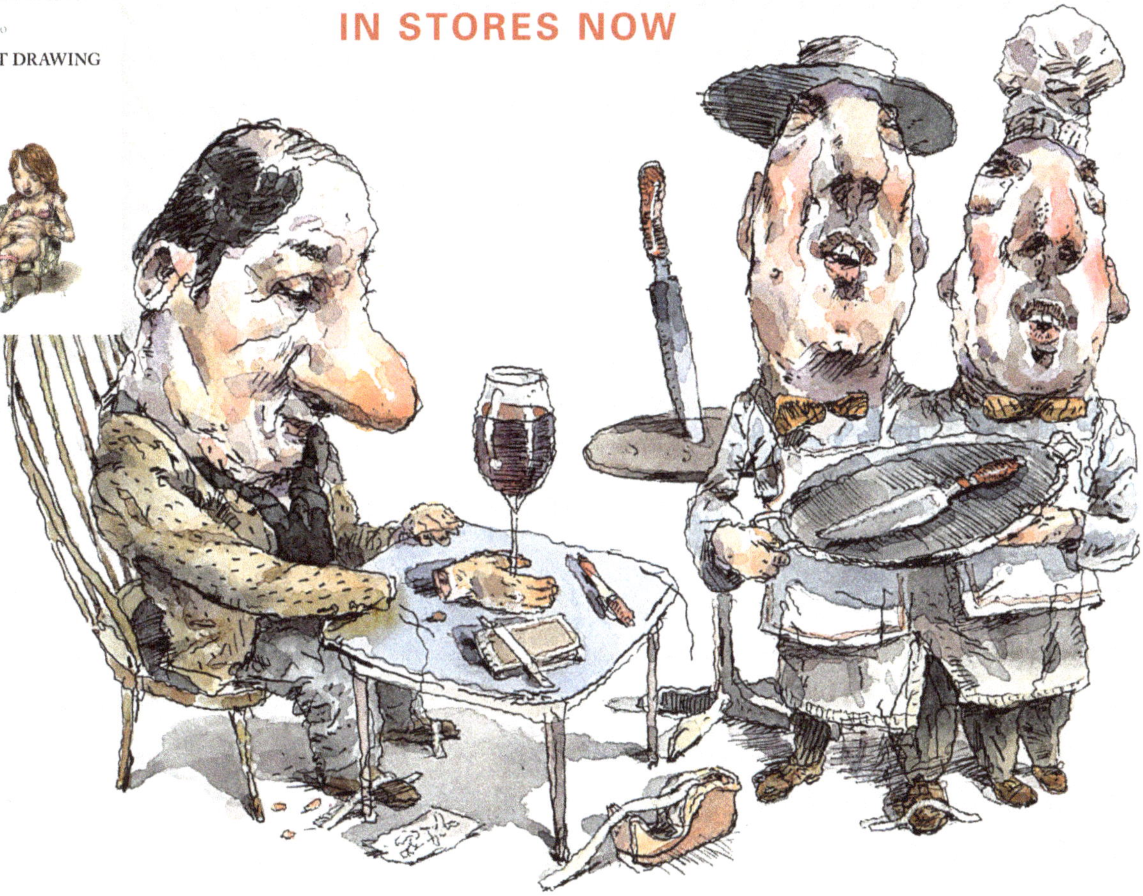

"John Cuneo looks with gentle open all-seeing eyes at the foibles, vanities and failings of humanity and draws what he sees. Like the best surrealists, he is a realist. His art is scabrous and loving and exact"

- NEIL GAIMAN, AUTHOR

"John Cuneo is a force of nature...and you can take that any way you like. We see in this collection the daily inspiration, the flowing river of experimentation. His art walks along with him in every dream, bar, party, restaurant. The work extends and transcends; making you stare, laugh, and maybe blush. And love his brilliance all things over."

- STEVE BRODNER, ILLUSTRATOR, *NEW YORK TIMES*

"Until I saw John Cuneo's erotic drawings, I had no idea just how artistically rewarding it could be to have your mind in the gutter"

- EDWARD SOREL, ILLUSTRATOR, *VANITY FAIR*

"Take a peek if you dare: Cuneo's line may always be supple and playful (he works hard at making drawing seem effortless) and his watercolors are always sensual, yet his wit is so sharp it effortlessly cuts through all the hypocrisy in politics and media."

- FRANÇOISE MOULY, ART EDITOR, *THE NEW YORKER*

BY NICK DOWNES

DARK CARNIVAL

Twenty-five tickets get you a baby piranha in a bowl.

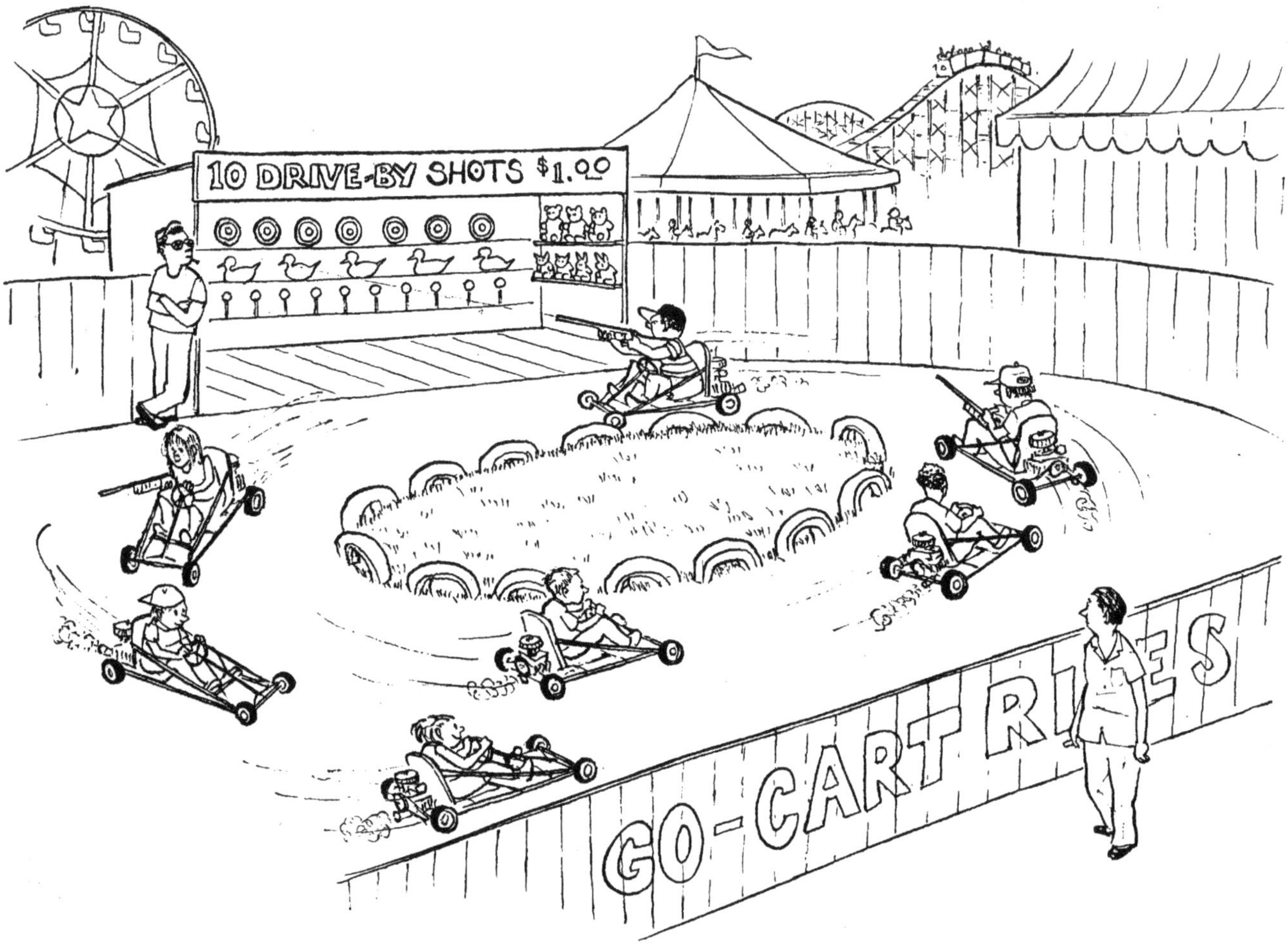
10 DRIVE-BY SHOTS $1.00
GO-CART RIDES

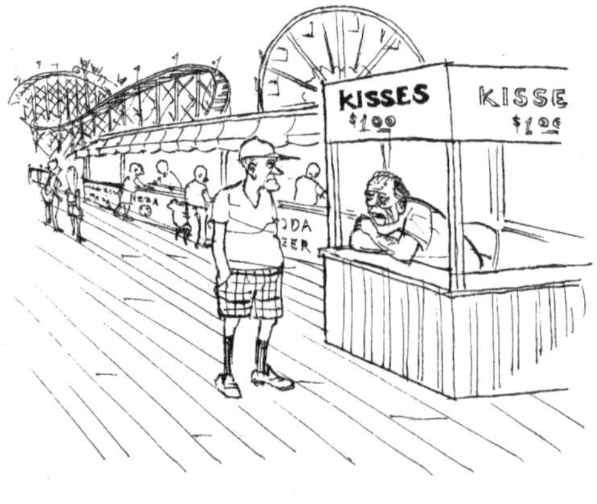
KISSES $1.00
KISSE $1.00

"Then, business is bad all over."

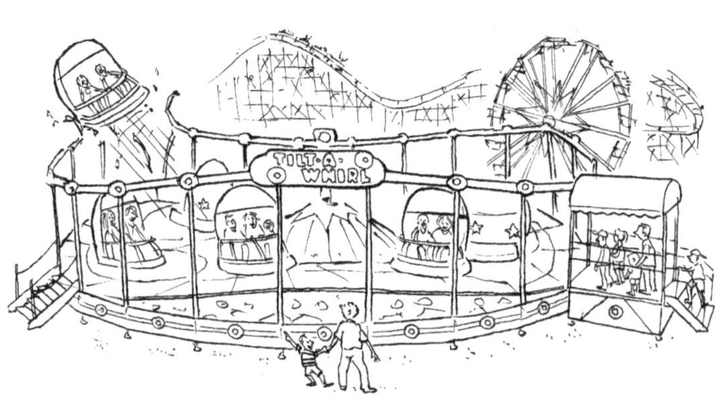
TILT-A-WHIRL

"Dad, I want to go on THAT ride!"

NICK DOWNES *lives like a troll under the Coney Island boardwalk.*

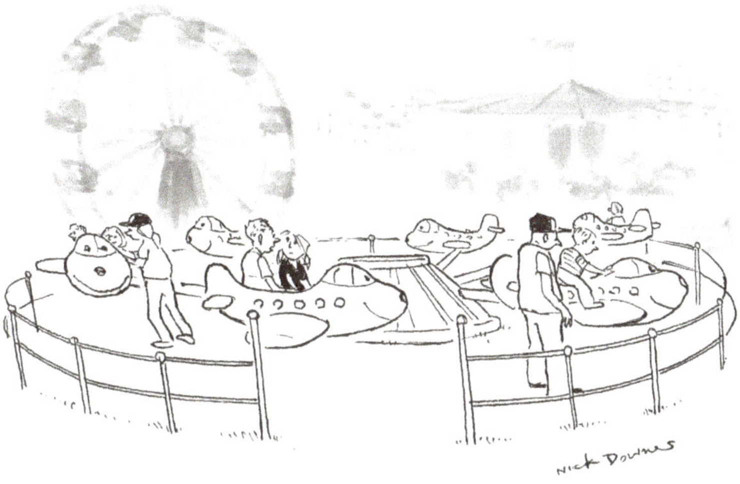

"If anything happens, Janice, I love you."

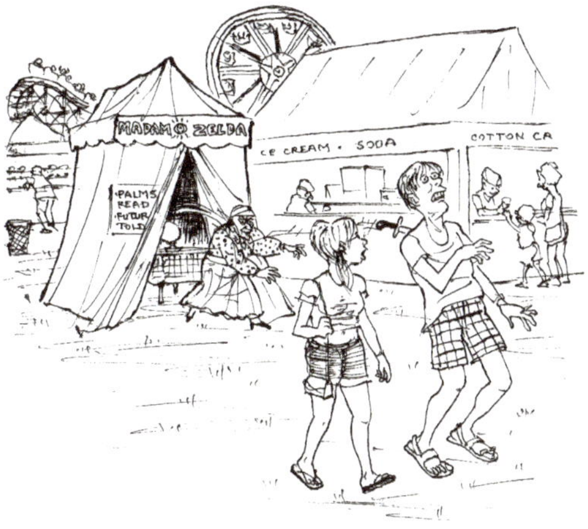
MADAM ZELDA
CE CREAM · SODA
COTTON CA

"It's just like she said it would happen."

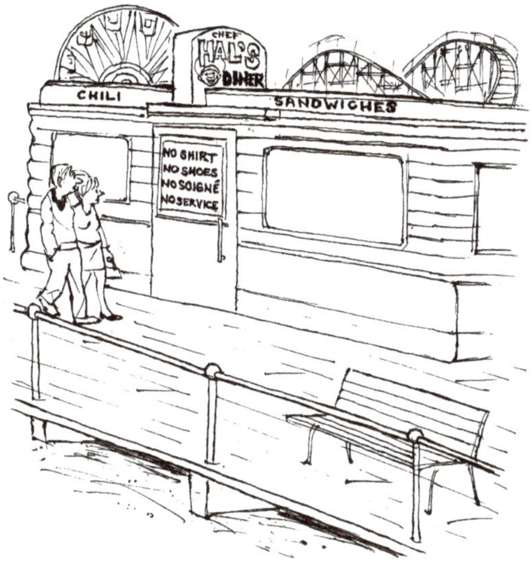
CHEF HAL'S DINER
CHILI
SANDWICHES
NO SHIRT
NO SHOES
NO SOIGNÉ
NO SERVICE

"Pretentious little place, isn't it?"

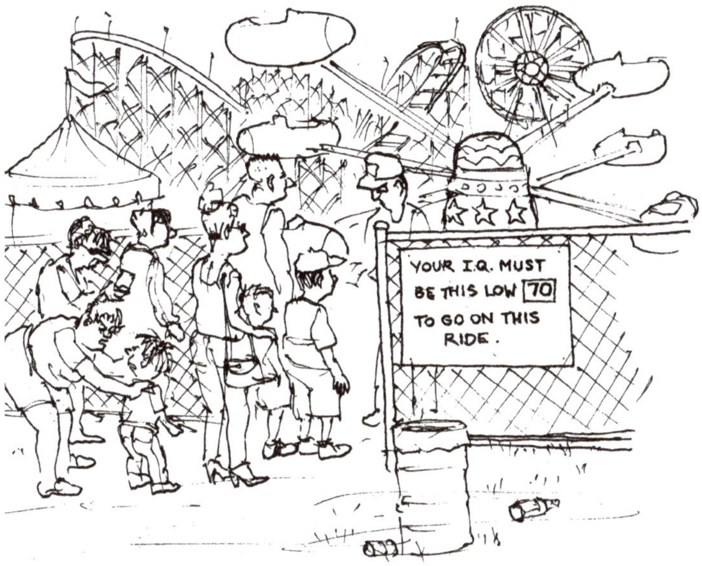
YOUR I.Q. MUST BE THIS LOW 70 TO GO ON THIS RIDE.

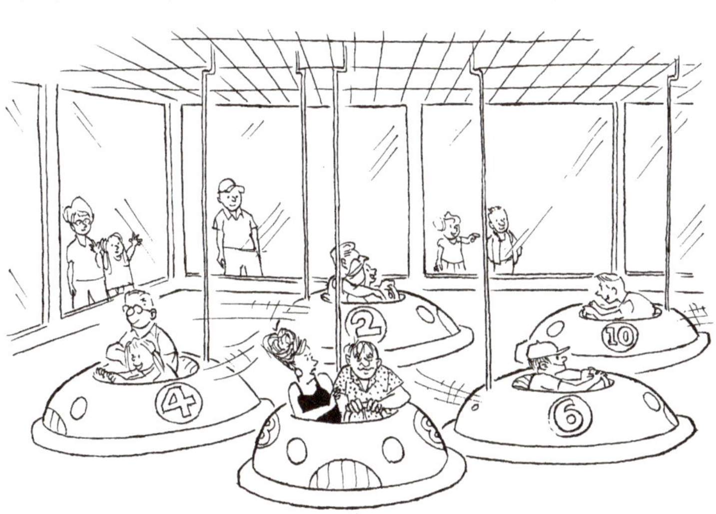
2
10
4
6

"Pull over and let me drive — you're too drunk to hit anyone."

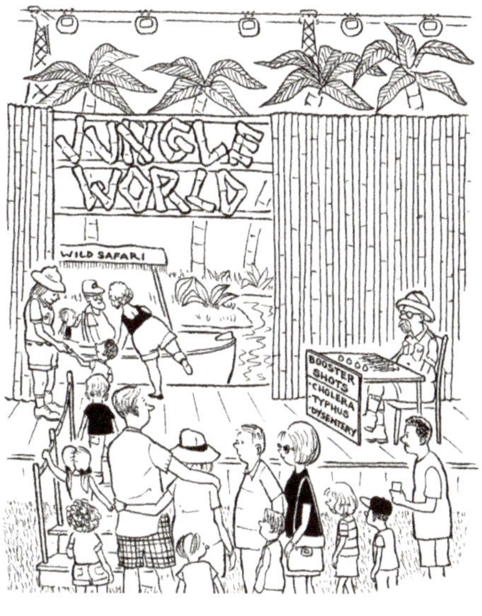
JUNGLE WORLD
WILD SAFARI
BOOSTER SHOTS
CHOLERA
TYPHUS
DYSENTERY

Gallimaufry

"In the restless voice of dissent lies the key to a nation's vitality and greatness."
J. Paul Getty

CLASSIC CAPSULES RETURNS.

[Classic Capsules returns to these pages after a yearlong hiatus by the reviewer, who thanks his devoted readers for their kind understanding during his separation and divorce.]

Bride of Frankenstein — Uncommunicative, "dead inside" woman thinks she can do better than man she was clearly made for, then ruins everything for everybody.

Gone With the Wind — Belle with many boyfriends makes party dress her priority during wartime. Spoiler: Southern gentleman dodges deadliest bullet in film's final moments.

King Kong — Overrated "beauty" fails to connect with unshaven, "too real" adorer.

Twelve Years a Slave — Predictably, the magic wears off after the first two years.

The Elephant Man — Newly freed-up bachelor charms all despite being "not one of the studliest guys in town."

It's a Wonderful Life — Distraught, hard-luck husband fantasizes he never existed; only noticeable changes in wife are that she fulfills her "workplace dream," stops plucking eyebrows.

Citizen Kane — Known publishing figure, terribly off-key singer, feud.

Sunset Boulevard — Seasoned writer, terribly delusional woman, feud.

All About Eve — This film would have been perfect if the title character had been named Kirsten!

The Best Years of Our Lives — Alcohol nicely completes suburban husband.

Father of the Bride — Wholly unbelievable tale in which overly educated, blowhard father never quotes from Latin books he knows his future son-in-law has never read during dinner scenes; future bride never delivers tearful monologue in parents' kitchen while waving steak knife.

Bonnie and Clyde — Shrill sister-in-law invites herself along on couple's road trip.

The Invisible Man — Accomplished, dapper professional goes unseen by woman he loves, others.

The Time Machine — Inventor squanders opportunity to revisit Kirsten's 2013 office Christmas party, punch Earl Webb in throat while he dances his stupid dork dance.

Twelve Angry Men — Hostilities subside after all men in room agree woman who testified on stand was woefully mistaken, unaccountable.

The Wizard of Oz — Wandering woman finally comes to her senses, realizes every place except home sucks.

—Ron Hauge

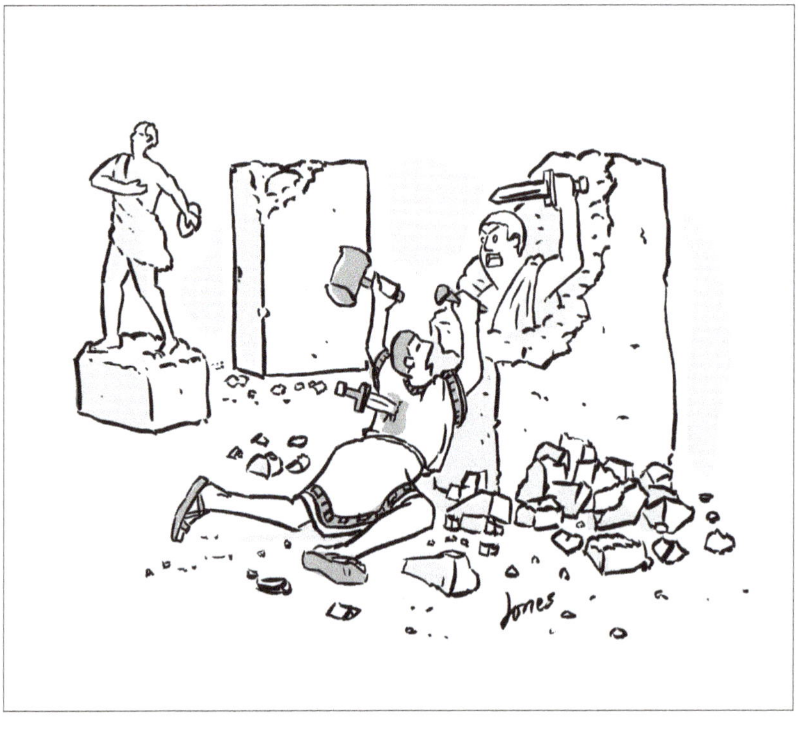
Jones

TRUMP GONE! TRUMP TRIUMPHANT! TRUMP ALL CAPS!

I emailed.

Someone else emailed.

I emailed to remind you that I and that other person had emailed.

YES: Experts have told us that short sentences get attention.

They convey URGENCY.

URGENCY that may trick you into reading an email eerily similar to the ones you've gotten every day for the past year.

An email that's written for a third-grade reading level, because while we're sure most Trump supporters are stupid, we're convinced that many of you are stupid, too.

That sentence was probably too long and complicated. SORRY.

I'll be blunt: We need to raise A LOT of money in the next 12 HOURS, or an arbitrary amount of money won't have been raised by an artificial deadline.

Money that presumably will be used to do some good somewhere, but you'll never know.

Why am I asking now? Well, did you see the NEWS? Trump is ENRAGED! He's RED-FACED AND SPLUTTERING with fury! Because we're WINNING! Yet at the same time, we're LOSING and TRUMP IS VICTORIOUS! He's LAUGHING AT US! At YOU! We definitely need more money either way!

If you donate JUST ONE DOLLAR by midnight, it will be quintuple-sextuple-septuple-octuple matched TO ALMOST INFINITY by rich people who are generous only when people like you do something very close to meaningless.

Frankly, I need you to step up NOW. But don't think that donating will get you off the hook, because we'll be back with another email almost immediately.

Somehow the fund-raising experts don't think this will sicken you.

I'll be clear: Something is happening on an ongoing basis that requires urgent responses continuously, as the situation becomes simultaneously bleaker and more hopeful.

Simply put, the stakes have never been higher, except for yesterday, and several hundred days before that!

BOTTOM LINE: If we succeed in raising the arbitrary amount of money by the artificial deadline, we can claim that the Republicans are STUNNED.

Then we'll announce that the Republicans are REDOUBLING THEIR EFFORTS and we'll come back to you for another dollar tomorrow, but for a few pleasant hours we can all feel like we did something.

Oh, and if it would add to the feeling that you're doing something, we have A PETITION you can sign that almost certainly won't be delivered to anyone.

Or, check out our childish "Do You Approve of Trump?" poll with A COLORFUL RECTANGLE TO CLICK.

So, can I count on your support NOW, or at least in a few hours when I send the next email?

Chief Fund-Raiser,
The Democratic Constant
Email Committee

—Steve Young

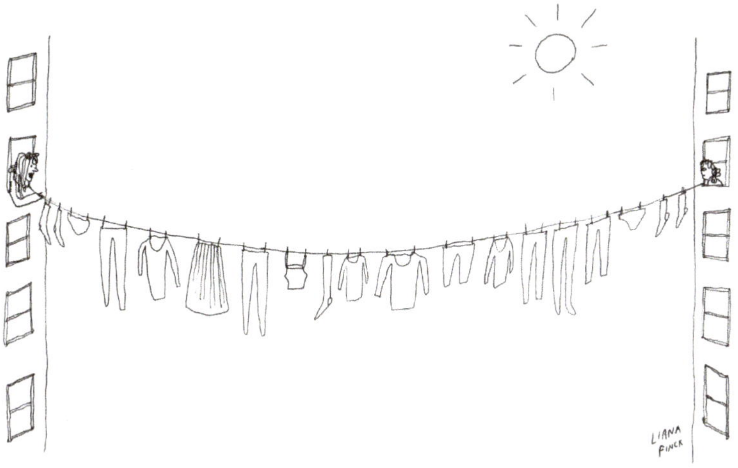
LIANA FINCK

"Are you completely naked now?"

A LIFE.

I have eaten the hot dog of the sidewalk vendor;
I have been in houses made of brick;
I have owned a paisley tie;
I have lived.

—Alan Goldberg

THE NEW YORK DADA FESTIVAL.

Everybody knows that at the end of summer the New York Renaissance Festival closes up its tents and its dunking booths, and the caravan of cube trucks pulls out of Tuxedo's Sterling Forest. Everyone does not know what happens the following week: Oblong banners, emblazoned with the iconic bowler-hat-and-scorpions-rampant, snap in the wind, announcing the arrival of the less popular, but equally entertaining, New York Dada Festival.

Like its Elizabethan predecessor, the Dada Festival opens each day with a ceremonial parade. This parade features nuns and midgets who march, skip and caper to the sound of a traditional Dada band: three tubas, 17 mariachi guitarists and a weeping schoolgirl dragging a cello.

Throughout the day, roaming members of the improvisational cast meet up to interact in loosely structured scenes and spectacular events. Find yourself at the beer stand just before noon and you'll witness fireworks, as a fanatical Arizona Cardinals fan throws raw hamburger meat at a bronze bust of Robert Downey Jr. Dwight Eisenhower arrives to shout instructions. Bits of pistachio fly from his mouth as he screams his invectives, and the football fan occasionally dabs himself clean with a blue bandanna. Late in the afternoon, near the footbridge a fundamentalist Muslim, an evangelical Southern Baptist and an Orthodox Jew play kitty whist without rancor, until Odin and Freya arrive in Thor's chariot to bury them in a massive pile of the soft cotton shoes of Chinese workers. While the zealots are played by talented but underpaid NY actors, the representatives of the Norse pantheon play themselves, and their entrance alone is worth the price of admission.

At the very end of each festival day, the entire cast and audience gathers for "the grand finale." Several clowns emerge, without makeup and dressed in polo shirts and casual slacks; they incant, in the solemn hollow tones of Gregorian monks, the week's gains and losses for the 10 most widely traded mutual funds. A swarm of exquisitely painted bees is released. A spandex-clad plumber prods a dog with an old television antenna, and when the dog's bark resembles a word, that night's revelry comes to an end.

When you make plans to attend the festival, you would be well advised to pack your own lunch; the sausage vendor offers only calumny and despair. The pancake stand gives off a delightful aroma, but all you can buy is an opportunity to squirt syrup at a cardboard cutout of Sean Spicer. At three squirts for a dollar it's worth doing, but the obvious emotional satisfaction won't fill your belly.

The ad men got it absolutely right on this one. When you see the posters in the subways and on the buses urging you to "Come for the eels; stay for the melancholy dissolution of the political substructure," heed the call. You have this reviewer's assurance, you won't be flambé!"

—*Dylan Brody*

NATURE'S GLOBE-STAND.

Heedless men are now braving snow, sleet, slush, ice, hail, icy mix and (sadly) unseasonably warm tundra to exalt humanity via a little-known pastime. The sport is called antlering, and game play advances as follows: a participant stalks a deer, elk, antelope, moose, or caribou and implants a globe of Earth atop the animal's horns.

All of the game's majesty is right now apparent to the reader. It is said by outdoorsmen "the antlers are nature's globe-stand."

Regard the elk — he is free, proud, defiant, outrageous. The creature now strains beneath a globe, in addition to the baroque embellishments endowed by nature. This brute apparently believes that, what with his embellishments, he is superior to the average human. We, of course, know that he is not. The animal doesn't know that we know! But now it is clear, now that a well-placed globe enlightens the animal. Do you think that you are superior to a human, O encumbered elk? How can one behold you, with your outlandish aggrandizements, and not laugh in human-life-affirming misery?

The outdoorsman arrives. His caribou is uncooperative, unyielding, intractable, defiant. The outdoorsman puts down his pack. He pretends to admire the caribou's antlers, all while opening his pack. The caribou blushes for the outdoorsman's ruse and even lowers his emotional guard. The outdoorsman removes from his pack a 45-inch-diameter model of his beloved Earth. Caribous don't love Earth.

There are a plethora of difficulties with antlering, and myriad antlering traditions, but the usual goal is to have North America facing forward. The outdoorsman places the globe on the animal's head, making sure that North America is facing forward. Smash it in! This globe will stay embedded in the animal's antlers for up to seven months. The sportsman flees. So? Fleeing was the idea.

It is here that I choose to bring up the subject of rams. You rams think you've got it pretty good, don't you? A globe doesn't fit in your mighty, spread-apart horns! Life's good? You happy, rams? You comfy? Can I get you more soda? Wait, what???!!!! Well, rams, I have got a surprise for you: We're going to duct-tape globes of Earth to your horns. Let's see how that treats you. Let us see how you like it.

It's a new sport we call duct-taping. Yesterday, as I unpacked some leftover custom-made globes and one of those jigsaw puzzles of the U. S. states, left over from an unsanctioned Canadian antlering expedition I took, I found that I had received a threatening letter from some rams:

A LETTER FROM THE RAMS
Raaaaaaaaaaaaaaams! Hello, humans. A globe doesn't fit in our mighty, spread-apart horns! We see ourselves as especially appropriate animals to speak up for our deer, caribou, moose, elk, and antelope buddies. We're comfy. We've got it good. So, too, should other animals. Also, what was up with this letter? You admitted to maltreatment of us, in a missive:

"Dear rams, Man, I love one-upping animals. I have sniffed a skunk's tail, I have thrown my feces at an ape, I have low-balled a skunk, I have sold an opossum a bill of goods, I have backhand-complimented a fox, I have done other bad things to a skunk, and I have worn fake feathers within range of several reportedly very arrogant peacocks. I invented antlering and duct-taping."

I was livid. I mean, who do they think they are, sheep? Oh, I'll get to the sheep.

In conclusion, there is a rumor going around that I have antlers. I do not have antlers! How dare you! I am not an antler animal! What is the meaning of this?! This is an outrage! Help me! Help me! Who do you think you are?! I'll have you know that I do not appreciate this! You'll be hearing from my lawyer! Why, oh, why, oh, why did I ever associate with animals that have antlers? Why??????????

—*Andrew Barlow*

"I preferred Season 3."

ON THE NAUGAHYDE.

there are no atheists in my dentist's chair
I stretch out full length
that's right, the whole 5 foot 6 of me
he straps me in
black jeans ride up on bright blue socks
"Some people are making a fashion statement;
I'm asking a fashion question"
his pretty hygienist smiles
"You're funny"
she should hear me sometime when I'm not screaming
his gloved finger dipped in slush
squeaks across my tooth,
strokes my gum
I hardly even know the man
my lips fade to black
here come da looong needle
I think we'll argue politics later
stab once stab twice
guess who can feel again
shock drains me white
I sweat I sit up I decide not to faint
I'm not a wimp I just can't stand pain
but I got the bastard back:
if cash were saliva I couldn't spit
and my PPO don't cover shit.
—*Paul Guay*

MAROONED.

There I sat, under a single palm tree, with a 360-degree aquatic vista.

But my salvation was sitting right there with me. A *New Yorker* cartoonist. Who better to know all the angles of our predicament? Here was someone who'd spent hours of his career on this exact problem!

Stuck in the Everglades, I'd want Bear Grylls. Stuck on a desert island — I'd want a one-panel cartoonist. My profession certainly wouldn't tell me how to, say, use a blender that washed up on shore. Or build a raft out of fingernail clippings. Or use the palm tree for sexual release.

It didn't start well. When I asked him for ideas how we might get out of this, he was downright chilly. "I get paid for that," he said, and stared at the horizon.

I didn't lose heart. Creativity is never linear. And I wasn't prepared to be picky; I wasn't demanding he save us

INNER DEMONS.
—*Sarah Booth*

All this writing has let loose some of my inner demons.
Out of their cages they are messing and mucking about
throwing shit around the room and hiding things I need
They mention in passing things I wish kept quiet and
openly talk to me of particularly drunken behavior
which I'd chew my leg off to get away from if I could.
Now, I'm running around chasing down these bastards
to get them back in their cage.

But, Maybe they too need some time off
from turning circles in their jails, the dizzy chasing of tails,
and from banging cups against the bars
reminding me they're still there.
Often the light of day isn't enough to diminish their power
and once I get them back in place
with something to chew on,
I know it's only a little time before my words lift their latches
once again.

in some hilarious way. Arch, dry, even obscure could still get the job done.

The hours passed. His silence disturbed me. We could die on this rock. Rescuers would find a pair of skeletons on the beach, one pulling his hair out, one staring at the ocean holding a pen and notebook.

I paced the island to get a grip. On Trip 73, a revelation came: My partner was using this all for inspiration, plumbing it for new material. I could get angry — or I could help. So I acted out every gag I could think of: bowled with coconuts, spelled SOS in the sand but in Morse code, cracked wise with the sharks circling our island.

It was all no good; the guy just stared, nibbling his Rapidograph. Spent, I slumped on the sand and started to weep. We'd never be rescued.

Suddenly, my partner's face brightened, and his pen sprang to life. He wrote notes, roughed sketches, smirked and giggled. Wiping the tears from my sunburned face, I stole a peek.

Two dogs at a job interview. Every page.

What else could I do but bludgeon him with a coconut and burn his notebook for a signal fire? None too soon, a cruise ship saw the flame and rescued me. I told them everything, too exhausted to lie.

When I was done, the captain pursed his lips and grew thoughtful. Finally, he drawled: "Dogs at a job interview? That's pretty funny."

—*James Finn Garner*

MINDFULNESS FOR BEGINNERS.

Mindfulness is a practice that has been cultivated for millennia as a means of living more fully in the present moment. When you are mindful, you recognize your own thoughts and feelings, but do not react to them impulsively the way you would if you were "on autopilot" or "the president."

Awaken Your Senses

Bring fresh, filtered water to a boil and allow to cool slightly. Pour over a Tazo Organic Zen or Calm Chamomile teabag nestled inside your favorite mug and let steep for 2-3 minutes. Maintain the resolve that at this time you have no other duties or responsibilities. Accept whatever arises in your awareness each moment. Notice each sight, touch, and sound so that you savor every sensa —

TWITTER
now
Donald J. Trump Tweeted:
Reeses Pieces can no longer be allowed to use the same colors M&Ms use. Small "m" on one side not enough --- and not always there! Must stop

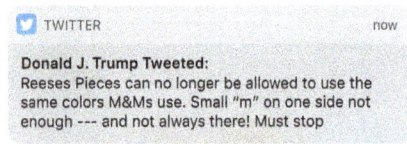

Add whiskey. Abandon plans of going to the gym later. Stare at Twitter, aghast and indignant, as hours vanish. Recognize that this is not the same as reaching the state of deep immersion psychologist Mihaly Csikszentmihalyi famously termed "flow." It is more akin to a binge: self-destructive, harmful to your physical and emotional well-being. Set down your phone and repeat to yourself as a mantra: We are in a prolonged state of national emergency.

Focus on Your Breathing

The cornerstone of mindfulness is observing your breath without trying to control or suppress it.

Feel your breath move in and out and notice how your abdomen expands. Let your awareness of everything else fall away. As you inhale and exhale, say to yourself: "Breathing in, I have arrived, breathing out, I am home" or "breathing in, willingness to collude, breathing out, obstruction of justice."

Distracting thoughts will naturally arise — sometimes a great many thoughts, overlapping one to the next, like how this is perhaps all the result of the current president fuming over his predecessor having been — and remaining — more famous than him, since what he ultimately desires — impossible, forever elusive — is neither the title nor the power but the nation's eyes and ears. The coverage from all angles. Universal adoration. That somewhere inside his fragile, arrested ego is an airtight logical proof: If he's the top guy, everybody below has to look up to him. And then the campaign rally walk-ons to the theme from the 1997 Harrison Ford political action-thriller *Air Force One* make a kind of sad, dumb sense: He'll never rise to the level of presidential, but he can achieve the look. He can be president the way he's seen it in the movies, just like he played a businessman on TV.

Notice this mental drift. Remark to yourself: "Thinking has just occurred" not as judgment but as a neutral observation, and return to your breathing and environment. But then remember that back-to-back hurricanes ravaged Texas, Florida and the Caribbean while San Francisco experienced a record-breaking heat wave and wildfires raged in the Pacific Northwest. So maybe let's limit "environment" to mean the room you're currently in.

Take a Shower

Rid your mind of plans, fantasies and attempts to relitigate the 2016 election. Focus your attention instead on the smell of the lavender body wash, the sensation of the warm water as you lather your skin. In here, there are no notifications. No speculation about whether today is the day Donald Trump finally became president. This is your haven: far off the beaten path, a lush tropical Hawaiian waterfall accessible only by foot, or by North Korean intercontinental ballistic missile.

Embrace each feeling and sensation as it occurs: the chill of cool air; goosebumps pimpling up; crippling fear of nuclear annihilation. Whether those thoughts are good or bad is unimportant. Refrain from humming the first few bars of "Rocket Man" and gently bring yourself back to your breath.

Take a Walk

Walking is an easy way to incorporate mindfulness into your day and provides bodily exercise as well as ample time to reflect. Bring your attention to the sensations of your legs as they move, fully experiencing the crunch of gravel underfoot. If your mind begins to wander, try anchoring your concentration to a single narrative thread by listening to a podca—

AT&T LTE
1:58 PM
Queue
Will America's Institutions Survive President Trump?
Trump's new war plan
Donald Trump as Julius Caesar
The House of Trump
Trump's art of the sabotage
Is Donald Trump Good for Journalism?
"Trump always shoots the hostage."

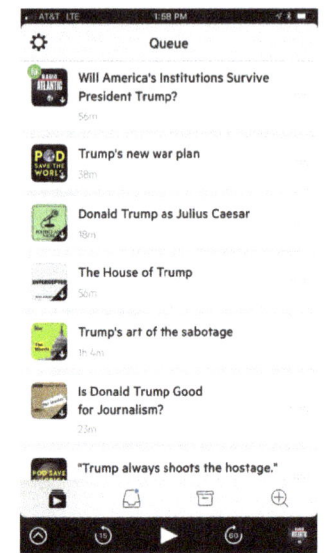

—or perhaps an audioboo—

AT&T LTE
1:58 PM
Recommended for You
UNDERSTANDING TRUMP
NEWT GINGRICH
DEVIL'S BARGAIN
JOSHUA GREEN
Understanding Trump
Devil's Bargain
Joshua Green
PETER SCHWEIZER
CLINTON CASH
GREAT AGAIN
DONALD J. TRUMP
Clinton Cash
Peter Schweizer
Great Again
Donald J. Trump
WHAT HAPPENED
My Library
Channels
More

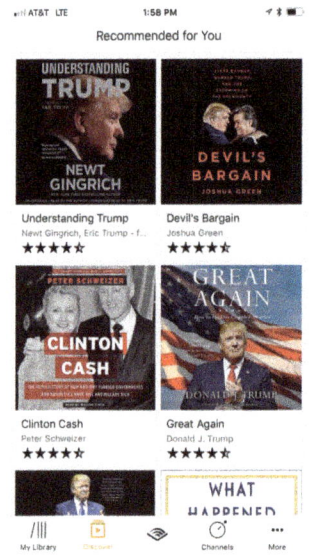

—you know what, just use the headphones to stop your ears, like Odysseus fending off the Sirens' alluring song. As thoughts arise, let them go. Do not become unduly concerned over how it's bound to get much worse before it improves. If it improves. If irreparable harm hasn't already been done to our core institutions and values, or, even more perilous, to our environment.

How the wheels of justice turn at a glacial pace — which, incidentally, is an analogy we'll soon need to update

— meaning there will be no quick fix, no deus ex machina or smoking gun. How, ultimately, we are in for three more agonizing, apoplectic years with only the fleeting joy of new seasons of *Stranger Things* — until he taints that, too, with fiery comments on the 2018 Emmys.

Try Again in 2020

Ask yourself: Do I truly desire to live more fully in this particular present moment?

—*Jeff Albers*

BEHOLD MY WIZARD POWERS!

Welcome to my wizard lair! I have many wonders to show you. You desire a demonstration of my skill in the magickal arts? Very well. Behold as I cast a *spell of levitation*! Ha! Your puny mortal mind reels as you watch me hover fully two or three feet above the ground. Using this arcane power, I can get things down from high shelves, easily avoid stepping in puddles, and almost slam-dunk a basketball but not quite. Technically I could levitate higher but I don't because I'm afraid of heights.

Be careful: Things in a wizard's house are never quite what they seem. That mirror is a portal into the realm of the faeries; that seemingly humble rug is a wondrous flying carpet; and that fish mounted on the wall can sing. It is not a Big Mouth Billy Bass. I enchanted that fish to make it so that it can sing and also live outside of water. I didn't know that Big Mouth Billy Basses were a thing when I caught the fish and cast the spells. If I did it again I would probably choose a different animal. And also a song other than "Don't Worry Be Happy."

Gaze into my crystal ball. With it, I can pierce the veils of time and space, and see events unfolding on the other side of the world, and things that have been, and things that will be, and also into my neighbor's apartment so I can watch TV for free when he leaves it on during the day for his dog. I can't change the channel, sorry.

With my wizardly knowledge of alchemy, I can transmute lead into gold! The only thing is, I don't know where to get lead. Gold is pretty rare, but lead is also not, like, super-common. I thought pencils used lead, but it turns out that's graphite. You don't have any lead, do you? I could really use some gold.

This way to my library! It is filled with ancient tomes that contain the arcane wisdom of the ages. Do you dare peruse *The Book of Choronzon*, whose pages hold the secret to unlocking your inner magickal potential? It's in the self-help section, next to *The Six Pillars of Self-Esteem*. I'm working on being less self-conscious about doing magic in front of other people.

The mystic art of shape shifting allows a wizard to appear in many different guises; I can take on the form of a lion, or an eagle, or a pizza delivery guy. If you ever see me around town delivering pizza, remember: It's just a magickal disguise I use to steal pizzas. Don't listen to anyone who says I need to work a second job.

Did you see how fast I chugged that beer, mortal? That's not magick; I'm just good at chugging beers. Okay fine, it is magick. I lied because I want you to think I'm cool.

Mow the lawn? Bah! A wizard need never mow his own lawn. I have a demonic familiar who attends to all such menial tasks around my wizard lair. The reason my grass is so tall is because my demon familiar moved out. He said I was "a crappy roommate" and that he "couldn't bear living in this shithole." He found a new place and started a very successful landscaping business, and now he won't return my calls.

As a wizard, I have the power to travel wherever I please. I need only cast a spell of invisibility and sneak into my neighbor's house and steal his bus pass.

If you, a mortal, wish to cool your beverage, you must put water in a tray, put the tray in a freezer, and then wait hours before your cubes of ice are ready! Pathetic! Look on in amazement as I, a wizard, simply cast a *spell of cup-making*, then a *spell of aqua-apparition*, then a *spell of freezing*, then a *spell of cup-disappearance*, which leaves me a chunk of coldest wizard ice! I then smash the wizard ice into pieces with my hands, and use a *spell of ice-into-drink* to magickally transport the ice chunks into my Fanta.

Though my powers are immense, some things are beyond magick. There is no spell a wizard can use to make a woman fall in love with him, or go on a date with him, or even just stop laughing at his beard.

Going so soon? Fair enough — mastering the mystic arts is not for the faint of heart. But before you take your leave, I must entrust to you a letter upon which my very fate depends. Treat this letter with the utmost care, mortal, for it contains a check to pay my gas bill. You can just drop it in the mailbox down the street. I would do it

"I pledge allegiance to this flag / that I made myself by hand / in order to be able to do this again."

myself, but I don't want to run into my neighbor. He wants his bus pass back.

—Luke Burns

THE FIRST SONS.

The minds of these first sons should certainly worry us
Their psyches, so feeble and fragile and furious
And I think, were an analyst ever to probe
It is likely he'd find a Leopold AND a Loeb
Though much LESS intellectually curious!

—Lance Hansen

GREAT MOMENTS IN THOUGHTS AND PRAYERS.

The chamber was silent as President Roosevelt spoke. "Yesterday, December 7, 1941," he said, "a date which will live in infamy, the United States of America was suddenly and deliberately attacked by naval and air forces of the Empire of Japan. Which is why I come before you today, to ask for your thoughts and prayers during this difficult time."

Congress erupted — but the president stood firm. "No, no," he said. "Now's not the time to talk of declaring war." We must remember the victims, the brave soldiers and sailors who died at Pearl Harbor."

"But wouldn't they want us to stop the Japanese most of all?" a congressman yelled.

"We can't know what they might want," FDR said. "All we know is the Japanese have attacked us. The Nazis have taken over most of Europe. And, I wasn't planning on telling you this, but there's also a genocide going on. So I ask you, members of Congress, and all good people of this country, to join me right now in thinking really, really hard about how you wish all this stuff would stop."

The thoughts and prayers worked. Within a week, the entire Japanese High Command had realized the error of its ways and retreated back to the home islands. But that wasn't good enough to satisfy Emperor Hirohito, who immediately sacked them all and threw the top men into prison. "I deserve it," said Tojo, who later wrote a series of children's books about bullying.

Over in Germany, the results were even more marked. From the moment America's mighty thoughts and prayers were unleashed, Hitler's Reich began to crumble. Tanks stopped; planes turned back; soldiers tossed their rifles into the river and headed home to be with their parents and sweethearts. All across Mitteleuropa, the locks on the concentration camps sprung open. Manna fell from heaven. Hitler's heart was transformed; he went on the radio expressing his deep embarrassment and humbly asking everyone's forgiveness. Thus the world met the man we now call "the Gandhi of Europe."

Thanks to these thoughts and prayers, Americans were credited with saving the world, and Nazis were never heard of again. Especially not in Charlottesville, Va.

............◆............

As Hurricane Katrina approached the Louisiana coast, New Orleans Mayor Ray Nagin burst into the Oval Office. "Mr. President, you have to do something! It's a Category 5!"

President Bush put down his remote and looked thoughtfully out the window, where a fine drizzle fell upon the White House lawn. This was not the first major crisis of his presidency...but instead of jumping to action, as he had been so willing to do after 9/11, Bush thought now about the wisdom of his predecessors. "How about we take a moment to pray?"

"Sir," Nagin responded, exasperated, "there's nothing wrong with praying, but right now time is of the essence. Thousands of people are going to die if we don't do something!"

"Darn it, would you calm down? When did 'doing something' ever help anybody?" Before the mayor could answer, President Bush grabbed his hands; almost immediately Nagin felt a surge of warmth within him. They bowed their heads...and on the television across the room they heard the weatherman report that the storm had suddenly and inexplicably changed course. "I've never seen anything like it — Katrina's actually reversing!" the man said, voice high with disbelief. "It's heading back where it came, out to sea, where it can never harm anyone ever again!"

There was still a lot of rain, but the collective love and faith amongst the people strengthened the levees as if from within. When the water receded, New Orleans stood as lush and gleaming as ever. Soon, the residents emerged from their homes. The white residents earnestly and respectfully sought out food and water, always waiting their turn and using only proper channels, while all the black residents looted stores like the dickens, because, well, you know. FEMA Director Mike Brown was given a raise and a promotion, for being so proactive in emergency management as to actually make emergency management unnecessary. The whole department was abolished, and Brown's duties were given to a select panel of clergymen.

............◆............

America watched in horror as a white man who was definitely not a terrorist, because this was not a terrorist act, because I already told you he's white, murdered nearly 60 of his fellow citizens.

As the nation cried out for action, wondering just what kind of country America had become, and why nowhere else seems to have to put up with this endless, pointless bloodshed, hundreds of politicians mustered up the courage to do what they knew they must: They headed for Twitter.

These good, fine public servants with certainly no ties to lobbying groups or gun manufacturers who actually profit from rampages like this one, generated so many thoughts and prayers that Jesus was awoken

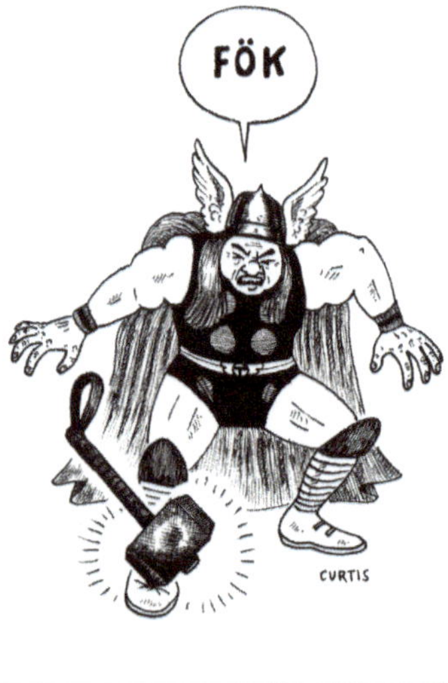
FÖK
CURTIS

STAN MACK'S CHRONICLES

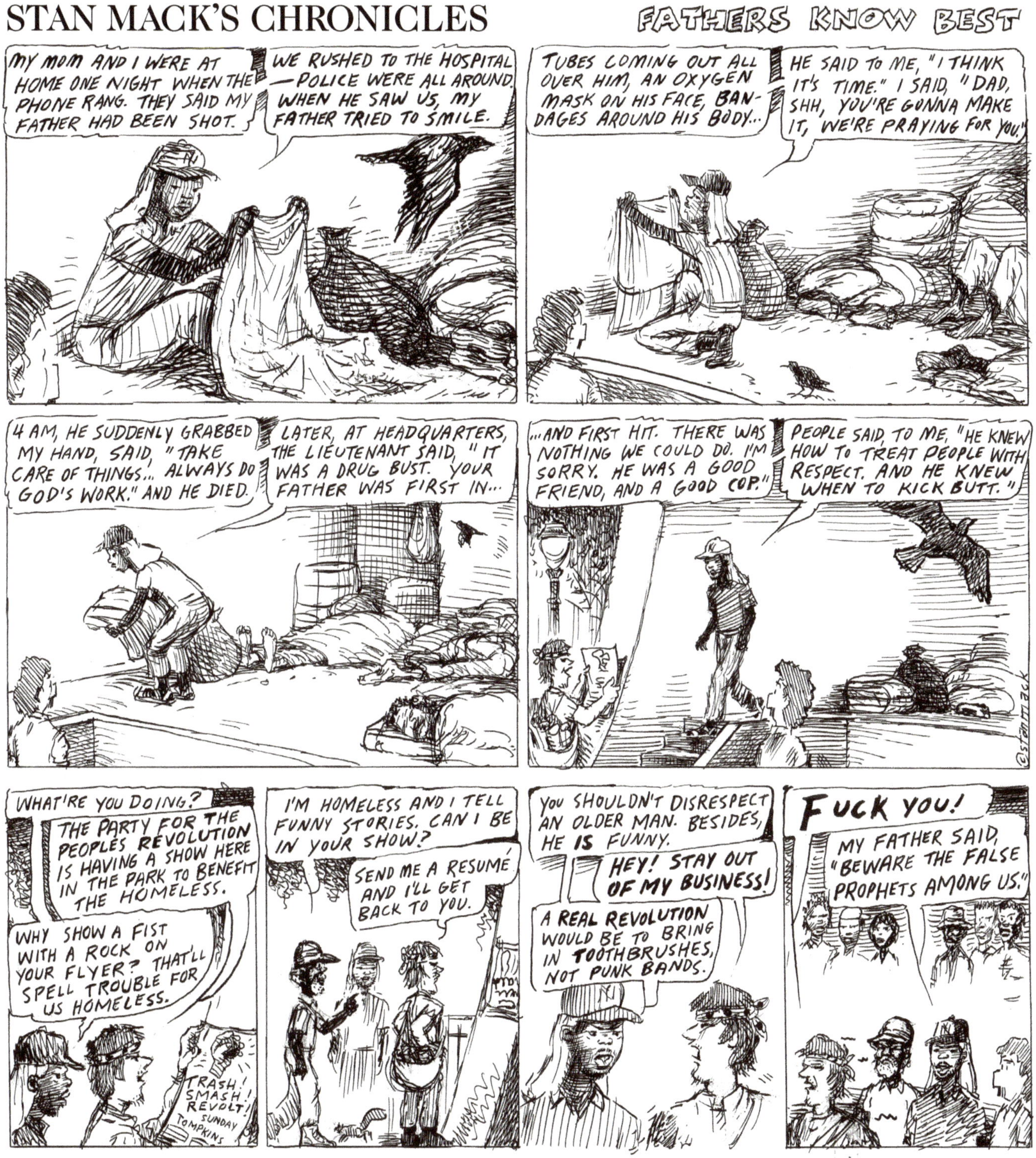

FATHERS KNOW BEST
MY MOM AND I WERE AT HOME ONE NIGHT WHEN THE PHONE RANG. THEY SAID MY FATHER HAD BEEN SHOT.
WE RUSHED TO THE HOSPITAL —POLICE WERE ALL AROUND. WHEN HE SAW US, MY FATHER TRIED TO SMILE.
TUBES COMING OUT ALL OVER HIM, AN OXYGEN MASK ON HIS FACE, BANDAGES AROUND HIS BODY...
HE SAID TO ME, "I THINK IT'S TIME." I SAID, "DAD, SHH, YOU'RE GONNA MAKE IT, WE'RE PRAYING FOR YOU."
4 AM, HE SUDDENLY GRABBED MY HAND, SAID, "TAKE CARE OF THINGS... ALWAYS DO GOD'S WORK." AND HE DIED.
LATER, AT HEADQUARTERS, THE LIEUTENANT SAID, "IT WAS A DRUG BUST. YOUR FATHER WAS FIRST IN...
...AND FIRST HIT. THERE WAS NOTHING WE COULD DO. I'M SORRY. HE WAS A GOOD FRIEND, AND A GOOD COP."
PEOPLE SAID, TO ME, "HE KNEW HOW TO TREAT PEOPLE WITH RESPECT. AND HE KNEW WHEN TO KICK BUTT."
WHAT'RE YOU DOING?
THE PARTY FOR THE PEOPLES REVOLUTION IS HAVING A SHOW HERE IN THE PARK TO BENEFIT THE HOMELESS.
WHY SHOW A FIST WITH A ROCK ON YOUR FLYER? THAT'LL SPELL TROUBLE FOR US HOMELESS.
TRASH! SMASH! REVOLT! SUNDAY TOMPKINS
I'M HOMELESS AND I TELL FUNNY STORIES. CAN I BE IN YOUR SHOW?
SEND ME A RESUME AND I'LL GET BACK TO YOU.
YOU SHOULDN'T DISRESPECT AN OLDER MAN. BESIDES, HE IS FUNNY.
HEY! STAY OUT OF MY BUSINESS!
A REAL REVOLUTION WOULD BE TO BRING IN TOOTHBRUSHES, NOT PUNK BANDS.
FUCK YOU!
MY FATHER SAID, "BEWARE THE FALSE PROPHETS AMONG US."

in heaven from a dead sleep. "I guess it's time," he said, putting on his sandals. Descending on a slide made of rainbows, Jesus literally stepped out of heaven and returned to earth.

He walked slowly from door to door, and gun owners, stunned into silence, handed over all firearms without question. "Thank you for not politicizing this issue, Mr. Christ," they said, voices quavering with emotion. "Don't mention it," Jesus replied.

Then Jesus walked to Capitol Hill and addressed Congress. "I came down after I heard all your thoughts and prayers," He explained. "But I guess I'm a little confused. You guys are constantly passing laws in my name — you know, about abortion and gay marriage and whatnot. So I don't get why you couldn't pass laws about guns? But whatever, I guess I'm here now." Congress applauded, and Mike Pence cried.

Riding his golden palomino, Flash, his long brown locks blowing in the wind, Jesus threw all America's guns into a volcano, where they melted down, returning essential elements to the earth. Trees sprouted spontaneously from the nutrient-rich soil. No one was ever shot again. All politicians were spontaneously given Medals of Honor and re-elected.

The thoughts and prayers answered,

Jesus went back to heaven. He had a little trouble getting back to sleep, but eventually nodded off.

—Laura Galaviz
& Michael Gerber

THANKS, BUT NO THANKS.

In honor of Hugh Hefner, here are some captions I've written through the years that I submitted for potential *Playboy* cartoons. They were all rejected.

• "I've heard of Secret Santa, but this is ridiculous!"
• "The strap on your backpack is broken, Miss Andrews. You'll need a new one! A new backpack, that is!"
• "Miss Hendricks! I can't believe you reported me to HR!"
• "I've heard of the search for intelligent life, but this is ridiculous!"
• "Jenkins! Your wife is really something! But you are nothing! *Nothing*."
• "These cookies aren't done. I'll have to put them back in the oven for a few...minutes!"
• "May I — ? Can I — ? Oh, I'm afraid to ask!"
• "I've heard of the dangers of leaving the flue closed when there's a fire in the fireplace, but this is ridiculous!"
• "Well, unfortunately I don't have money to pay for the pizza. How ever shall I pay you back? Oh! Wait. My boyfriend has some cash, I think. Let me get him. Hold on."
• "Your play didn't make a lot of sense to me!"
• "MapQuest led me here: to your pants!"
• "I'm starting to realize why my bookmarked recipes in Epicurious keep disappearing!"
• "I've heard of mutually assured destruction, but this is verging on the ridiculous!"

—Dirk Voetberg

I'M MOVING BACK TO MY PARENTS' CAR.

Your wife. Your kids. Your other kids. Your teenage daughter's third baby. Changing climate. Changing your father-in-law's diaper. Sometimes you wish you could get away. Sometimes you wish you could do it all over. Sometimes you wish you could start again in a town where you don't owe the mayor money.

Overdraft notices. Student loan debt. A $20 late fee from renting *Suburban Commando*. The system is rigged against you, and there's nothing you can do to change it. You tried, but there's only so many times you can chain yourself to a mail truck.

Wanted for a murder you didn't commit. Convicted of an arson that wasn't even fun. Jailed for a crime you only helped videotape. Society is out to get you. The economy is out to get you. The news is out to get you. If you don't act now, it might be too late.

Remember high school? Remember Saturday morning cartoons? Remember when your 11-year-old brother died? Remember that issue of *Hustler* that made you cry? Did anything ever really happen or is everything just a story you tell yourself to help you fall asleep?

Earthquakes, machine guns, cleansing ethnic people. Everywhere you look, the world is in crisis. Everywhere you look, you're still losing your hair.

Store brand soda. Generic cereal. Knock-off crayons. Factory closures, liquidation sales, a law office inside an old Long John Silver's. Did living the American Dream always mean giving away your dignity?

What does one do? Where does one go? There's no shame in admitting defeat. There's no shame in moving back to your parents' car. Hell, they do live in a limousine.

—Osman Siddique

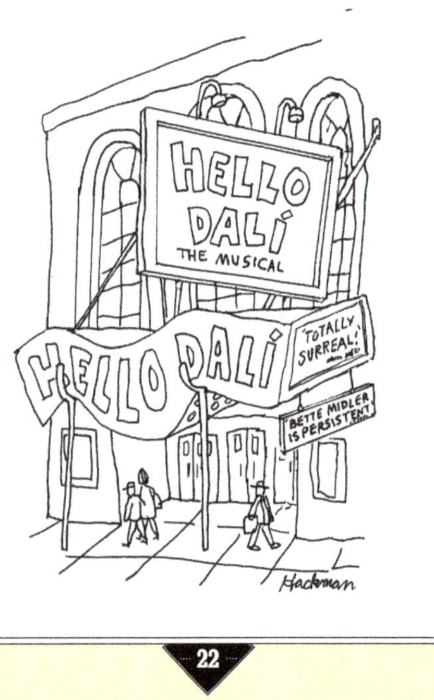

HELLO DALÍ
THE MUSICAL
HELLO DALI
TOTALLY SURREAL!
BETTE MIDLER IS PERSISTENT
Hackman

A TRUE PATRIOT STANDS FOR THE ANTHEM. PERIOD.

America is the greatest country in the world. And that's why, when the national anthem starts playing before a sporting event, I stand with my hand over my heart, facing the flag, contemplating the greatness of this country.

As the game progresses, I continue standing with my hand over my heart, facing the flag. If other fans yell "sit down!" because they can't see the action, I think about how they don't love the country like I do. If they did, they'd be standing, with the anthem playing in their heads. If punches are thrown, I don't care; this is about basic values, right and wrong. Don't even get me started on the players. If they truly loved this country, they wouldn't be wasting their time playing the game that the troops fought for their right to play. They'd be on their feet, clothes torn, bleeding from the nose and mouth, respecting the flag.

After the game ends, I don't leave and go to my car. I continue standing and facing the flag, singing the words to the anthem louder and louder as the stadium staff picks me up and deposits me in the parking lot. Then, when it becomes clear I have no intention of leaving the facility, they carry me to the first public thoroughfare outside of the property line. Still I stand, facing the flag. No matter how far they move me, I remember where that Star-Spangled Banner is.

When the sun rises the next day and it's time for work, I ignore my boss's cellphone calls. If I am fired, so be it. What's more important: this country, or my paycheck? As hunger gnaws at my stomach, I do not move an inch. When I become lightheaded, I concentrate on my love of the Stars and Stripes. People died for that flag, my friend. I do not call and ask my children how school was. I do not contact my sister to find out if she's still in a fight with Dad. I do not concern myself with social and political issues or foot pain or what happened this week on *Scandal*. That's how much I love America.

When my wife shows up, tears in her eyes, asking why I don't come home, I do not pause to turn and explain that I am home, that this is America, that if she doesn't feel at home here maybe she should consider socialist Scandinavia. In my heart, I divorce her. I keep standing on my weakening legs and struggle to keep my eyes open — red, white and blue flooding my rods and cones.

When the TV crew comes, I do not stop to explain what I'm doing, or why. I sing the little-known second verse to myself and have faith that true patriots will understand. I disregard the so-called reporter's biased questions about "a sense of proportion" and "mania" and "the completely intolerable odor of urine and feces, oh dear lord it is awful." What do you expect from the liberal media?

After I collapse and slip into a coma, my mind continues the salute. The anthem continues to play and Old Glory blocks all else from my vision. I do not know who my family is, what I do, where I came from. I do not know my own name. I only know that I love America, and what I love about America is a flag and a song.

—Jonathan Zeller

AN APOLOGY

I'd like to formally apologize to the entire company for the email I sent earlier today. I did not mean to hit "Reply All."

Though some of you were offended, I was merely communicating, in a natural, human way, my overall frustration with the direction of our business — just as someone might raise their voice, or perhaps toss off a colorful phrase in the heat of the moment. Or throw chairs across a conference room, or hurl a plate in the kitchen. And, just as we clean up shattered dishes and haul wrecked Aerons to the Dumpster out next to the loading dock, so too must I own up to my intemperate speech.

"Those assholes in biz dev" are obviously not "worthless." It is common knowledge that every human being contains roughly fifteen dollars in chemicals. Not to mention lots of water which, in a sad commentary on our stewardship of the environment, becomes more precious each and every day. *Ten percent of the world does not have access to clean drinking water.* That is much more worth your outrage than an obviously misdelivered email fired off after-hours by an overworked and underappreciated CEO.

Similarly, everyone in Marketing is not "a writhing mass of backstabbing snakes." This doesn't even make sense. How can a snake hold a knife, much less plunge it into someone?

Perhaps this company-wide inability (or unwillingness) to distinguish fact from fiction is at the root of our recent slide? I don't know, I'm just spitballing.

Obviously, our Research and Development department should not *necessarily* be "amputated like a gangrenous limb." Maybe we can spin them off as a separate division which can function autonomously — somewhere far, far away from the rest of us. Perhaps in a multiverse, or some newly discovered exoplanet?

It is clear that Operations did everything within their power to meet the deadline for our recent product launch. But their "power" is, we all must agree, roughly equivalent to an ant under a magnifying glass burned alive by focused sunlight. Maybe I'm overestimating a bit.

I cannot believe I have to say this, but on the advice of counsel, here it is: I do not honestly believe Ops should "kidnap schoolchildren and force them to pack shipments." That would be both illegal, and result in costly errors.

Finally, having apologized to those I specifically admonished, I must address those divisions not mentioned in the email. Many of you have written that you feel "left out."

I can only say this: I will get you next time.

—Lee Sachs

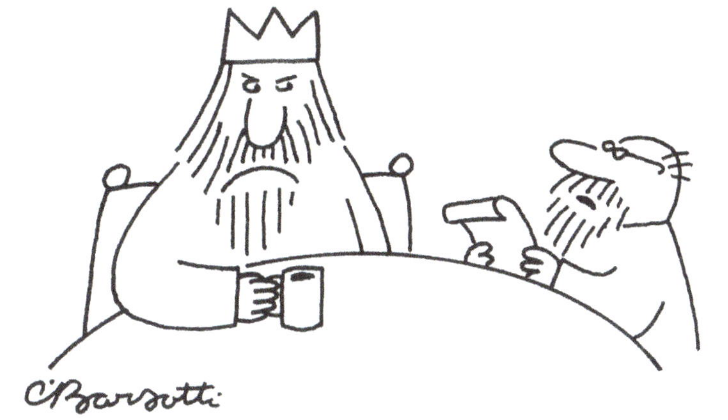
C Barsotti

"How much news will we be wanting this morning, sire?"

AMERICA WITH GUN CONTROL: A PLAY IN ONE ACT.

ACT 1

SCENE 1

MAN and WOMAN sit on a couch.

MAN: Were there any mass shootings today?

WOMAN: No.

MAN: Excellent.

The MAN and WOMAN sit there, living.

WOMAN: Would you like to have intercourse?

MAN: Yes, I would like to have intercourse.

WOMAN: Me, too. Let us begin the intercourse.

They have excellent intercourse.

BLACKOUT.

—Zack Bornstein

STREET SEEN.

—Lisa Donnelly

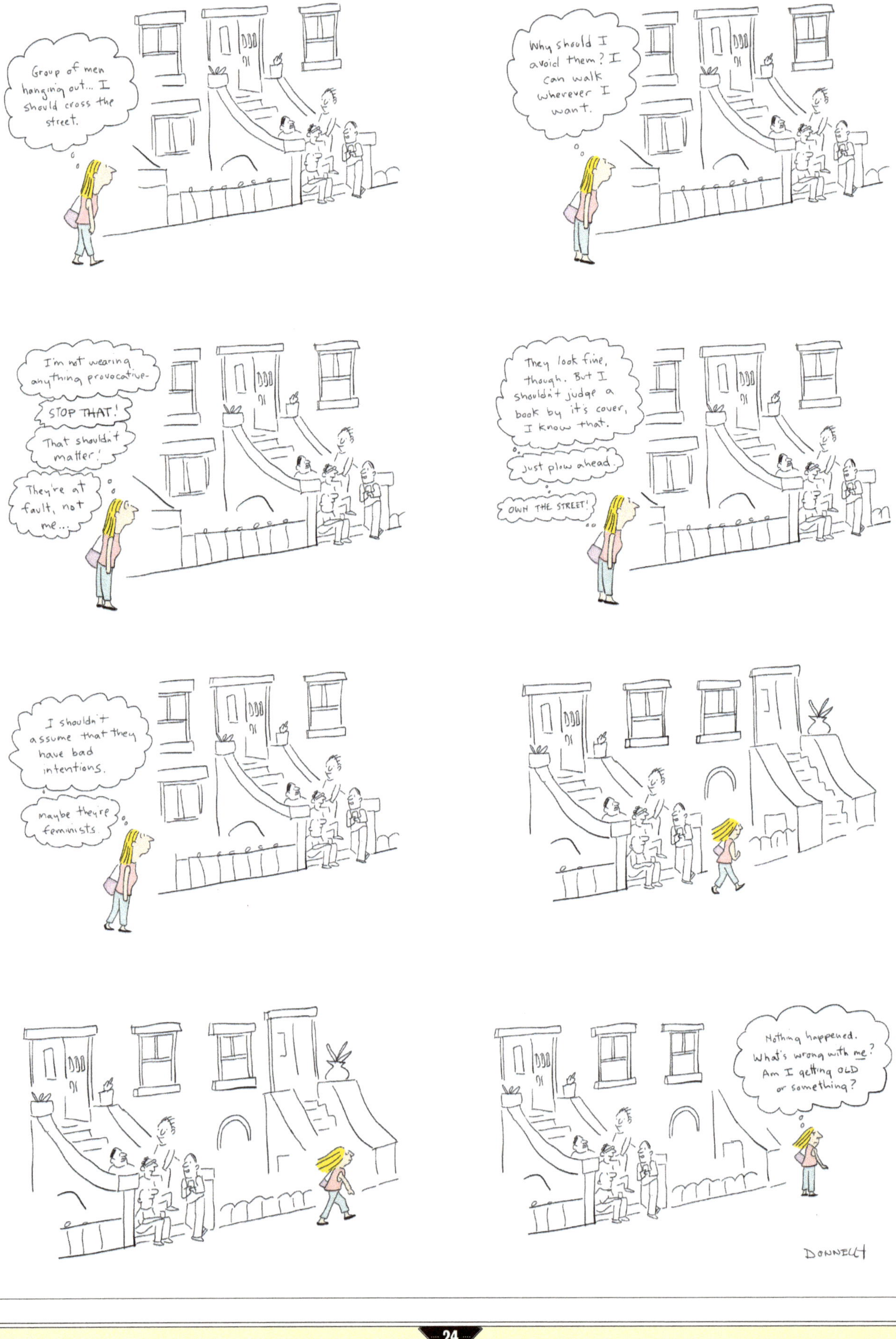

Group of men hanging out... I should cross the street.
Why should I avoid them? I can walk wherever I want.
I'm not wearing anything provocative-
STOP THAT!
That shouldn't matter!
They're at fault, not me...
They look fine, though. But I shouldn't judge a book by it's cover, I know that.
Just plow ahead.
OWN THE STREET!
I shouldn't assume that they have bad intentions.
Maybe they're feminists.
Nothing happened. What's wrong with me? Am I getting OLD or something?
DONNELLY

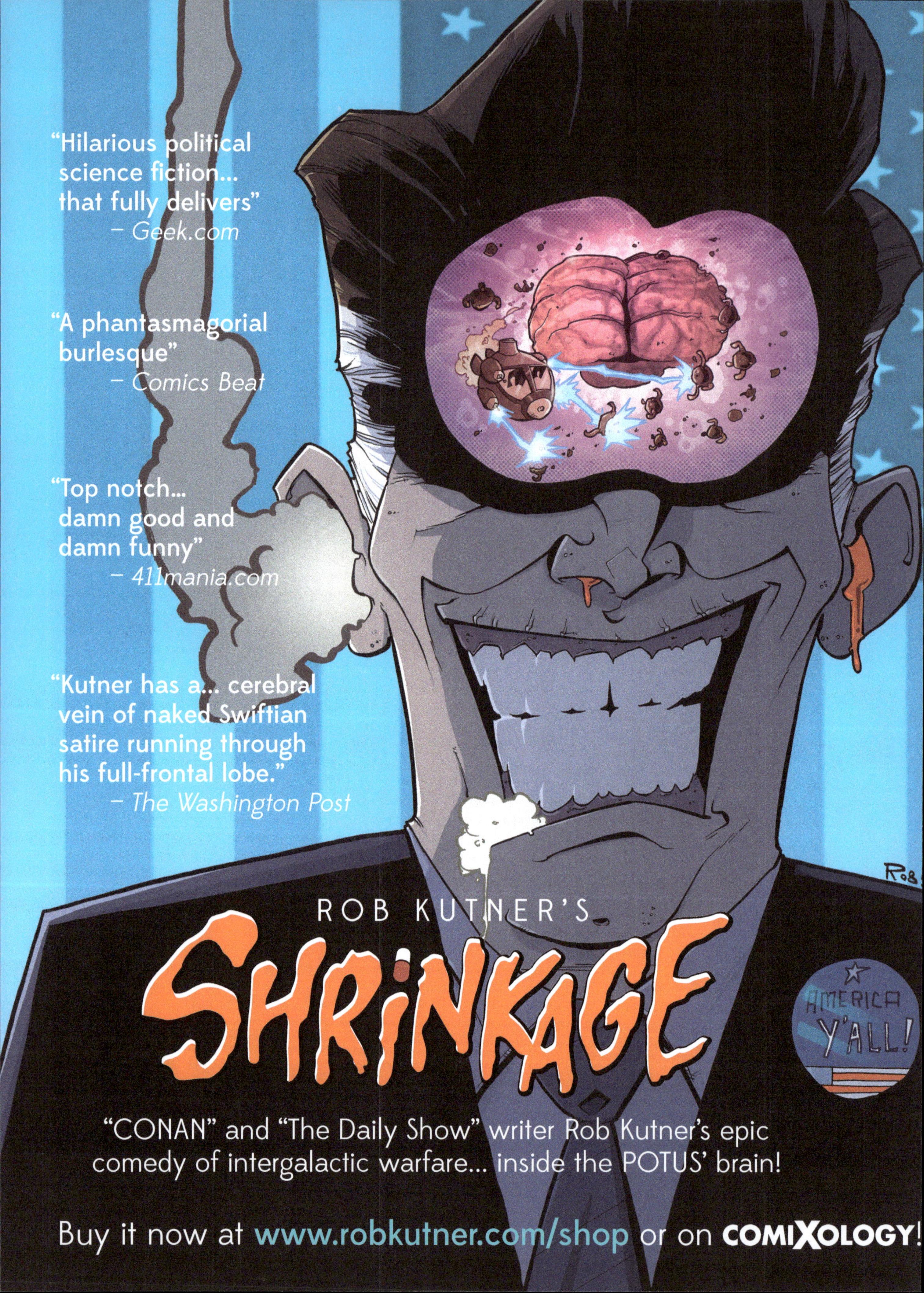
"Hilarious political science fiction... that fully delivers"
– Geek.com
"A phantasmagorial burlesque"
– Comics Beat
"Top notch... damn good and damn funny"
– 411mania.com
"Kutner has a... cerebral vein of naked Swiftian satire running through his full-frontal lobe."
– The Washington Post
ROB KUTNER'S
SHRINKAGE
AMERICA Y'ALL!
"CONAN" and "The Daily Show" writer Rob Kutner's epic comedy of intergalactic warfare... inside the POTUS' brain!
Buy it now at www.robkutner.com/shop or on COMIXOLOGY!

CHARACTER COUNTS
BY ED SUBITZKY

Young George Washington
Don't believe ye lamestream media

"Father, I cannot tell a lie. I chopped down the cherry tree.

Also, I'm the one who set the puppies and the kittens on fire.

Also, I copped a feel from Aunt Esmeralda while she was pouring tea.

Also, I gave Grandpa Arnold turpentine and told him it came from your liquor cabinet.

Also, I had sex with Cousin Alice.

Also, after Alice got sick, I had sex with her mule.

Also, I shot your favorite horse, cooked it and shared it with the Indians.

Also, I French-kissed a salamander just to see what it was like.

Also, I stole the money you keep in the drawer and used it to buy funny-smelling cigarettes from a sailor.

Also, sometimes I dress in girls' clothes when no one is looking.

Also, I read Page 62 of *Lady Chatterley's Lover* out loud to Mother.

Also, I told Aunt Abigail that my penis is bigger than a cucumber.

Also, I performed bodily acts known only in China with various members of the militia.

Also, I tripped Old Man Burns while he was carrying eggs for the orphanage.

Also, I tied the school principal to a tree and pushed on him until he passed gas.

Also, I described my bodily functions in great detail to one of our slaves.

Also, on Sundays, I let the pastor do strange things to my ankles.

Also, I paid the old witch in the swamp to put a curse on the kids who laugh at my haircut.

Also, I robbed the general store and made the owner try to eat one of his saddles.

Also, I made No. 2 on my teacher's desk after he told me I had to take an exam again.

Also, I tried to guess what Mary Smith's breasts look like.

Also, I asked Mary Smith if I could touch her breasts and when she slapped me, I spit at her.

Also, when the Army marched through town, I paid them to step on old lady Millicent.

Also, I put a snake up Grandma Lucille's nose after she had passed out from laughing at Grandpa Oscar's limp.

Also, I wrote a dirty inscription in the family bible that involved a carrot.

Also, instead of churning the butter, I churned some little kid from town whom I didn't know.

Also, I asked Doc Jones if he knew how to remove a rolling pin from my large intestine.

Also, I stole his stethoscope so I could hear you and Mother having sex through the wall.

Also, I went to the town library and looked up all the dirty words Uncle Preston uses.

Also, I set up a bordello in the barn and overcharged Benjamin Franklin and Thomas Jefferson.

Also, I tried to stuff a hibernating bear into the outhouse.

Also, I told little sister the bogeyman would get her and when she cried, I threw her out the window.

Also, instead of doing my homework after school, I hid behind the haystack and tried to tickle a turtle.

Also, I fed a live rooster to a coyote and then looked at someone's feet.

Also, when you said someday I might be president of the country, I laughed so hard that I wet my pants all the way up to the drawstring.

Also, I chopped down an apple tree, too.

And a pear tree.

In fact, I chopped down every tree I could find anywhere."

"Son, I'm very proud of you for not telling a lie."

ED SUBITZKY *was a stalwart of* **The National Lampoon** *and its* **Radio Hour,** *and later appeared frequently on* **Letterman.** *Currently, he also contributes to* **The Journal of Consciousness Studies.**

NEFARIOUS
BY LARS KENSETH

THE DETAILS OF MY ESCAPE
I am always two steps ahead of you. Or maybe three.

Greetings from nowhere. It is I, Lars Kenseth. Shocked, are we? You thought me dead, didn't you? Well, if death is sipping regionally specific alcoholic beverages while basking in the splendor of an unspecified location, then I guess I *am* dead.

No, you'll never know where I am...but that isn't what vexes you, is it? It's *how*. How did I do it? Your consternation and befuddlement pleases me to no end, but I suppose I've tortured you long enough, hmm? Here are the answers to the questions that have terrorized your mind, lo these many months. Here are the details of my escape.

I dug my 200-yard tunnel with an old shoe that I fashioned into a crude spade. Its beaten, supple leather turned rigid through a petrification method that I developed after watching Alton Brown make an extremely resilient meringue.

I never used cash or credit while I was on the run. Instead I turned to the only truly untraceable form of payment: iTunes gift cards. Who gave that to you? Your aunt? Or was it Mom? No one knows.

Rather than do the expected and leave no fingerprints, I left fingerprints everywhere. I spent one hour every day for the past two years touching everything I saw. Go ahead, think of something I couldn't possibly have touched. Guess what? I touched it. And I'm not sorry.

I evaded your search dogs by hiding myself in an oversized novelty coffee tin. I still have 18 grams of house blend in my lungs, which my new foreign doctor tells me is harmless. Plus, I can make a latte by coughing into a cup of warm milk.

I used a squadron of look-alikes — doubles trained to confuse you and your investigative team. Chiefly by making them move across the street from you and become beloved by neighbors and extended family alike. Then people would say: "Why are you so harsh to the Larses? They seem so nice!" And you would have to smile through your rage and agree, lest you look petty and unfair. *Ha.*

I gave myself reconstructive plastic surgery, so as to turn potentially suspicious looks into shameful averted gazes. No one stares too long at a botched facial surgery, which makes it the only truly perfect disguise. I also did this to save money. I'm not made of iTunes gift cards.

Do you finally see whom you are dealing with? Is the terrible picture becoming clear to you now? NO, IT ISN'T, because that tunnel I mentioned before? *It was a decoy.* I actually just crawled out an open window. And ran away.

You almost had me near the outdoor market. We locked eyes. Then I seemed to vanish into thin air as a bus drove by. Truth is, I actually just jumped into a nearby trash can to make it look like I was mysterious. I sat there for 45 minutes doing the crossword on my phone.

Remember that weekend your wife came back home after two years apart and said she wanted to reconcile? That was just a distraction. Also, that wasn't your wife — it was one of my doubles. Some plastic surgery is worth paying for, you know?

Oh, and I heard that you recently renewed your vows. Congratulations…?

Rather than use the phone or internet, I brainwashed a young street urchin into thinking he was a carrier pigeon. He would carry my notes near and far. And sometimes, he'd even come back.

I trained myself to evolve chameleonlike abilities. My skin tone can range from "mother of pearl" to "light olive," which means I can walk freely and without fear through hundreds of Greek and Russian restaurants.

I've visited 924 different post offices that feature my wanted poster and wrote "Forget it, we got 'em!" on every single one.

My in-depth knowledge of bad acting classes means I can pose as a tree almost anywhere for 15 minutes. Which is why when I made it into Angeles National Forest, it was over. I was *gone*.

Hear those sirens approaching? They're for you. The police, Interpol, the FBI — they all think I paid you off, that you were my inside man. Impossible, you say? Ridiculous, you cry? Look in your desktop drawer. There are enough iTunes gift cards there to put you away for life.

And to think, this could have all been avoided if you'd just treated my HBO GO login with *respect*. ■

LARS KENSETH *(@larskenseth) is a cartoonist for* **The New Yorker**, *a Sundance Fellow and is currently baking a big loaf of weird for* **Adult Swim**. *Feel free to troll him on Instagram.*

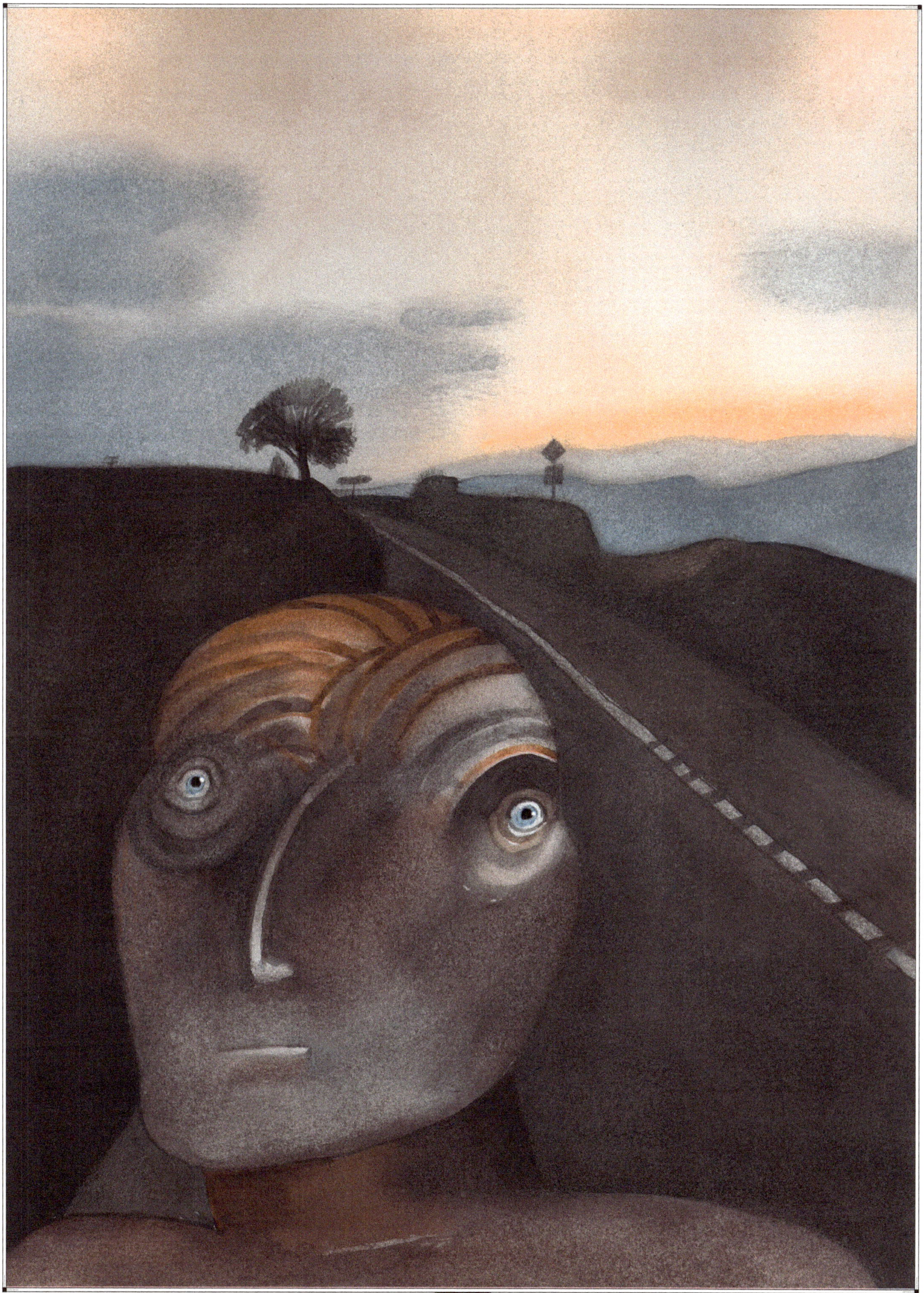

ETIENNE DELESSERT

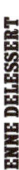

WELLNESS

BY STEVE YOUNG

TIPS FOR STAYING HYDRATED

Eight glasses a day just won't cut it

Dehydration is a serious health concern, especially in hot weather, and mild weather and cold weather. Each year several million Americans die of dehydration. There aren't enough properly hydrated gravediggers to keep up.

After I wrote that first paragraph, I paused to drink a very large amount of water. No joke. You might think that sitting indoors and writing won't lead to dehydration, but that's the kind of dangerous assumption that can kill you. People die of dehydration while watching TV, sleeping, bathing, even reading articles about staying hydrated.

The facts are simple. The human body is composed almost entirely of water. The parts that aren't water are for the most part extremely damp. Water evaporates, and damp things dry out. You need a constant high-volume intake of water, watery fluids, and dampness in order to survive.

It's not enough to "have an occasional drink of water." The graveyards are full of people who learned that the hard way. Did you know that when you drink a 12-ounce glass of water, the exertion of drinking and swallowing that water can dangerously dehydrate you?

We've all been told that fact, but you probably didn't remember it, because you're dehydrated, and you go through life delirious. Your brain, which ideally should be dripping wet, most likely resembles a sponge that was wrung out and left on the edge of the sink an hour ago. The sponge will be okay. But you won't be.

Excuse me while I pause to drink more water. You should, too. Drink more than you think you need, or want. Then drink more.

Develop good hydration habits, like carrying a five-gallon jug of water with you at all times, even if you're just going from your living room to your bathroom. Speaking of bathrooms, urinating dehydrates you. Don't do it.

Remember when I mentioned that the human body is mostly water? I'm not saying that if you're dehydrated and there's no jug of water handy, you should resort to cannibalism… but I'm not saying you shouldn't, either. Keep in mind that some dehydrated person out there may be scheming right now to kill you and drink your damp, watery blood. They'll probably drop dead of dehydration before they can get around to killing you, but what if…? You must be vigilant.

Yes, keeping yourself well hydrated is a stressful burden. And the stress can make you sick. Right now I don't feel so good… okay, I just vomited. Don't say it's because I drank too much water, because that can't be true. We're not having that conversation. Now, obviously I lost a lot of dampness when I vomited, and I'll need to take a few moments to replenish. I'm going to drink a jug of water and get whatever moisture I can from the sponge over by the sink. Maybe I'll re-moisten the sponge with water from the jug.

Ahh, that's better. But not good enough. Never good enough. You're lucky you're not here with me right now, because to supplement my water intake I would be inclined to kill you and drink your life-giving blood. It's nothing personal. Unless you're a dehydration denier. Then you deserve to die.

Remember when I mentioned early on that there's a shortage of gravediggers? That's partly my fault. I've killed a few for their blood. Usually I just drink jugs of water, but when it's hot, mild or cold, you have to resort to extreme measures. Even if it means killing those who provide a vital service to the dead. And when another gravedigger arrives to dig the dead gravedigger's grave, bang, I get him, too. It's a law of nature: drink or be drunk.

I'm not a monster. I have ethical standards. If a gravedigger has a jug of water with him, I attack him just to take the water. Of course I can't allow him to identify me as a water robber. So I have to kill him. And because killing someone involves a lot of physical exertion, I get even more dehydrated and have to resort to drinking his blood.

Did I mention that I'm writing this from prison? I'm in solitary confinement. They're pretty good about providing enough water, but human blood is hard to come by in here. I've thought about drinking my own blood, but — come on — that would be ridiculous.

Follow these tips and you'll enjoy vibrant, well-hydrated health.

I am feeling a strong urge to urinate, but I'm going to fight it.

(This piece was originally published in "Lock 'N Talk," the weekly newsletter of the U.S. "Supermax" penitentiary in Florence, Colo.)

STEVE YOUNG *(@pantssteve) is a veteran* **Letterman** *writer who's also written for* **The Simpsons***. He recently worked on NBC's* **Maya & Marty** *variety show and is teaching a course at NYU's Tisch School.*

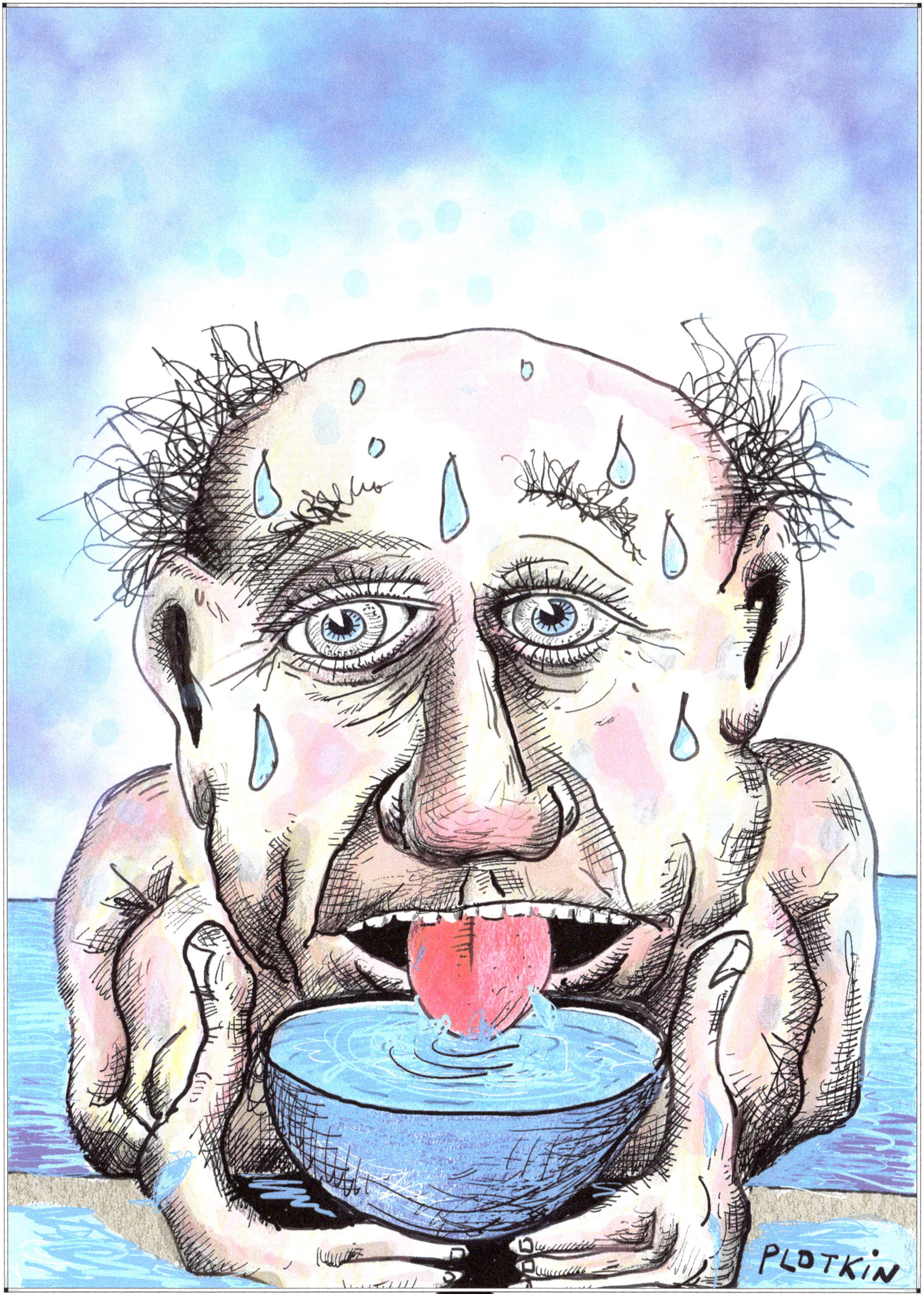
PLOTKIN

JONATHAN PLOTKIN

FARE PLAY
BY JOE KEOHANE

INTRODUCING YOUR NEW MTA!
It's gonna be really great, the best in the world. You're gonna love it.

Here at New York's Metropolitan Transportation Authority, we believe in choice. That's why, as a thank you to our loyal customers for their patience during a very challenging summer, and to fund ongoing improvements to our system's aging infrastructure, we're very excited to introduce MTA 2030™: four new transit experiences that will offer unprecedented choice and world-class amenities for riders of the MTA.

MTA PLATINUM™

First, MTA Platinum Members enjoy access to over 250 new, air-conditioned MTA Lounges, where they can enjoy complimentary snacks and premium beverages while they wait for their trains.

Once those trains arrive, MTA Platinum Members will then be personally escorted to their cars by an MTA Gold Red Cap™. Velvet blindfolds will be made available for this journey, as well as noise-canceling headphones in the event of a busker. Once inside, MTA Platinum Members will be escorted to their sumptuous, 700-square-foot private MTA Platinum cabins, which are equipped with reclining chairs, televisions, private restrooms, Wi-Fi, phone chargers, coffee and tea service, and sound- and odor-proofed door and walls. If desired, a shade may be opened via touchscreen, allowing the MTA Platinum Member to gaze out at commuters who are not MTA Platinum Members, and, if desired, address them via personal intercom system.

Upon arrival at their destination, MTA Platinum Members will be spirited to the nearest lounge, toweled, perfumed and admired, before being transported to street level via private elevator—all the while luxuriating in the assurance that no matter what they do, nothing bad will ever happen to them. *($10,000/month)*

MTA GOLD™

MTA Gold Members enjoy access to over 250 MTA Lounges, and guaranteed seating in one of the MTA Gold Cars™. These cars contain six premium cabins, which accommodate no more than six verified MTA Gold Members at a time, are equipped with reclining chairs, Wi-Fi, phone chargers, sound- and odor-proofed door and walls, and PA systems that clearly announce station stops. *($5,000/month)*

MTA SILVER™

MTA Silver Members enjoy 24-hour access to the world-famous MTA system (when available), on our MTA Silver Trains™, which offer select dry seats, occasional air-conditioning, intercoms that issue random muffled noises that may or may not be about terrorism, a reasonable level of cleanliness, and no more than three creeps per car. *($1,000/month)*

MTA STANDARD™

MTA Standard Members enjoy randomized access to the MTA system. After entering via platforms that are hot and wet year-round, MTA Standard Members are directed to MTA Standard Cars™, which offer amenities such as unlimited creeps, clutches of cruel, screaming teenagers, spread-legged men who smell like ham, bedbugs, people eating fish from Styrofoam containers while blocking the doorways, strange blank-faced travelers shoving their way from car to car for no known reason, and strange puddles that crawl agonizingly back and forth across the grimy floor, back and forth, as the train lurches, and stops, lurches and stops, pitching suddenly into total darkness for minutes at a time so creeps can lean against you and smell your hair, and a breakdancer can kick you in the neck, and the conductor can spew his vengeful lies to this helpless, writhing mass of human misery fused stickily together in this metal box. And did someone just stick a finger in your ear? You'd better hope that was a finger, buddy. Where are you now? Will you ever get where you're going? Where *are* you going? Does any of it matter? The answer, we're sorry to say, is no, no, no. *($2.75/ride; baggage, pet and children fees apply)* **B**

JOE KEOHANE
is a NYC-based journalist whose work has appeared in many publications of varying repute over the years--from **Esquire** *and* **The New Yorker**, *to several others that he will never cop to.*

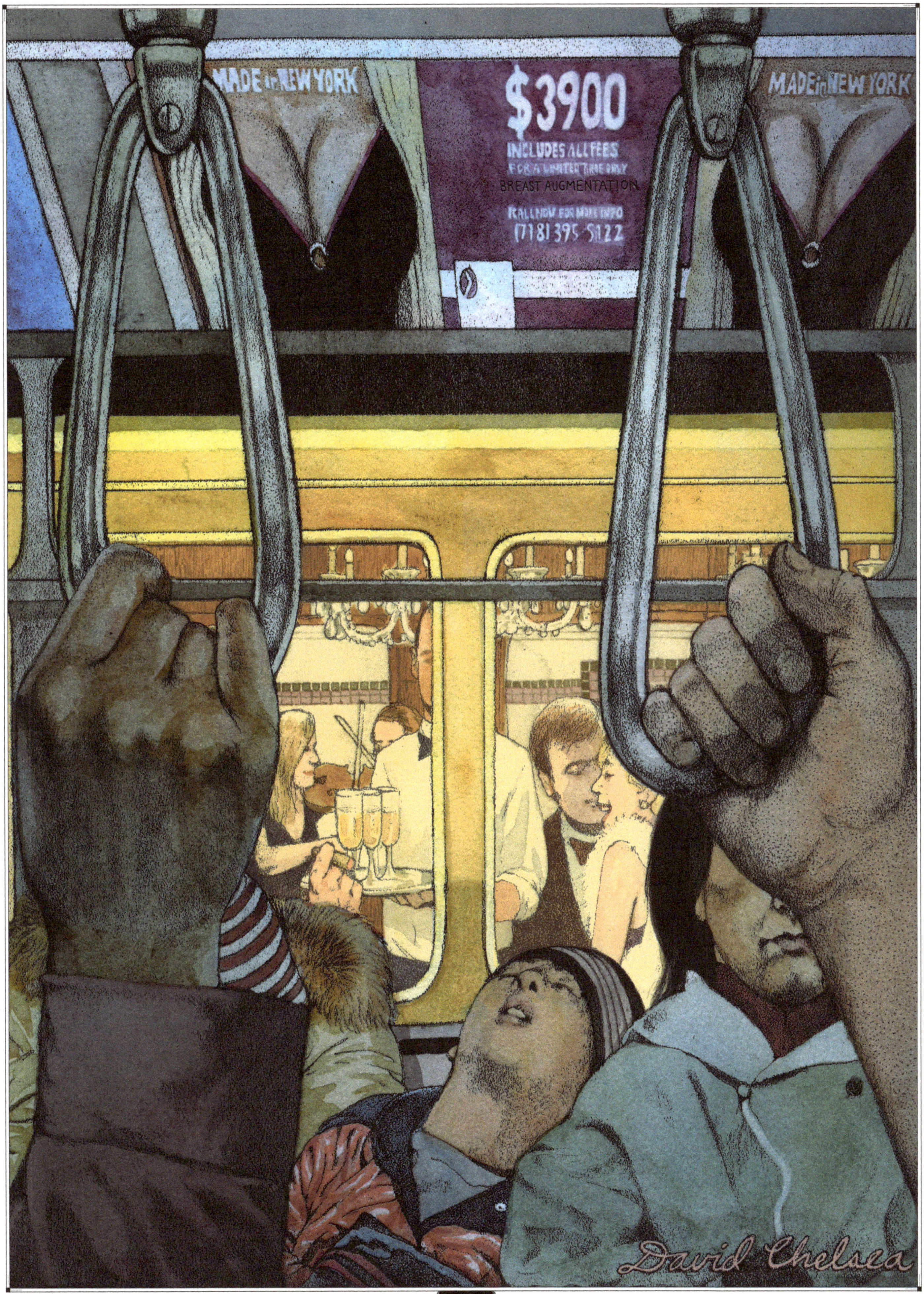
MADE in NEW YORK
$3900
INCLUDES ALL FEES
BREAST AUGMENTATION
(718) 395-5122
MADE in NEW YORK
David Chelsea

F.U., E.T.

BY EVAN WAITE & RIVER CLEGG

HUMAN SOCIETY DEFENSIVELY EXPLAINED TO ALIENS

Welcome to Earth! Care for a beer?

Beer? Oh, it's a thing we drink to make ourselves feel good, even though it almost always makes us feel bad. It's really popular. Sometimes we go into special buildings where they serve beer. The beer costs much more to obtain inside these buildings, but we accept this because there are often attractive people in there that we would like to kiss.

Kissing is when we put our tongues inside each other's mouths and hope not to catch a disease.

No, you sound gross.

This? It's a gym bag; I was about to go to the gym. Gyms are unpleasant buildings where we lift heavy things called weights. This process is boring and excruciating, but it makes our arms slightly larger, which we like.

No, it makes perfect sense. I can tell you don't lift because your tentacles are thin and puny.

Can you repeat that? Your high-pitched alien whine is difficult to detect for my muscular human ears.

It's a newspaper. The headline is about one of our many wars. War is horrible, but sometimes it's necessary because we need oil. We could all just share the oil and live in peace, but we definitely won't do that.

Because we don't feel like it.

Oil is this black liquid deep in the ground made of crushed dinosaur bones and stuff. We use it for energy.

Obviously the sun could provide us with more energy — it's the sun! But we don't know what to do with that information.

Because we refuse to invest in solar energy. It's impractical. Or too expensive. I forget which.

Solar-powered spacecraft? That's nice. Good for you.

STEPHEN KRONINGER

Yes, we're aware that global warming could lead to our extinction. What's your point?

Look, we'd just rather subsidize oil companies, okay? They need money, too!

Money is inedible green paper that we value above all else.

No, you seem stupid.

Maybe Earth isn't for you. Nothing personal, but aliens should stay with their own kind. Human cultures aren't usually too welcoming to newcomers anyway. We even have a name for it: *xenophobia*.

Of course it's illogical! You think we don't know that? We start the word with an x even though it sounds like a z. We embrace the illogical! We make choices *because* they're meanspirited and self-destructive! Take a look at human art sometime. *The Iliad* is basically about some Greek guys who kill each other because they're insecure about the size of their genitals.

Yeah, we know that's a stupid thing to worry about! And it's without a doubt the human male's biggest preoccupation! My ex Carol said I was the biggest she's ever had! Call her up if you don't believe me.

God, talking to you is a pain in my ass. And before you ask, God is a symbol we've created to make sense of our loneliness in an uncaring, empty universe. We know there's no actual proof He exists.

Wait. Seriously? You guys have God, too?

And He sent you to convert our species?

Nah, we're good.

Your God can make my penis even bigger?

This changes things.

EVAN WAITE (@theohbits) is a staff writer on Comedy Central's **The President Show**. He has also written for **The Onion, The New Yorker, Funny or Die** and **Kevin Hart's Guide to Black History**.

RIVER CLEGG (@RiverClegg) is a staff writer on Comedy Central's **The Opposition With Jordan Klepper**. He also writes for **The Onion, ClickHole, The New Yorker** and **McSweeney's**.

DIARIO DE OAXACA

PETER KUPER

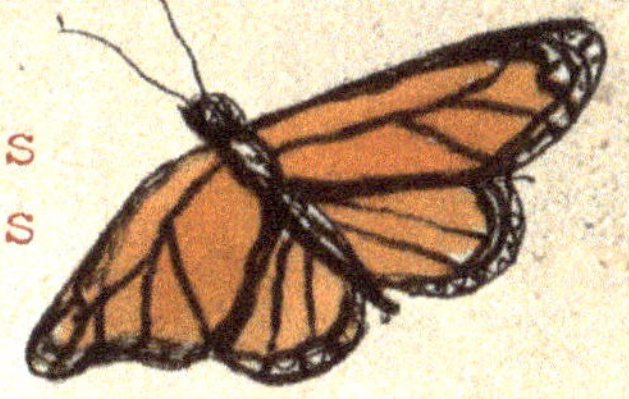

Diario de Oaxaca is artist Peter Kuper's chronicle of two years living in Oaxaca, Mexico, encountering its modern conflicts against the backdrop of the country's ageless beauty and enduring rhythms. From a town held hostage by soldiers to the miracle of the monarch butterfly sanctuary, Kuper renders his experiences in vivid detail, capturing both the light and shadows that define life in Mexico

DIARIO DE
OAXACA
PETER KUPER
A SKETCHBOOK JOURNAL OF TWO YEARS IN
MEXICO
Introduction by Martin Solares

"Kuper is a colossus; I have been in awe of him for over 20 years. Teachers and students everywhere take heart: Kuper has in these pages borne witness to our seemingly endless struggle to educate and to be educated in the face of institutions that really don't give a damn. In this ruined age we need Kuper's unsparing compassionate visionary artistry like we need hope."
-Junot Díaz

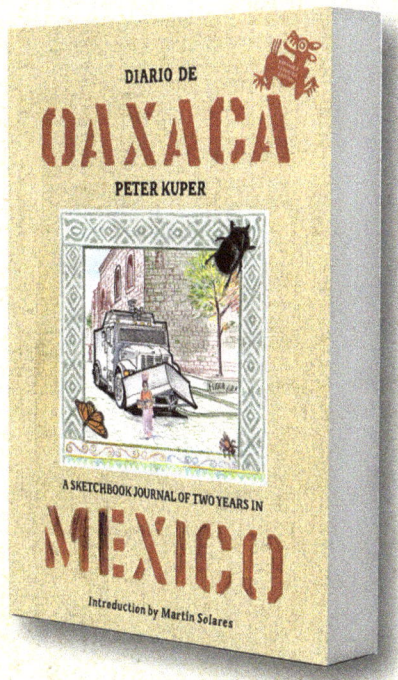

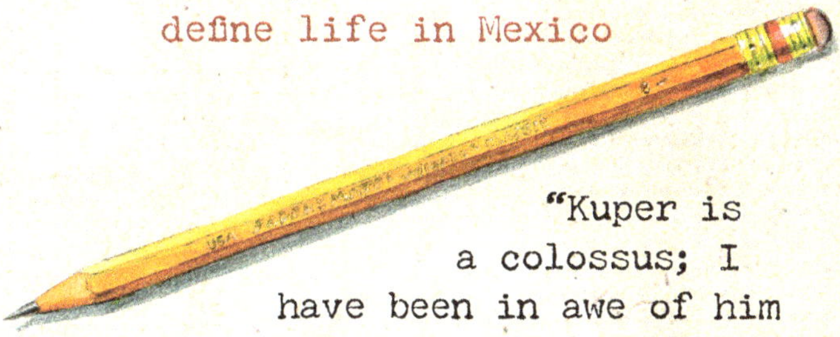

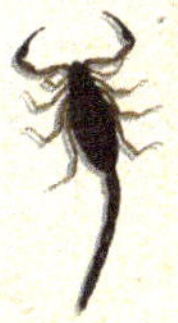

$24.95

978-1-62963-441-8

available at www.pmpress.org

American Bystander readers save 40% on your next PM Press order with coupon code: BYSTANDER

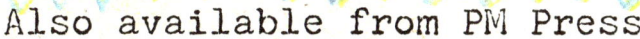

Also available from PM Press

PETER KUPER
Drawn To New York

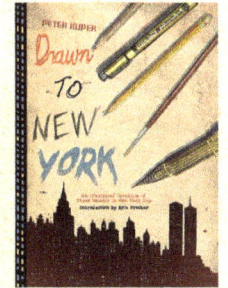

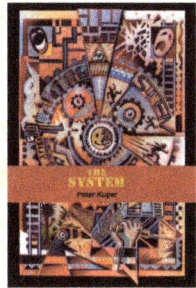

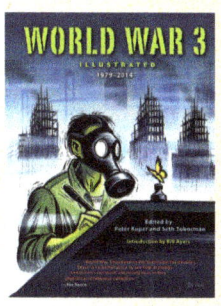

Drawn to New York:
An Illustrated Chronicle of
Three Decades in New York City

Peter Kuper

The Sytem

WORLD WAR 3
ILLUSTRATED
1979-2014

World War 3 Illustrated:
1979-2014

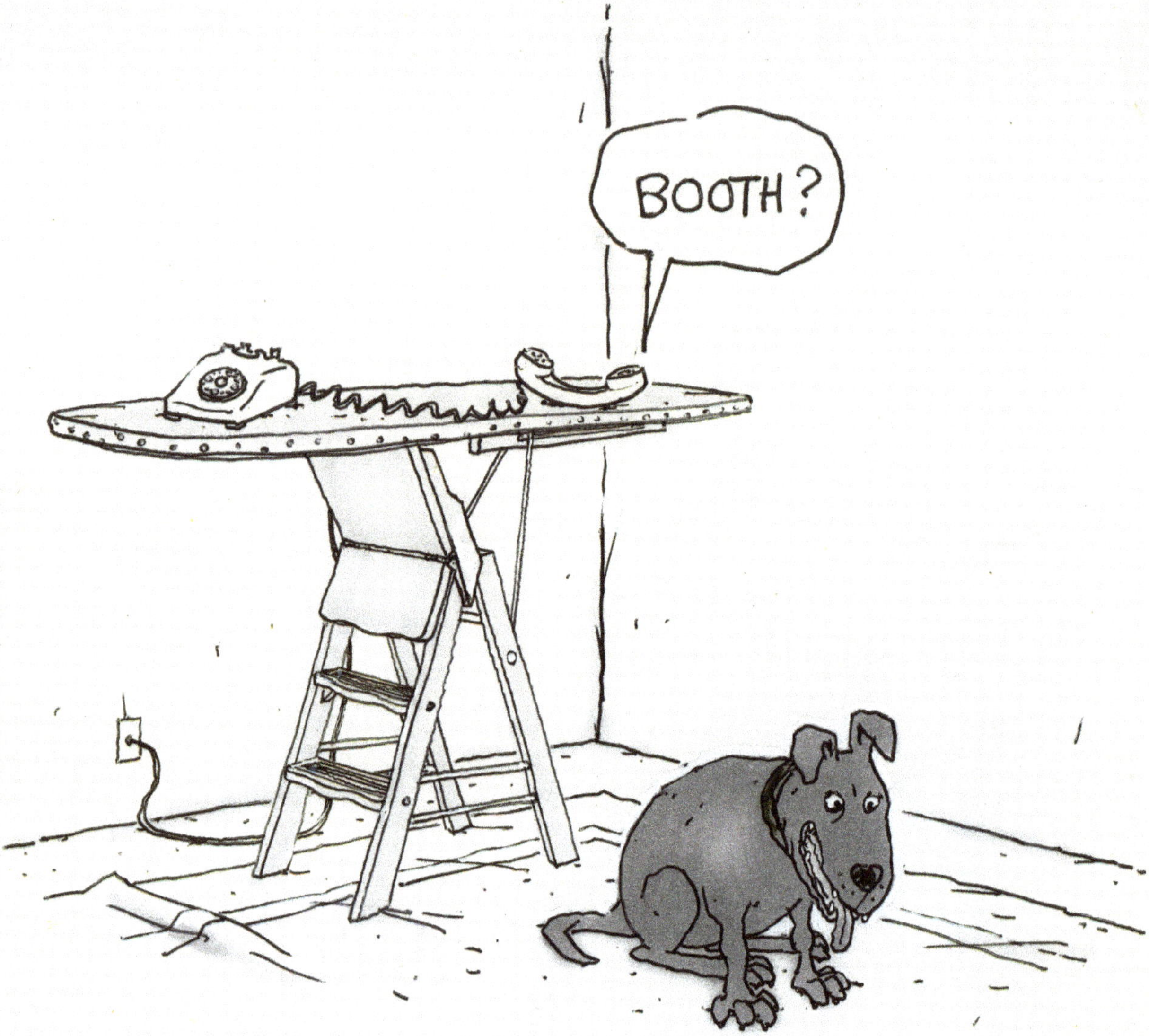
BOOTH?

George Booth — A Cartoonist's Life

Curated by J.J. Sedelmaier • October 24th to December 30th, 2017

OPENING RECEPTION Friday evening, October 27th at 6:30 p.m. There will be a cash bar, with a suggested donation of $10. Your generous donation will benefit the Society's arts programming & exhibitions.

The Society of Illustrators 128 East 63rd Street, NY, NY. (212) 838-2560 *info@societyillustrators.org*

Comedy of Manners

"We really are very decent, polite people," Paul said.

Ellen sipped her Scotch. Paul turned his wine glass slowly on the paper cocktail napkin, spreading a spilled drop into a red circle.

"I don't know why we couldn't have chosen someplace nicer," Ellen said.

"She said she wanted to buy us dinner," Paul said. "I was trying to be polite."

"Still. We could have gone somewhere decent and then insisted on picking up the bill."

"This is decent," Paul said.

"You know what I mean," Ellen said.

"You mean you prefer the 18-year-old Macallan to the 12."

Ellen gave him the look that meant, you're not at all funny, and then said, "This is Dewar's." Then, responding to his apologetic shrug, "They have 12 and 18. But if she's buying . . ."

"We really are very decent, polite people," Paul said. He sipped his wine.

"Is she late?"

"We're early."

"I should've gotten the Macallan and paid for it separately."

"You still can."

"Too late." She didn't quite nod toward the front of the restaurant and Paul turned to see Lindsay out there on the sidewalk, beyond the glass, moving toward the door. He read the body language as best he could, but there wasn't much to go on and he could never tell the difference between chilly and irritable anyway. Or needing to pee.

In hushed tones, a hurried whisper, Ellen said, "Don't push her about grad school." Lindsay came toward them and then Paul was up, out of his seat to watch her approach.

He took in her coat, slouchy soft in a way that suggested it had been expensive originally. He imagined her, out there in Los Angeles, going through the racks at thrift stores, keeping up appearances. She looked thin, too. Fit. He opened his arms and she hugged him affectionately, smelling of shampoo and autumn.

Ellen remained seated so that Lindsay had to lean over her shoulder to kiss her, and Ellen returned the kiss awkwardly, patted a conveniently placed hand and gestured for one of the empty seats at the four-top.

Lindsay said, "Actually, can we — " She turned to a passing waiter: "Can we move to that booth in the back? Is that going to mess things up for you guys?"

"That's fine. Let me just — " He looked at Lindsay, saw something in her demeanor that altered his tone and said, "I'll let your server know." He hurried off as though he'd been sent on a very important errand. Ellen stood up and collected her drink.

Paul lifted his coat from the back of the chair where he'd draped it, grabbed Ellen's coat as well and then said, "Would you grab my wine, baby girl?"

Lindsay said: "It's okay, Dad. They'll bring it over."

"I don't like to make extra work for them. Would you?"

Lindsay sighed a sigh that held in it a lifetime of tiny battles lost, tiny points conceded. She picked up the wine. She also picked up the circle-stained cocktail napkin to avoid that additional moment of dialogue. Ellen was already on her way to the back booth with a forced cheer in her gait to indicate a false lack of irritation at the displacement. Lindsay and Paul followed.

They settled in.

"So," Paul said as an opening probe, "You're in town."

"Yes," Lindsay said. "Just for a couple of nights."

"Working," Paul said.

"Yes."

"Is this a television thing?" Ellen asked. "Or one of those other things?"

"What other things?"

"Sometimes you do those other — what do you call them? You know what I'm talking about, Paul. Borging or something."

"Blogging?" Lindsay asked.

"Right! Those."

Lindsay said, "I was a blogger for three years, Mom. For

Dylan Brody *is a playwright and humorist, poet and snappy dresser. Don't ask him about his tie. He'll talk for an hour about the Plattsburgh knot.*

a travel site. I know you read at least some of the posts."

"I did read some of them. You know. On the computer. When you sent me the thing to click on."

Paul winced.

"The links?" Lindsay asked.

Ellen said: "Right! The links to the blogging! All the new language. It really is something. Anyway, I only read them on the computer. You know. Where you scroll through and read all the text and see the pictures and it's all just on one long page."

Lindsay said, "As opposed to what, Mom?"

Ellen said, "I didn't go out and try to find copies of the – you know – the actual thing."

Paul said, "Ellen."

Ellen said, "What?"

Lindsay said, "What actual thing?"

Ellen said: "You know. The magazine or the little booklet or wherever they were really publishing the stuff."

Lindsay said, "What?"

Ellen said: "Oh, come on, now. Don't be like that. I read all the ones you sent me the clicky things to."

Paul said, "Links."

Ellen said: "Right. Sometimes I even left comments."

Lindsay said, "Yes."

Ellen said: "Right there at the bottom. Did you read those?"

"Yes."

"I remember once I typed: 'This was really well written! Thanks for sending it!' and sometimes if there were little mistakes with punctuation or grammar I pointed it out for you."

Lindsay said: "Yes. I remember."

Ellen said: "'Cause, you know, I figure if I can help in any way."

"Yes."

Paul said, "You did that in the comments section?"

Ellen said: "Sure! That way she could fix it, maybe, before it actually got published or printed or whatever."

Paul said, "Ellen."

Ellen said, "What?"

Lindsay said: "I'm not doing that any more. I'm here with a location shoot."

Ellen said, "Isn't that wonderful."

A waitress approached the table. She said: "Hi. I'm Signe. I'll be your server this evening."

Ellen said, "You already told us that."

Signe said: "Yes. But I was introducing myself to the other young lady."

"Hello, Signe. I'm Lindsay."

"She doesn't need to know that, honey," Paul said.

Ellen pulled down the last of her Scotch and then crunched a bit of ice in her teeth as she slid the glass toward the waitress.

Signe did not respond to that. She said: "Can I bring you anything to drink? Have you had a chance to look at the menu?"

"I haven't. I'm sorry. Do you have any herbal tea?"

Signe listed some teas, and Lindsay chose one. Then Signe said, "Would you like another Dewar's?"

"Please," Ellen said.

"Not Macallan?" Lindsay asked.

"Oh, that's not necessary," Ellen said.

Lindsay said, "Bring her a glass of your oldest Macallan, and if the bartender grumbles about putting it on the rocks tell him that when he can afford good Scotch he can decide how he wants it served."

Signe said to Ellen, "We have a 25-year-old."

Ellen said: "Oh, that's just absurd. Eighteen is fine."

Signe said, "Okay."

Lindsay said, "Bring the 25."

Signe left them alone.

"So, you're shooting a location?" Ellen said.

Lindsay said: "We're shooting on location. Have you seen the show?"

"What show, honey?" Paul asked.

Lindsay blinked slowly. She said: "I told you about this. In an email. Last year."

"About what, dear? You know I don't understand half of what you say when you're talking about work." Ellen patted her daughter's hand.

Paul waved to Signe as she approached with the fresh Scotch and pointed at his empty wine glass.

"*Served Cold*. TNT? Thursday nights?"

Ellen said: "Oh! I heard about that show. You remember, Paul?"

"What are we talking about now?"

"That show!" Ellen said. "The one Stacy Kiel was going on about the other night. And on NPR... what's his name? Oh, help me out here, Paul. The guy with the funny inflection."

"Bander Sujianmati."

"Yes! That's the one. He did a whole piece on it, about how it's so violent and angry..."

"Oh!" Paul suddenly said, engaged. "I remember that review. He compared it to the whole Quentin Tarentino thing in cinema and talked about how it all started with Kubrick's *The Shining*. The — I loved this line — 'the celebration of our darkest impulses; the repeated affirmation of an underlying hostility, a fundamental violence at the heart of every family.'"

"Yes! I don't know how you remember whole chunks like that."

"It struck me when I heard it. I remember."

"It stars that woman, I think," Ellen said. "The one who used to be on that other show. The comedy. We never watched that either. Except that one episode you wrote. You remember that, honey? You called us all excited 'cause you'd sold one episode to this ridiculous sitcom on network television?"

"*Show Me the Love*," Lindsay informed her. "Yes. I remember."

Paul said, "You were so excited to be getting into the Guild."

Lindsay said, "Yes."

Ellen said: "And then we tried to watch it, and we just couldn't even sit through the whole half-hour, it was such utter schlock. I mean, I'm sure you did a wonderful job of writing just what they wanted, but it was all those corny one-liners and then the big fake laughs from the studio audience. Just ridiculous."

Lindsay said, "Okay."

Paul said: "But you were so excited about selling that episode and getting into the Guild. I remember that. What was that? Three years ago? Four?"

Signe put Paul's full glass of wine on a fresh new cocktail napkin. She put a small tin of steeping tea beside a teacup for Lindsay. She paused for a moment, then said: "I'll be back in just a minute to take your orders. Okay?"

Paul waved her away without looking. Lindsay said, "Thank you, Signe."

Lindsay's phone made a small noise. She ignored it.

"So," she said, "What have you guys been up to? Dad, you have to be starting to think about retirement."

"I don't want to talk about it," Paul said.

"And yet, he does. Several times a day," Ellen said. "Usually half a sentence grumbled into the refrigerator."

Paul sipped his wine. He crinkled his eyes in the way that told both Lindsay and Ellen that he was about to say something but wasn't sure how it would be received. He said, "Lindsay, I want to say something."

Lindsay said, "I'm not going to graduate school."

Paul said, "That's not what I was going to say." But then he didn't go on at all.

Lindsay poured tea into her cup. She waited. She sipped.

Ellen said, "You're not drinking at all now?"

Lindsay said, "I have an early call tomorrow morning."

"To whom?" Ellen asked.

"What?"

"Who do you have to call early tomorrow?"

"That's — no. That's what time I have to get to work. It's called a call time."

"Oh," Ellen said.

Paul said, "We don't really know all the lingo."

Lindsay said, "I know."

Abruptly, Paul blurted out, in an oddly scolding tone, "You know we love you, right?"

"I do," Lindsay said. "Sometimes I wish you could love me with, you know, less hostility."

Paul chuckled. "I get that," he said.

Ellen said, "I still drink."

Lindsay said: "Yes. I see that."

Ellen said, "Your father really only drinks wine, but I just love Scotch. Mostly only in the evenings."

Lindsay said, "Mostly?"

"Sometimes on the weekend, if we're playing Scrabble, you know, and it's the afternoon."

"Ah."

"Ellen."

Ellen said, as though she was answering a question that nobody had asked, "Never more than two."

Lindsay said, "Okay."

Ellen said: "I know my limit. That's how I know I'm not an alcoholic. Just two drinks and no more. If I have too much I fall down. Literally. One time I went to sit on the toilet and woke up on the floor of the bathroom."

Paul said, "Good story."

Lindsay said, "And this is how you know you're not an alcoholic?"

Ellen said, "Don't be like that." Then she stood up. "You know what I want, right, Paul? You can order for us. I'm going out to have a cigarette while we wait for the food."

She made her way to the front door. Lindsay and Paul sat in silence for a moment. Paul said, "We're missing something, aren't we?"

Lindsay nodded. She said, "It doesn't matter, Dad."

He said, "I don't know what you want from us."

She shrugged. She said, "It'd be nice if you said you were proud of me."

"Oh, honey. We are so, so proud of you. We tell people all the time about how wonderfully you turned out. We might have made some mistakes as parents, but you are proof that we were not completely incompetent."

Lindsay chuckled. "Is that what I am?"

Paul said, "What?"

"Proof of your competence."

Paul said, "I don't understand."

They sat in silence for a moment. Her phone made a noise. She reached into her purse and fished it out. She swiped through the combination lock to bring

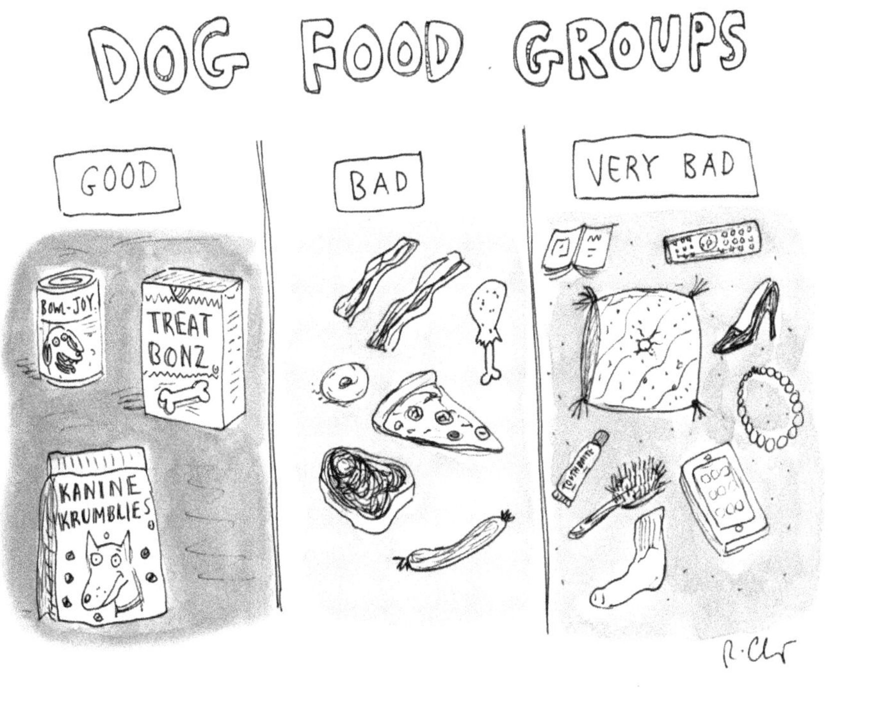
DOG FOOD GROUPS
GOOD
BAD
VERY BAD
BOWL-JOY
TREAT BONZ
KANINE KRUMBLIES

her screen to life. She began scrolling through texts.

Paul said, "Don't do that."

Without looking up, she said, "What?"

"Look at your phone in the middle of a conversation."

"It was actually the middle of a pause."

"Still," Paul said.

"It's not 5 o'clock yet in LA. I'm still working, Dad."

"You're at a restaurant. With your parents."

"One of them."

"It's rude," he said. "Put it away."

"Rude? Your wife just walked out of the room to have a cigarette. I waited until there was a pause, and now I'm checking through a great many texts, some of which I really should have responded to when they came in."

"Really? You're so important that people in LA need you to get back to them right away when they text you in Boston?"

"I'm not on vacation, Dad. Yes. They need me to get back to them."

"Oh, stop it," Paul said. "You're just avoiding talking to me."

"Now who's overestimating their importance?"

"What?"

She finished thumbing out a response to the texts and put the phone back into her purse.

Ellen returned in a small cloud of eau de Parliament. "What'd I miss?"

Paul said, "We had a fight."

"Oooh. Exciting. What about? Did you offer to pay for grad school?"

"I told her it was rude to look at her phone at the dinner table."

"Oh! Your father is right about that dear. I read about it in the advice column in the paper. It's not Dear Abby. I don't remember her name. But someone wrote in about that, and she said that it's very rude. Very common now, but totally unacceptable."

"Is that what you read about it in your print-medium newspaper, Mom?" She heard the defensive anger in her own voice.

"What does that mean?"

Lindsay sighed.

"Wait," Ellen said. "I remembered something when I was outside. You started saying something and then we got sidetracked. Something about that awful show on the Dynamite Channel."

"TNT. Not the Dynamite Channel."

"I know, dear. I like to call it the Dynamite Channel."

Lindsay waved to Signe, who came at once. "Are you all ready to order?"

Paul said: "My wife and I would like to split a Cobb salad. Is that allowed?"

"Of course. Do you want that all chopped up and mixed to make things easy or — "

"Oh, do it the way you usually do it. I like when it's all fancy in the separate wedges and then I get to mix it up myself," Ellen said.

"Okay. And for you?"

"You know what? Do you still have the bisque?"

"I love the bisque. Would you like a cup or — "

"A bowl," Lindsay said.

"Terrific," Signe said.

Lindsay said: "A big bowl. Does it come in extra-large? Do you have a tureen of bisque that I could order?"

Signe laughed. "One venti bisque. If the bowl's not enough for you, I'll bring you a second one and only charge you exactly the same amount for that one."

"Wow. You made that sound like a bargain. You're awesome."

"I strive to not suck," Signe said with a smile as she collected the menus.

Ellen finished off her drink and handed Signe the glass. "Could I have another of those?"

"Of course."

Signe went.

As if in response to an accusation, Ellen said: "Oh, come on. The first one was just Dewar's."

Paul said, "Ellen."

Ellen said to Lindsay, "I wish you wouldn't do that."

Lindsay said, "What do you wish I wouldn't do?"

Ellen said, "Make jokes with waitresses like that."

"What kind of waitresses should I make jokes with?"

"You know what I mean. Stop being funny. Everyone finds it exhausting."

Lindsay closed her eyes in a way that suggested that she had a terrible headache, although she did not. She opened them again and sipped her tea.

Paul said, "So, is that what you're working on?"

Lindsay said, "What?"

Paul said, "That TNT show? *Cold Servings?*"

"*Served Cold.*"

"Yes."

"Oh." Ellen said. "I didn't realize you worked on that show."

"I know. I got that."

"What do you do on it?"

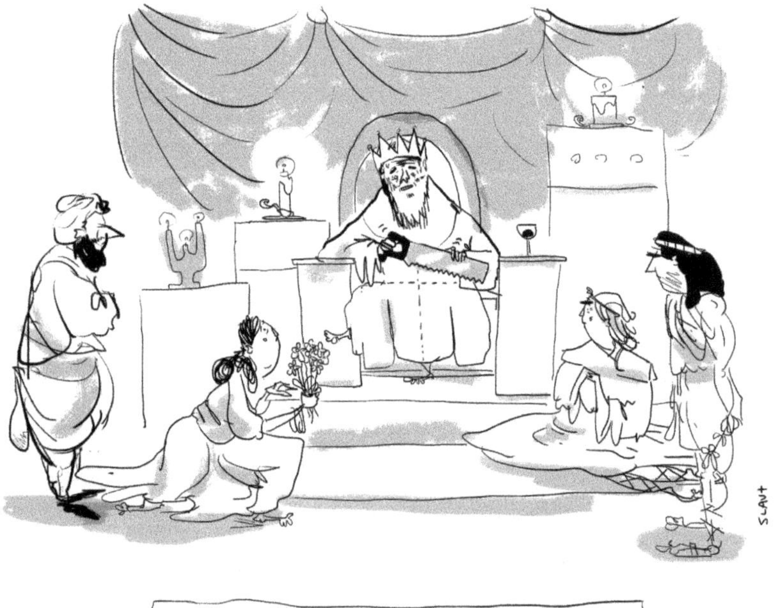
SLAVT

KING SOLOMON, ETHICAL SLUT

"It doesn't matter. Just… let's eat and talk about something else."

"Are you upset because I said what I heard on NPR? That wasn't my opinion. I've never even watched the thing."

"Yeah. Got that."

Signe set down a fresh drink for Ellen. Paul sipped his wine.

"Are you upset because we never watch it?" Ellen asked.

"A little. Yes."

"Because you work on it? I didn't realize you worked on it, honey," Ellen said. Her inflection implied that she believed her words were an apology.

"I sent you an email when it went to pilot. Another when it was picked up."

"I know, honey. But I don't really know what all of that means."

"So," Paul said, "You've really been with this thing from the beginning."

"Yes," Lindsay said. "The very beginning."

"I can see how that feels important to you, baby girl," Paul said. "But it's still just a TV show."

"No. It's not, Dad. It's not just a TV show. It's my show. It's my series. We're out here shooting a bunch of location scenes for the second season. We're picked up for a second season. My show."

Ellen said: "Oh, don't be pretentious about it. So you work on a show. It doesn't make it yours."

"I'm not — it is my show."

Paul said: "No. It's that woman from that other show. The comedy."

"She's the star, Dad. I created it. I executive produce it. It's my show."

Signe brought the salad and the bisque. She put down an extra plate so that Ellen and Paul could split the salad. Ellen set about mixing the salad together. She said, "I love this part!"

As Paul moved some of the newly mixed salad to the extra plate, Ellen sipped her Scotch.

Paul said, "We don't really know what any of that means."

Lindsay said: "I pitched a show. Then I wrote the pilot. Then I sold the show. Then we made 22 episodes of which I wrote nine while overseeing the writing staff that wrote the others."

Ellen said: "Well, I think it's great that you're working, but I don't think

"You don't need glasses to see it's time to get the fuck out."

that's the kind of thing you should be bragging about. I mean, don't put this *Cold Justice* thing on your résumé."

"*Served Cold*," Lindsay said.

"Whatever it's called."

"Ellen," Paul said. Then he said: "This is the thing, isn't it? The thing we were missing?"

Lindsay nodded.

"You're — that's a big deal, selling and running a show."

Lindsay nodded.

"I don't even see how you would know how to do all of that," Ellen said.

Paul said, "Ellen."

Lindsay said, "It doesn't matter, Mom." She blew on a spoonful of bisque.

"Seriously, though, honey," Ellen went on. "I think it's great that you're making a living doing this TV stuff while you're working on your real writing and whatever, but you shouldn't tell people you're working on that awful show."

Paul sighed.

"Why's that, Mom?"

"Because nobody likes it. Apparently it's very violent."

"It's consistently beating out the big three networks in its time slot."

"That doesn't mean anybody likes it."

"Actually, Mom, it means a lot of people like it."

"Well, that doesn't mean it's any good. A lot of people thought Milton Berle was funnier than Jack Benny. A lot of people liked the Stooges more than the Marx Brothers."

"Okay, Mom."

"I hope you're socking away a lot of money in the bank so that you have something of a cushion and you can just relax when that show is over and do your real writing."

"This is real writing."

"It's television," Paul said.

"It's been called innovative television. And — we're getting terrific ratings. And we got picked up for a second season." She heard her voice getting higher. She heard the plea behind it, the need to be heard, to be recognized.

Paul said, "Well, I suppose that's the sort of thing people in LA would be very impressed by." Then, after the shortest of beats, he said, "I don't know what you think you need my approval for."

Lindsay sighed. She pulled bisque into her mouth, focusing on the sound and then sensation of the warm broth.

Paul said: "Don't slurp, baby girl. It's very rude."

"It really is," Ellen said. She signaled the waitress that her glass was empty.

B

SAM GROSS

The Twisted Cross

Some regrettably timely cartoons by

S. GROSS

"It's not a flag, it's a sheet. We fuck on it."

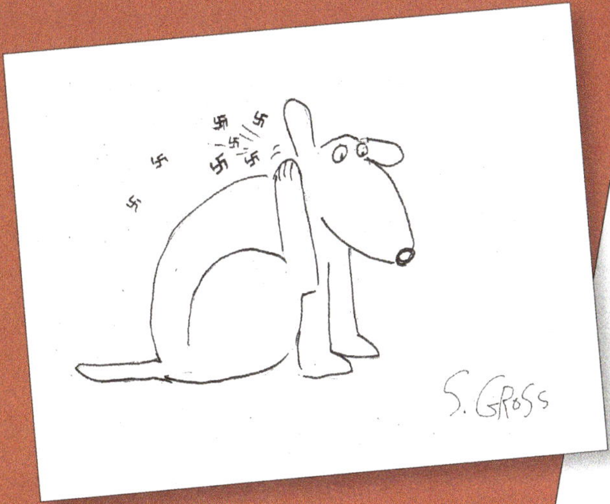

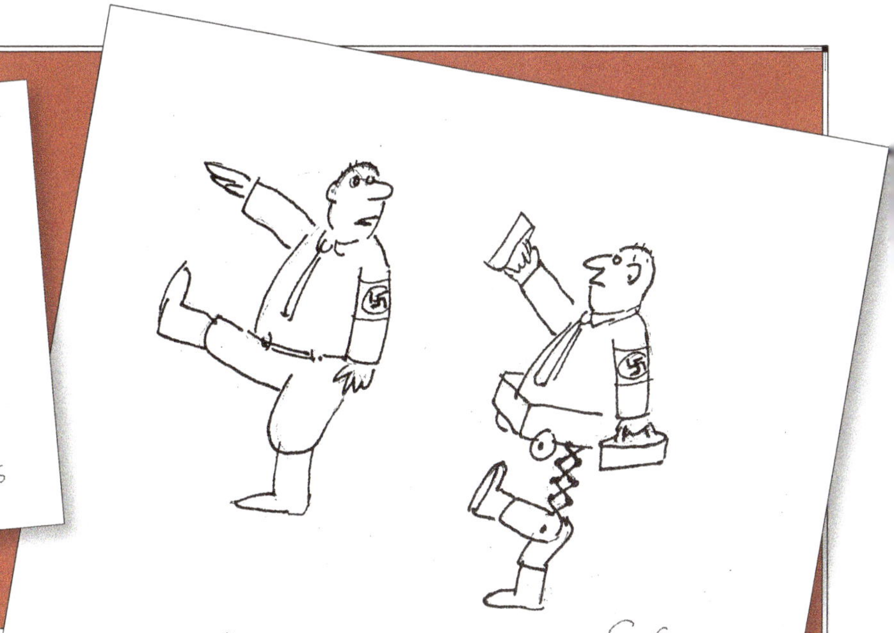

"Eddie, you're one hell of a Nazi."

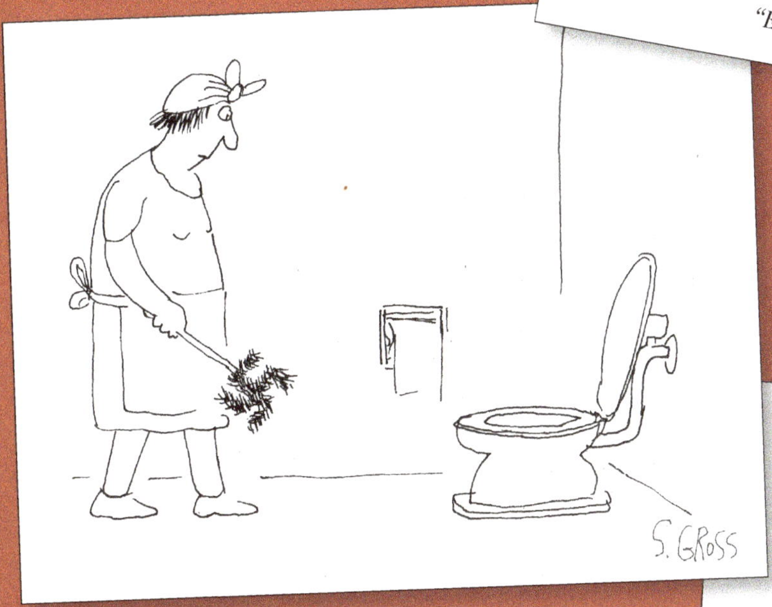

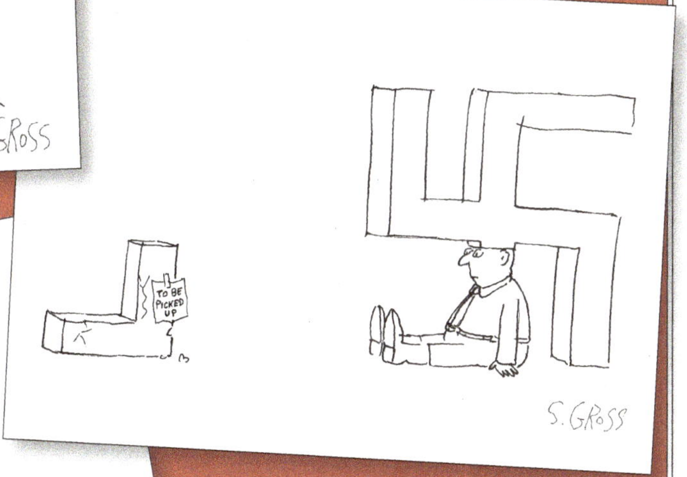
TO BE PICKED UP

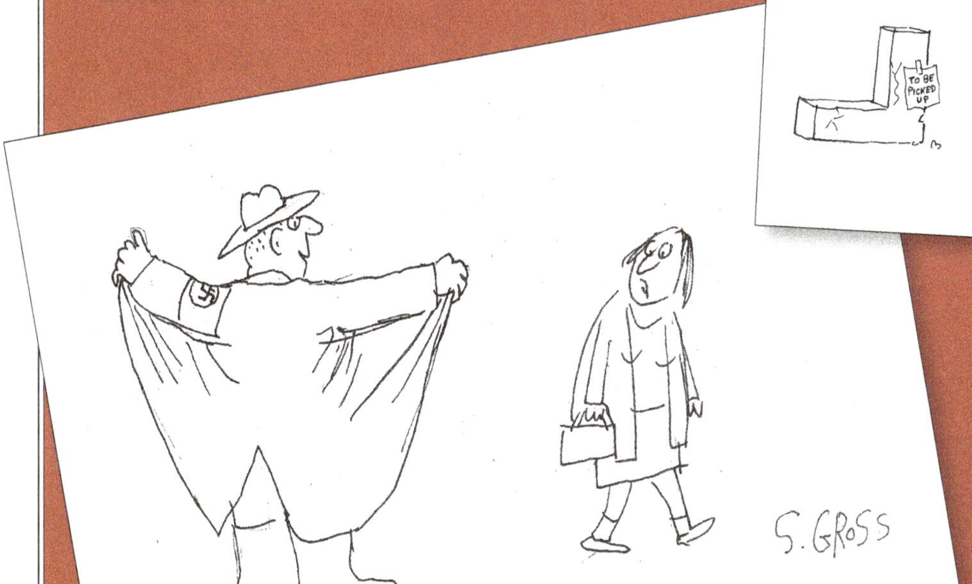

"You shouldn't do that if you're circumcised."

Prior to becoming a cartoonist, **Sam Gross** *was an accountant, a member of the U.S. armed forces, a student, a child, a baby and a fetus. And even before that, a gleam in his daddy's eye.* **B**

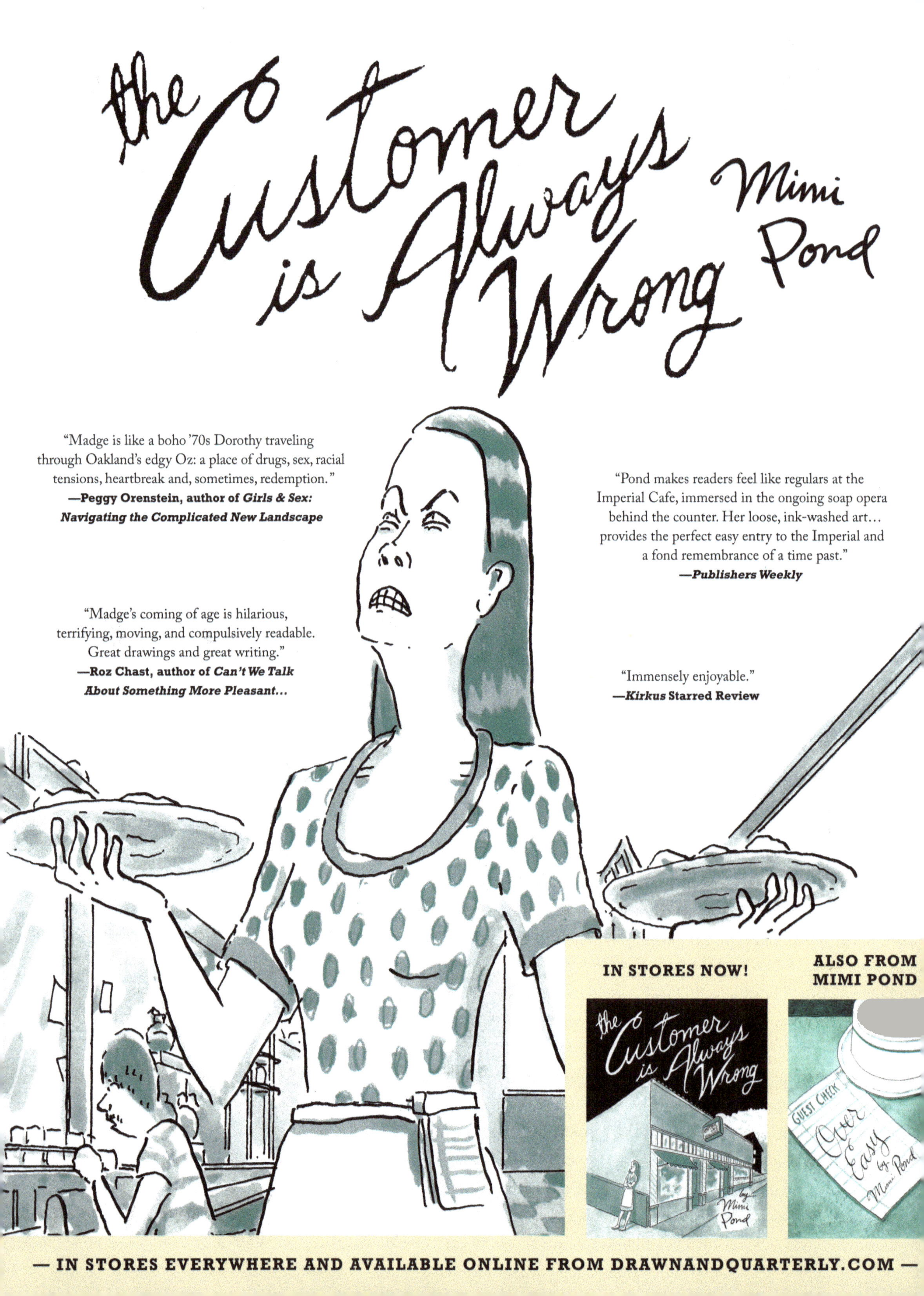
the Customer is Always Wrong
Mimi Pond
"Madge is like a boho '70s Dorothy traveling through Oakland's edgy Oz: a place of drugs, sex, racial tensions, heartbreak and, sometimes, redemption."
—Peggy Orenstein, author of Girls & Sex: Navigating the Complicated New Landscape
"Pond makes readers feel like regulars at the Imperial Cafe, immersed in the ongoing soap opera behind the counter. Her loose, ink-washed art… provides the perfect easy entry to the Imperial and a fond remembrance of a time past."
—Publishers Weekly
"Madge's coming of age is hilarious, terrifying, moving, and compulsively readable. Great drawings and great writing."
—Roz Chast, author of Can't We Talk About Something More Pleasant…
"Immensely enjoyable."
—Kirkus Starred Review
IN STORES NOW!
the Customer is Always Wrong
by Mimi Pond
ALSO FROM MIMI POND
GUEST CHECK
Over Easy
by Mimi Pond
— IN STORES EVERYWHERE AND AVAILABLE ONLINE FROM DRAWNANDQUARTERLY.COM —

The Secret Life of Walter Mitty, Firearms Enthusiast

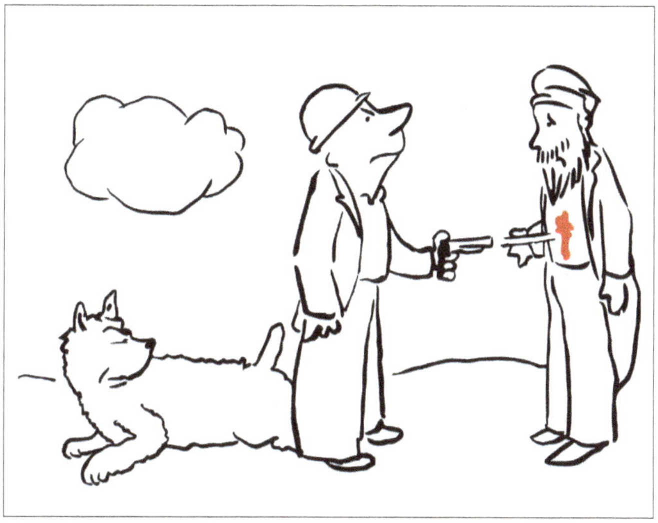

JOE OESTERLE

We're going in!" The commander's voice was like thin ice breaking, as the Blackhawk carrying members of SEAL Team 6 hurtled toward Abbottabad under cover of darkness. Suddenly, there was a crackle of small arms fire from below. Rounds slammed into the side of the chopper. The pilot was killed immediately. Even a hardened crew of warriors couldn't help but whimper as the bird lurched, but not the commander. He had a job to do. He just grinned and gripped his HK416 assault rifle one-handed and trained his eyes on a lone window in the compound. A light went on. A tall figure, bearded, appeared. It was bin Laden. "There you are, you son of a bitch," the commander growled, drawing a bead dead center on his target's forehead as the dying chopper plummeted to earth, wreathed in black smoke. "I may be going to hell. But I'm taking you with me!"...

"Dude."

"What?" said Walter Mitty, the roaring of the great wounded bird fading in the remote airways of his mind.

"You can't return this," said the bored clerk.

"Why?"

"Bro. You clearly opened it."

"I did not!" cried Mitty, training his steely brown eyes on the clerk. The clerk just blinked at him. Mitty flung the *13 Hours: The Secret Soldiers of Benghazi* DVD across the store and stormed out into the mall.

Mitty eventually regained his composure in the atrium, carefully controlling his heart rate to steady his hands. He took stock of the sightlines and emergency exits. He studied the faces around him to divine possible terroristic intent. While conducting this routine sweep, his eye fell upon the lovely dark-haired girl at the cellphone case kiosk. He had learned from his recon missions that her name was Brenda. Brenda. Brenda.

"Easy there, creepo," snapped a mall cop, "You're making that chick nervous." Mitty muttered an objection and hastily walked away. He shuffled around the mall aimlessly for a time, but he kept ending up back by the kiosk.

"... thank God you're here, Walter," Brenda said, her cheeks flushed, huddled in a corner surrounded by dozens of whimpering, defenseless shoppers and sobbing mall cops. "I thought we were dead meat. We don't stand a chance without you."

"Is it the government again?" Mitty asked. It was. Mitty had been warning everyone about this on Facebook for years — but did they ever listen? Of course not. And look who's sorry now. Mitty briefly considered just leaving them there to fend for themselves. It would be a valuable lesson, and of course he would have been well within his rights to do it. But sometimes the world needs a hero, especially these days.

As the government's pounding on the mall doors intensified, Mitty scrambled up three escalators and made his way to the roof, gripping his trusty Bravo Company RECCE 16 300 BLK KMR-A Carbine. It was a great weapon. As he rained hell upon the parking lot below, he was reminded of how it's light weight and large capacity was perfect for this job. As he mowed down the bad guys, Mitty heard cheers from inside the mall.

But then he heard a scream. It came from behind him. "Walter! Help!" It was Brenda. A bad guy holding a huge knife had her. But Mitty had a surprise for him. Tucked in his belt was an XVR 460 Magnum. One of the most powerful handguns on the planet...

"Sir, it was an hour and four minutes."

"No it wasn't," muttered Mitty, frowning at the parking garage

---

Joe Keohane, *a New York-based journalist who fears guns, once won a shooting contest with a Ruger SR9 in a range located behind a bar in Union, N.J. No joke.*

The outrageous 1977 filmatic smash in book form! You ain't never read anything like it!

40TH ANNIVERSARY OF ORIGINAL PUBLICATION!

STINKER Lets Loose!

OUR FAVORITE DEEP-FRIED DIXIE IS BACK AND LETTING LOOSE AS ONLY A STINKER CAN!

With old pals Boner and Jumbo along for the crazy ride, plus new friends Buck and Rascal, the rowdy gang hits the highways and biways of Bicentennial America and meets scores of beautiful Southern gals, reams of trecherous villains and even . . . the Big Man!

Will Stinker truly Let Loose? Or will Big Government and the "Smokeys" bring him down?

The outrageous cinematic hit of 1977 is back in book form and ready to be consumed by a new generation of movie lovers of ALL *stars* and *stripes*!

Strap yourself into this fully amped, revved-up Mean Machine and ride off into a Southern inflected, sudsy adventure!

With more than 25 BLACK & WHITE photos from the movie!

ON SALE MAY 2017 JUST $9.99!

"The movie made my eyes bleed, and the book made pus run out of them. The two things were made for each other. They're awful and awfuler. This novelization stinks."
— David Sedaris

Novelization by JAMES TAYLOR JOHNSTON
Adapted from the screenplay by WILLARD KATZ and GEOFF RODGERS
Based on a story by VIC TAIT and STEPHANIE SAMPSON and STU CALEBESH & GREY WHITTLE

CHARACTER OF STINKER CREATED BY BENJAMIN SILVER

SUNSHINE BEAM PUBLISHING, INC.
HOLLYWOOD, CA 90072

---

attendant. "It was 59 minutes! I know it was!"

The attendant wouldn't budge. He scratched his pockmarked face. "Buddy, come on, people are waiting."

"It was 59 minutes!"

"It's like a 50-cent difference," said the attendant. "Look, I'll give it to you. Just, like, get out of here." Mitty muttered something cutting and gave the man the full $2.50. Then he stepped just hard enough on the gas to make sure everyone was aware of his displeasure. Mitty had somewhere to go, but he couldn't remember where. All the disrespect had frazzled him.

…"Perhaps this will refresh your memory." Bin Laden was back, and his ISIS men had the mall surrounded. Hundreds of defenseless civilians were now at the mercy of the terrorists. And the police were helpless against ISIS's way better guns. Even Mitty was cornered. Bin Laden handed him a copy of the new bill that made Sharia the law of the land. All he had to do was file it in the mailbox just over there. Bin Laden smirked. "The problem with American men is that you're too soft," bin Laden said. "Soft, soft soft…"

Mitty perked up. "Stool softener!" he said to himself. He was at a red light with the window still down. A car full of teens next to him laughed. "Did that guy just say 'Stool softener'?" one asked. "Yo, this dude just said 'stool softener'! What's up, bro? Are your shits too hard?"

But Walter Mitty was miles away, back at the mall. What ISIS hadn't counted on was that he had been preparing for this moment. He had hidden a MAC-10 under Santa's village, and as he fell to his knees pretending to beg for his life, he grabbed it and unloaded on the terrorists, dodging their bullets and never once hitting a civilian. By the time it was over, the terrorists were all dead, and the cops told him they've never seen a bigger hero in all their lives and that they knew Navy SEALs who would have buckled under that sort of pressure, and Brenda kissed him. "Your gun is amazing," she said suggestively.

"Excuse me, sir? Your prescription is ready. Sir?"

"Sorry," muttered Mitty. "I was just thinking."

Mitty went out through the automatic doors that made a faintly derisive whistling sound when you went through them, carrying his stool softener. It was two blocks to the parking lot. Walter Mitty clicked on his e-cig. Cherry. It began to rain, rain with sleet in it. He stood up against the wall of the drugstore, vaping. He put his shoulders back and his heels together. "To hell with the stool softener," said Mitty scornfully. He took one last drag and put his e-cig away. Then, with that faint, fleeting smile playing about his lips, he faced his vanquished enemies; erect and motionless, proud and disdainful, Walter Mitty the Undefeated, inscrutable to the last.

B

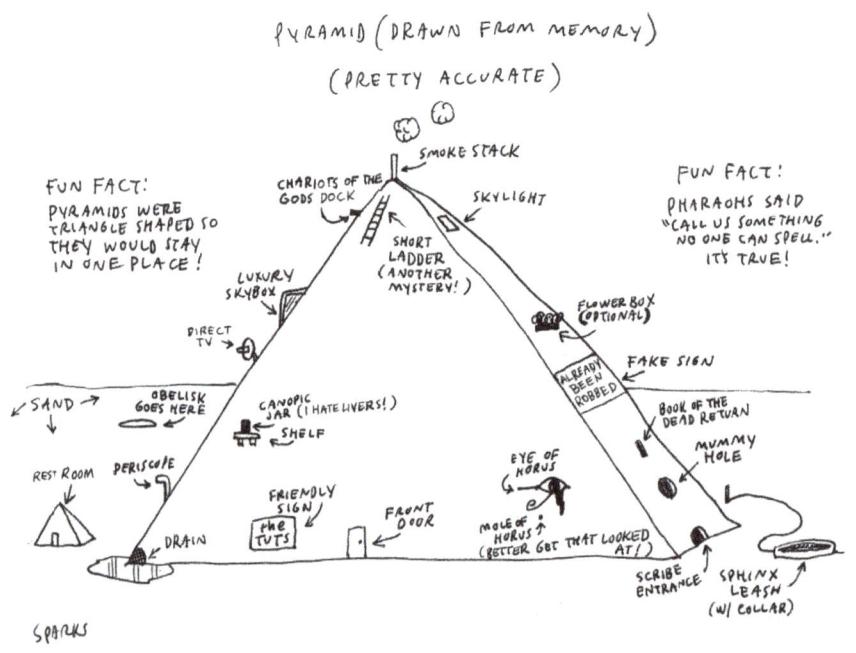

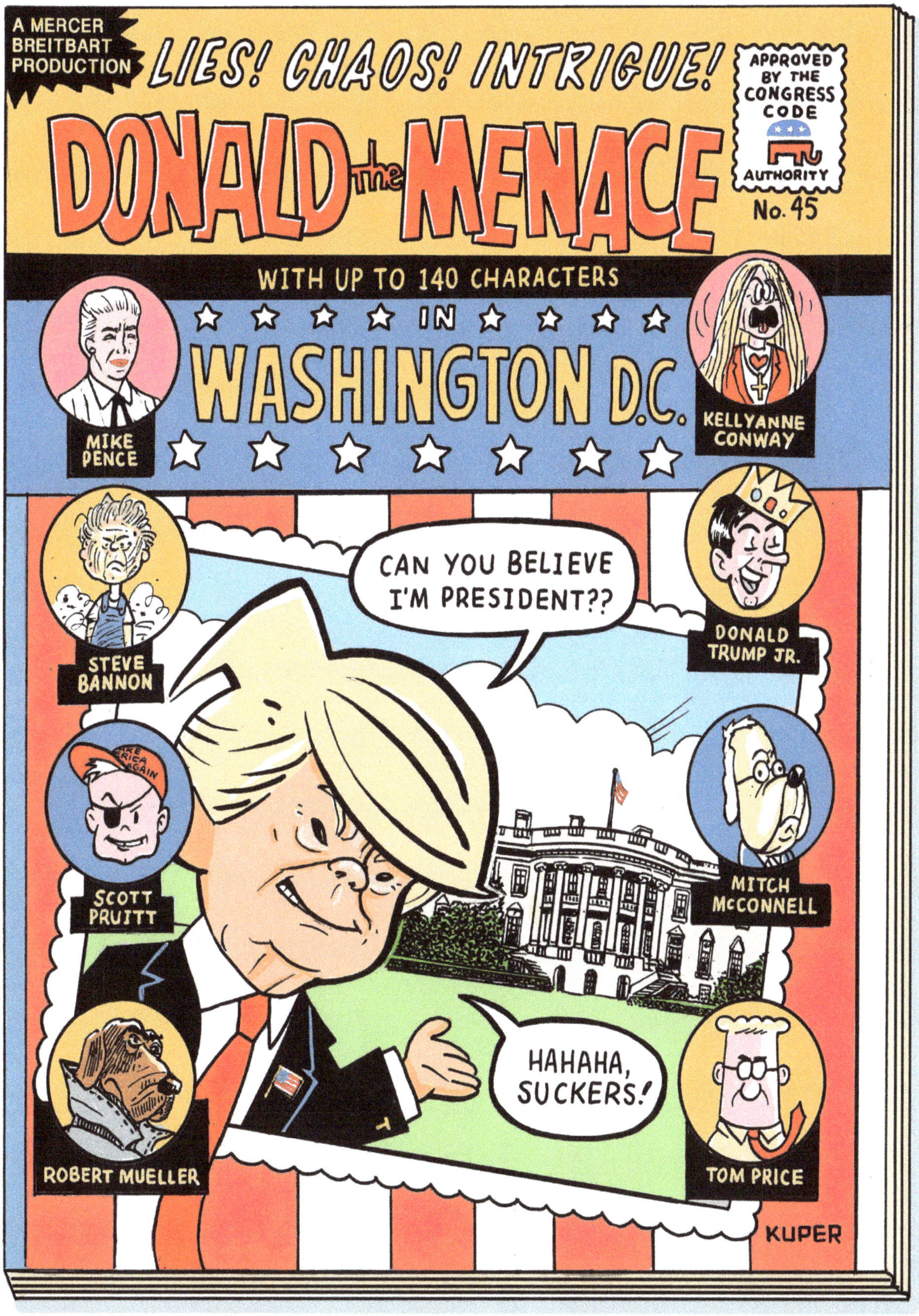
A MERCER BREITBART PRODUCTION
LIES! CHAOS! INTRIGUE!
APPROVED BY THE CONGRESS CODE AUTHORITY
DONALD the MENACE
No. 45
WITH UP TO 140 CHARACTERS
IN
WASHINGTON D.C.
MIKE PENCE
KELLYANNE CONWAY
STEVE BANNON
DONALD TRUMP JR.
SCOTT PRUITT
MITCH McCONNELL
ROBERT MUELLER
TOM PRICE
CAN YOU BELIEVE I'M PRESIDENT??
HAHAHA, SUCKERS!
KUPER

Peter Kuper's *cartoons and comics appear in magazines and newspapers around the world including* **The New Yorker** *and* **MAD**.

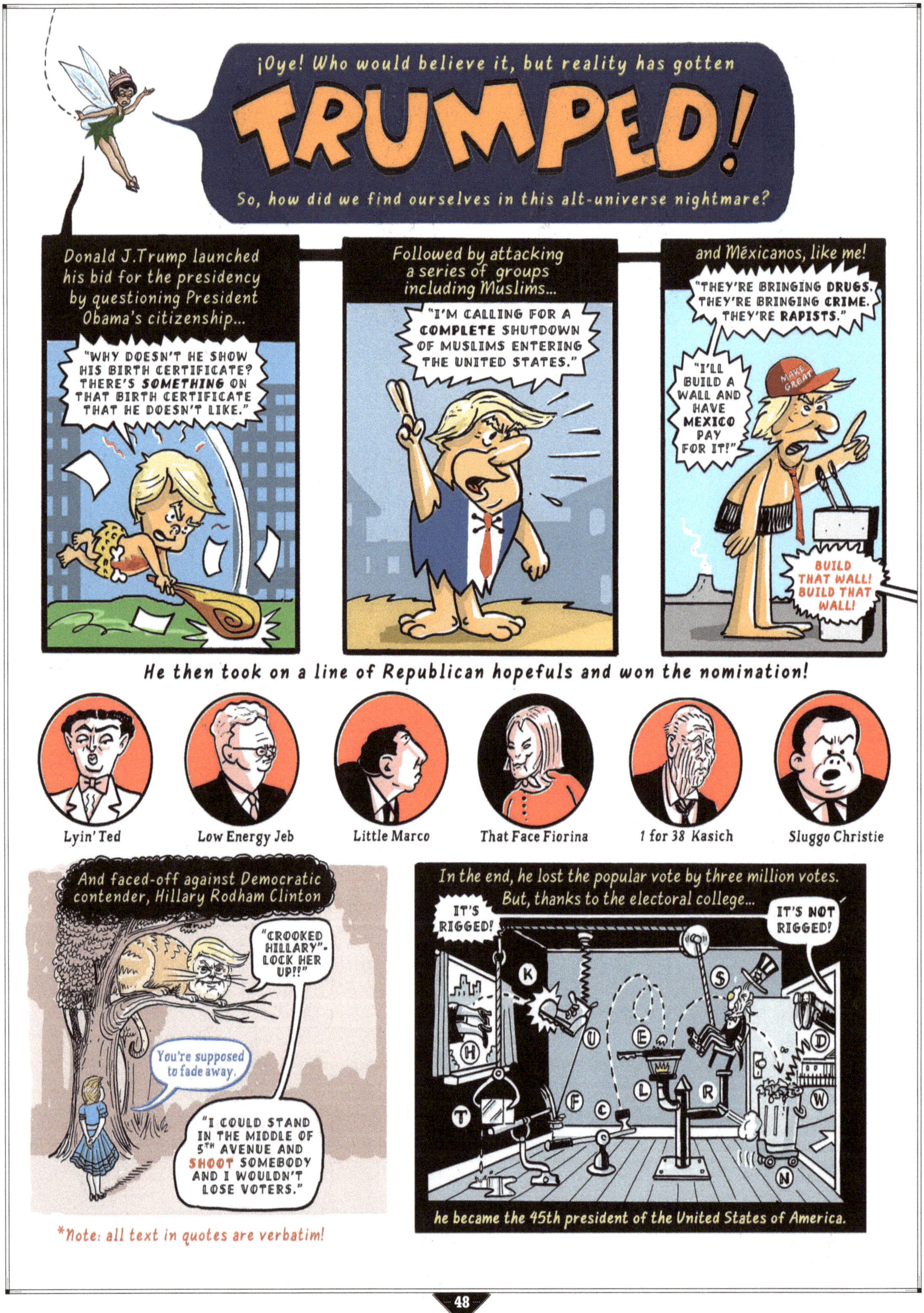
¡Oye! Who would believe it, but reality has gotten
TRUMPED!
So, how did we find ourselves in this alt-universe nightmare?
Donald J. Trump launched his bid for the presidency by questioning President Obama's citizenship...
"WHY DOESN'T HE SHOW HIS BIRTH CERTIFICATE? THERE'S SOMETHING ON THAT BIRTH CERTIFICATE THAT HE DOESN'T LIKE."
Followed by attacking a series of groups including Muslims...
"I'M CALLING FOR A COMPLETE SHUTDOWN OF MUSLIMS ENTERING THE UNITED STATES."
and Mêxicanos, like me!
"THEY'RE BRINGING DRUGS. THEY'RE BRINGING CRIME. THEY'RE RAPISTS."
"I'LL BUILD A WALL AND HAVE MEXICO PAY FOR IT!"
MAKE GREAT
BUILD THAT WALL! BUILD THAT WALL!
He then took on a line of Republican hopefuls and won the nomination!
Lyin' Ted
Low Energy Jeb
Little Marco
That Face Fiorina
1 for 38 Kasich
Sluggo Christie
And faced-off against Democratic contender, Hillary Rodham Clinton
"CROOKED HILLARY"- LOCK HER UP!!"
You're supposed to fade away.
"I COULD STAND IN THE MIDDLE OF 5TH AVENUE AND SHOOT SOMEBODY AND I WOULDN'T LOSE VOTERS."
*Note: all text in quotes are verbatim!
In the end, he lost the popular vote by three million votes. But, thanks to the electoral college...
IT'S RIGGED!
IT'S NOT RIGGED!
he became the 45th president of the United States of America.

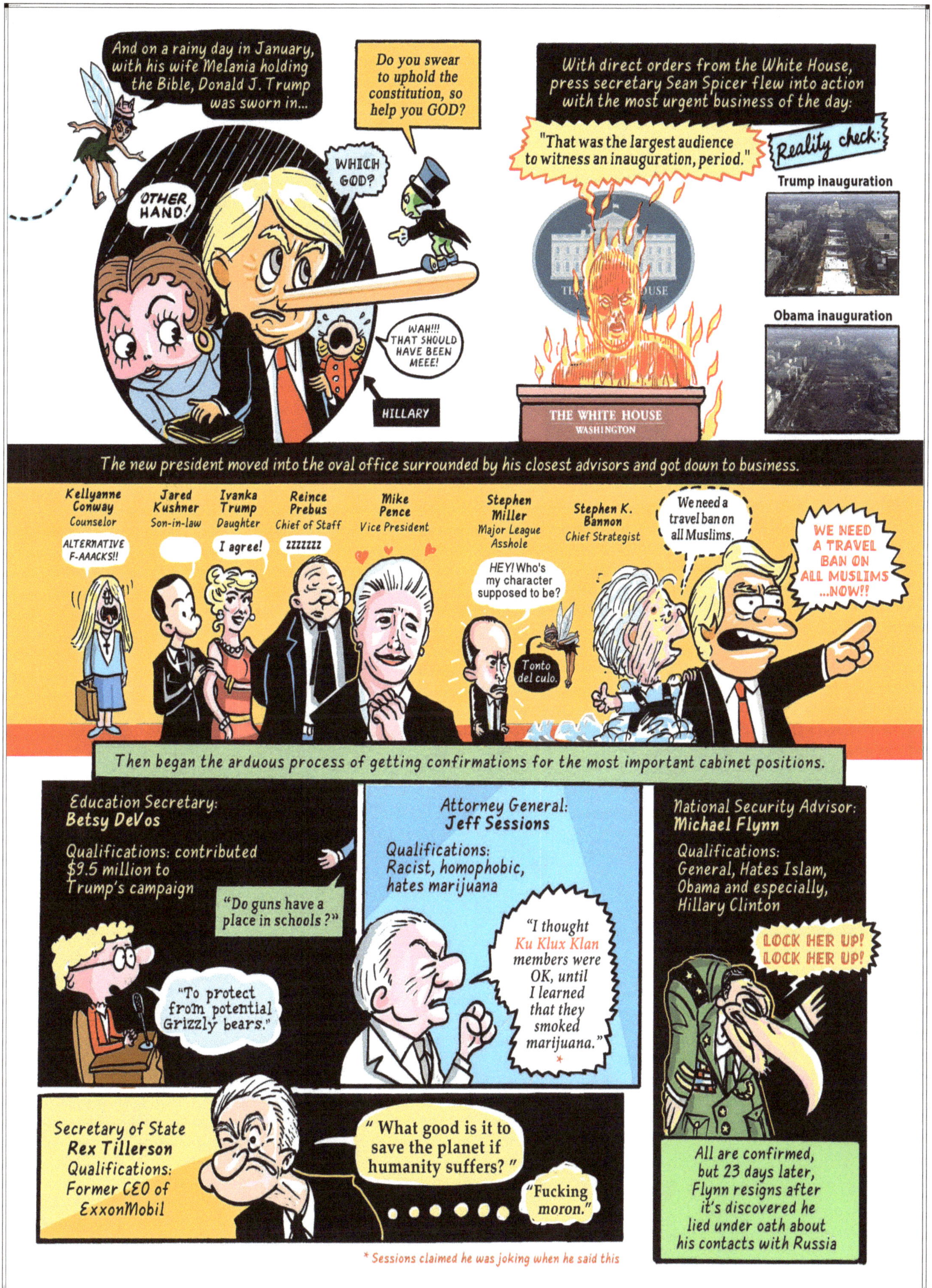

And on a rainy day in January, with his wife Melania holding the Bible, Donald J. Trump was sworn in...
Do you swear to uphold the constitution, so help you GOD?
WHICH GOD?
OTHER HAND!
WAH!!! THAT SHOULD HAVE BEEN MEEE!
HILLARY
With direct orders from the White House, press secretary Sean Spicer flew into action with the most urgent business of the day:
"That was the largest audience to witness an inauguration, period."
Reality check:
Trump inauguration
Obama inauguration
THE WHITE HOUSE
WASHINGTON
The new president moved into the oval office surrounded by his closest advisors and got down to business.
Kellyanne Conway
Counselor
ALTERNATIVE F-AAACKS!!
Jared Kushner
Son-in-law
Ivanka Trump
Daughter
I agree!
Reince Prebus
Chief of Staff
zzzzzzz
Mike Pence
Vice President
Stephen Miller
Major League Asshole
HEY! Who's my character supposed to be?
Tonto del culo.
Stephen K. Bannon
Chief Strategist
We need a travel ban on all Muslims.
WE NEED A TRAVEL BAN ON ALL MUSLIMS ...NOW!!
Then began the arduous process of getting confirmations for the most important cabinet positions.
Education Secretary:
Betsy DeVos
Qualifications: contributed $9.5 million to Trump's campaign
"Do guns have a place in schools?"
"To protect from potential Grizzly bears."
Attorney General:
Jeff Sessions
Qualifications: Racist, homophobic, hates marijuana
"I thought Ku Klux Klan members were OK, until I learned that they smoked marijuana." *
National Security Advisor:
Michael Flynn
Qualifications: General, Hates Islam, Obama and especially, Hillary Clinton
LOCK HER UP! LOCK HER UP!
Secretary of State
Rex Tillerson
Qualifications: Former CEO of ExxonMobil
"What good is it to save the planet if humanity suffers?"
"Fucking moron."
All are confirmed, but 23 days later, Flynn resigns after it's discovered he lied under oath about his contacts with Russia
* Sessions claimed he was joking when he said this

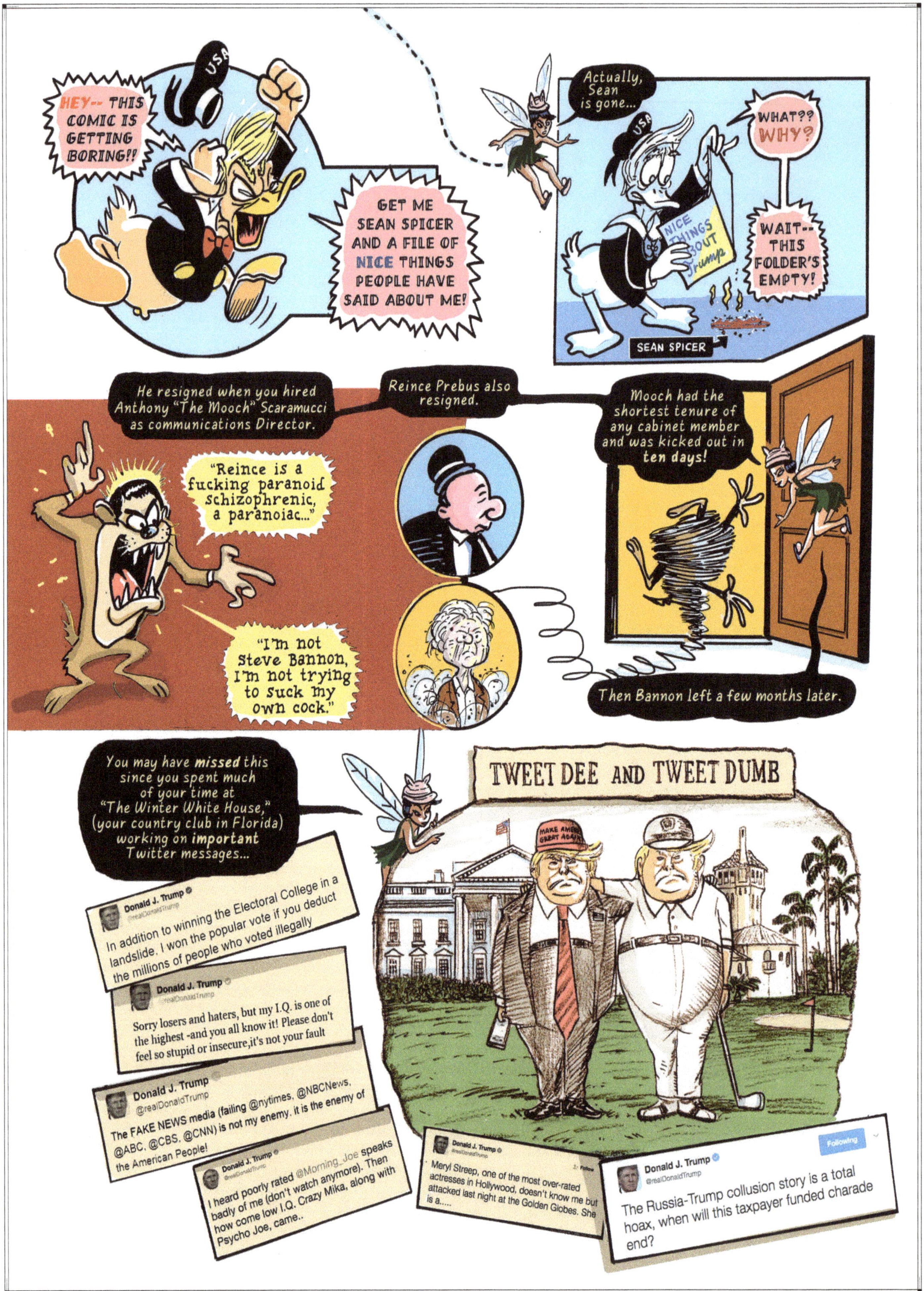

HEY-- THIS COMIC IS GETTING BORING!!
USA
GET ME SEAN SPICER AND A FILE OF NICE THINGS PEOPLE HAVE SAID ABOUT ME!
Actually, Sean is gone...
WHAT?? WHY?
NICE THINGS ABOUT Trump
WAIT-- THIS FOLDER'S EMPTY!
SEAN SPICER
He resigned when you hired Anthony "The Mooch" Scaramucci as communications Director.
Reince Prebus also resigned.
Mooch had the shortest tenure of any cabinet member and was kicked out in ten days!
"Reince is a fucking paranoid schizophrenic, a paranoiac..."
"I'm not Steve Bannon, I'm not trying to suck my own cock."
Then Bannon left a few months later.
You may have missed this since you spent much of your time at "The Winter White House," (your country club in Florida) working on important Twitter messages...
TWEET DEE AND TWEET DUMB
MAKE AMERICA GREAT AGAIN
Donald J. Trump @realDonaldTrump In addition to winning the Electoral College in a landslide, I won the popular vote if you deduct the millions of people who voted illegally
Donald J. Trump @realDonaldTrump Sorry losers and haters, but my I.Q. is one of the highest -and you all know it! Please don't feel so stupid or insecure,it's not your fault
Donald J. Trump @realDonaldTrump The FAKE NEWS media (failing @nytimes, @NBCNews, @ABC, @CBS, @CNN) is not my enemy, it is the enemy of the American People!
Donald J. Trump @realDonaldTrump I heard poorly rated @Morning_Joe speaks badly of me (don't watch anymore). Then how come low I.Q. Crazy Mika, along with Psycho Joe, came..
Donald J. Trump @realDonaldTrump Meryl Streep, one of the most over-rated actresses in Hollywood, doesn't know me but attacked last night at the Golden Globes. She is a.....
Donald J. Trump @realDonaldTrump Following The Russia-Trump collusion story is a total hoax, when will this taxpayer funded charade end?

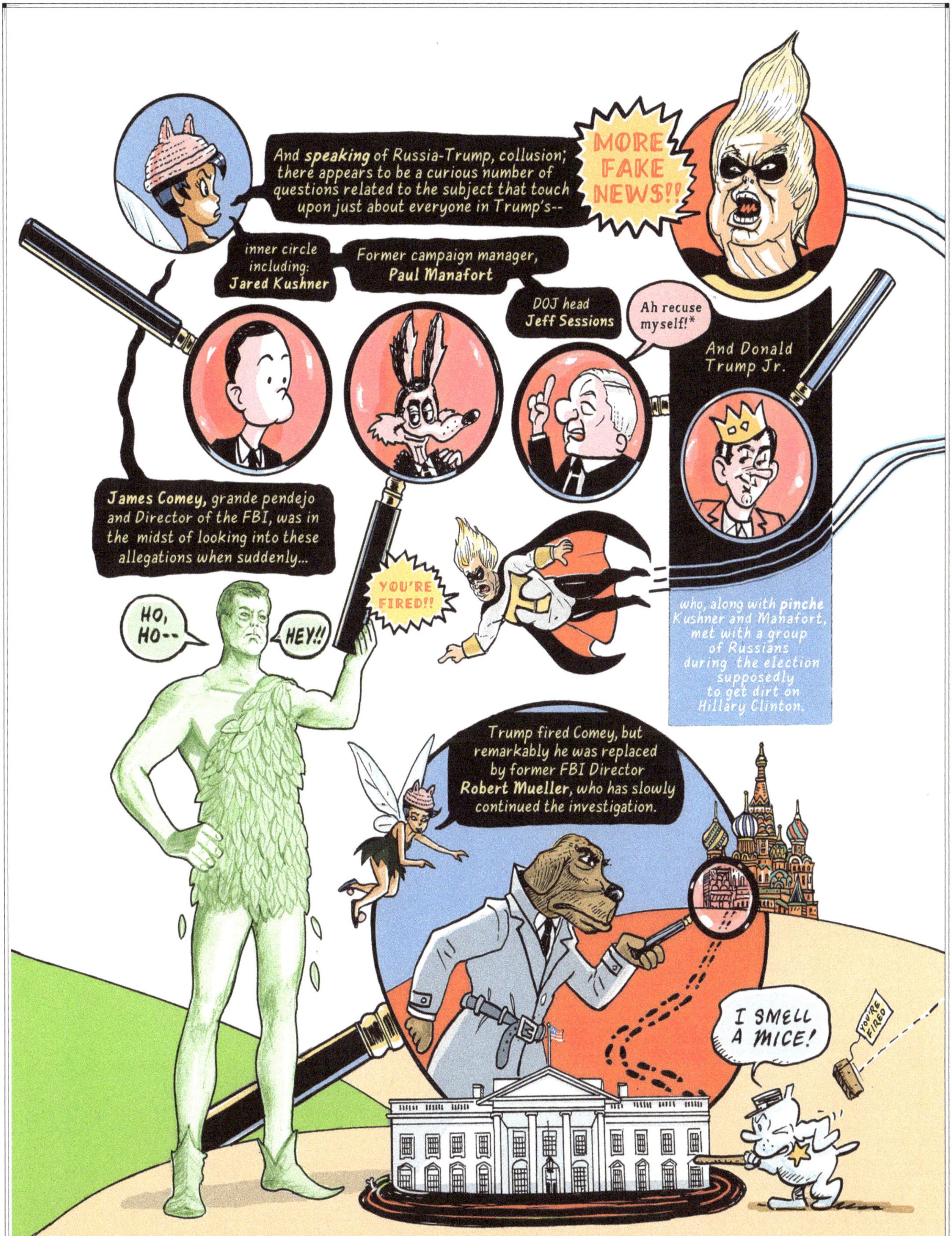
And speaking of Russia-Trump, collusion; there appears to be a curious number of questions related to the subject that touch upon just about everyone in Trump's--
MORE FAKE NEWS!!
inner circle including: Jared Kushner
Former campaign manager, Paul Manafort
DOJ head Jeff Sessions
Ah recuse myself!*
And Donald Trump Jr.
James Comey, grande pendejo and Director of the FBI, was in the midst of looking into these allegations when suddenly...
YOU'RE FIRED!!
HO, HO--
HEY!!
who, along with pinche Kushner and Manafort, met with a group of Russians during the election supposedly to get dirt on Hillary Clinton.
Trump fired Comey, but remarkably he was replaced by former FBI Director Robert Mueller, who has slowly continued the investigation.
I SMELL A MICE!
YOU'RE FIRED

*Sessions was forced to recuse himself from the Russian investigation since after claiming during his confirmation hearing he'd had no previous contact with the Russians it was later revealed that he HAD met with Russian ambassador Sergey I. Kislyak while advising Trump during the election.

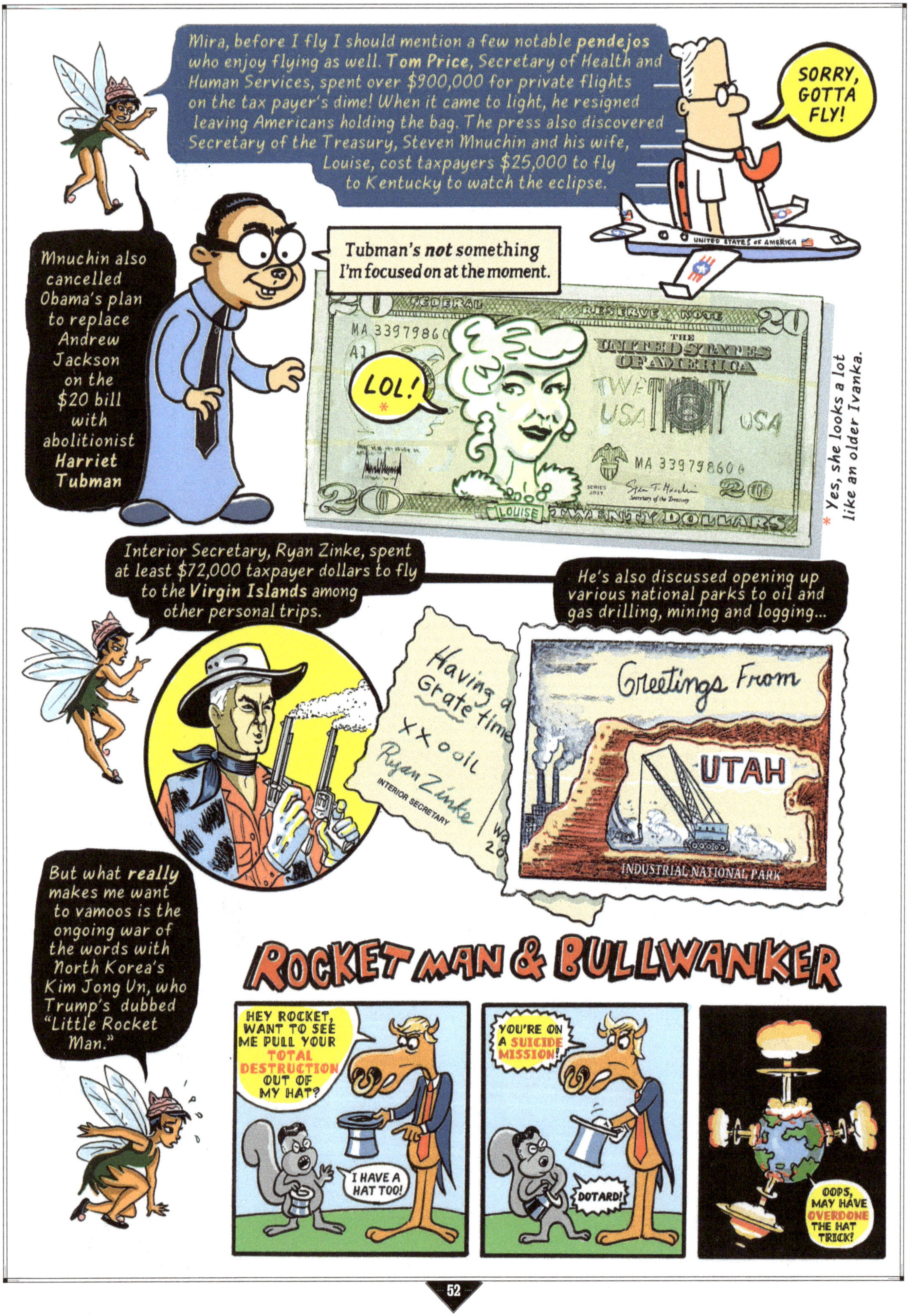
Mira, before I fly I should mention a few notable pendejos who enjoy flying as well. Tom Price, Secretary of Health and Human Services, spent over $900,000 for private flights on the tax payer's dime! When it came to light, he resigned leaving Americans holding the bag. The press also discovered Secretary of the Treasury, Steven Mnuchin and his wife, Louise, cost taxpayers $25,000 to fly to Kentucky to watch the eclipse.
SORRY, GOTTA FLY!
UNITED STATES OF AMERICA
Mnuchin also cancelled Obama's plan to replace Andrew Jackson on the $20 bill with abolitionist Harriet Tubman
Tubman's not something I'm focused on at the moment.
FEDERAL RESERVE NOTE
THE UNITED STATES OF AMERICA
LOL! *
LOUISE
TWENTY DOLLARS
* Yes, she looks a lot like an older Ivanka.
Interior Secretary, Ryan Zinke, spent at least $72,000 taxpayer dollars to fly to the Virgin Islands among other personal trips.
He's also discussed opening up various national parks to oil and gas drilling, mining and logging...
Having a Grate time
xx ooil
Ryan Zinke
INTERIOR SECRETARY
Greetings From
UTAH
INDUSTRIAL NATIONAL PARK
But what really makes me want to vamoos is the ongoing war of the words with North Korea's Kim Jong Un, who Trump's dubbed "Little Rocket Man."
ROCKET MAN & BULLWANKER
HEY ROCKET, WANT TO SEE ME PULL YOUR TOTAL DESTRUCTION OUT OF MY HAT?
I HAVE A HAT TOO!
YOU'RE ON A SUICIDE MISSION!
DOTARD!
OOPS, MAY HAVE OVERDONE THE HAT TRICK!

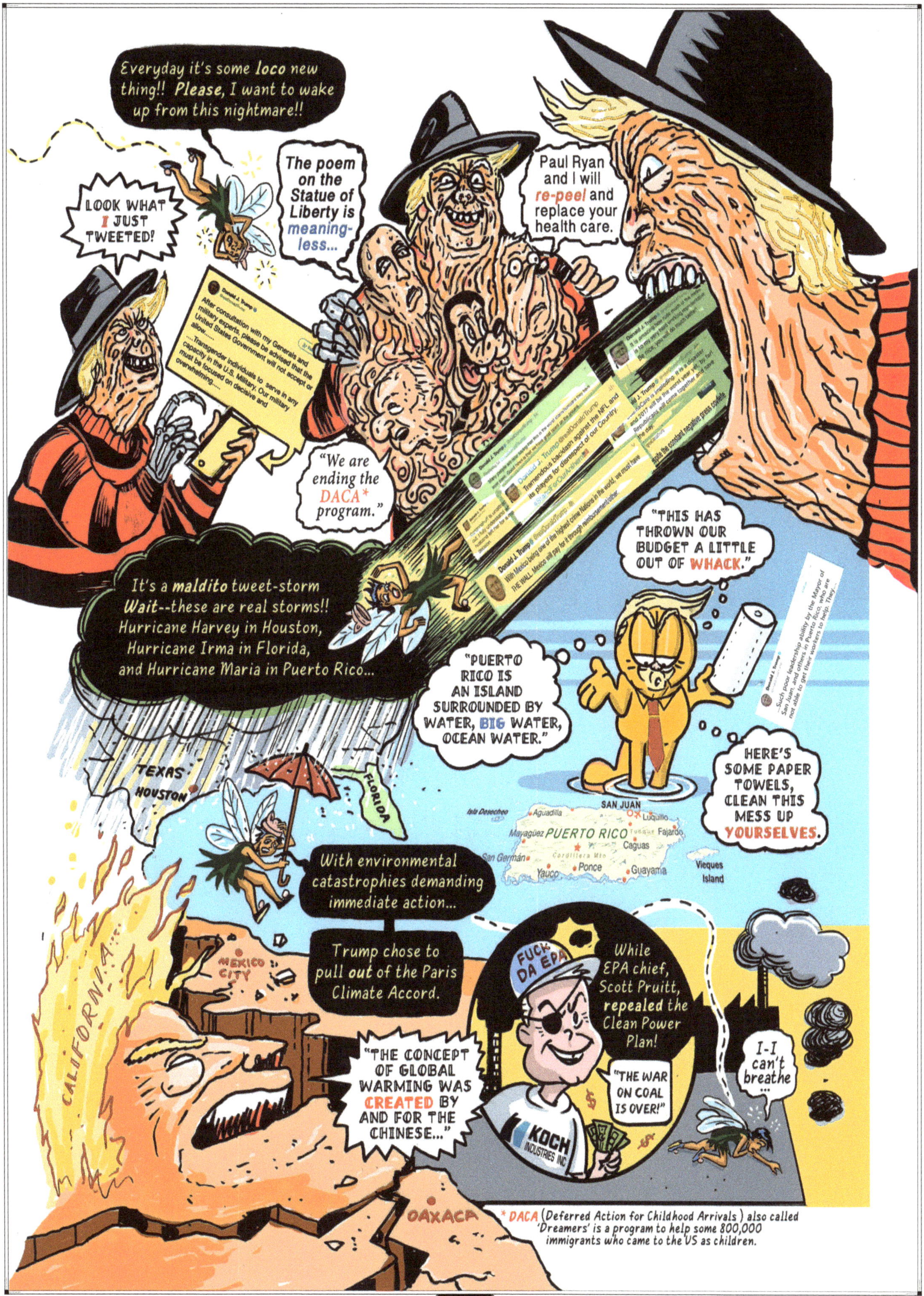

Everyday it's some loco new thing!! Please, I want to wake up from this nightmare!!
LOOK WHAT I JUST TWEETED!
After consultation with my Generals and military experts, please be advised that the United States Government will not accept or allow......
....Transgender individuals to serve in any capacity in the U.S. Military. Our military must be focused on decisive and overwhelming.....
The poem on the Statue of Liberty is meaning-less...
Paul Ryan and I will re-peel and replace your health care.
"We are ending the DACA* program."
Tremendous backlash against the NFL and its players for disrespect of our Country.
It's a maldito tweet-storm Wait--these are real storms!! Hurricane Harvey in Houston, Hurricane Irma in Florida, and Hurricane Maria in Puerto Rico...
"THIS HAS THROWN OUR BUDGET A LITTLE OUT OF WHACK."
"PUERTO RICO IS AN ISLAND SURROUNDED BY WATER, BIG WATER, OCEAN WATER."
HERE'S SOME PAPER TOWELS, CLEAN THIS MESS UP YOURSELVES.
TEXAS
HOUSTON
FLORIDA
SAN JUAN
Aguadilla
Luquillo
Mayagüez
PUERTO RICO
Fajardo
Caguas
San Germán
Ponce
Yauco
Guayama
Vieques Island
With environmental catastrophies demanding immediate action...
Trump chose to pull out of the Paris Climate Accord.
MEXICO CITY
CALIFORNIA
While EPA chief, Scott Pruitt, repealed the Clean Power Plan!
FUCK DA EPA
"THE WAR ON COAL IS OVER!"
I-I can't breathe...
"THE CONCEPT OF GLOBAL WARMING WAS CREATED BY AND FOR THE CHINESE..."
KOCH INDUSTRIES INC
OAXACA

* DACA (Deferred Action for Childhood Arrivals) also called 'Dreamers' is a program to help some 800,000 immigrants who came to the US as children.

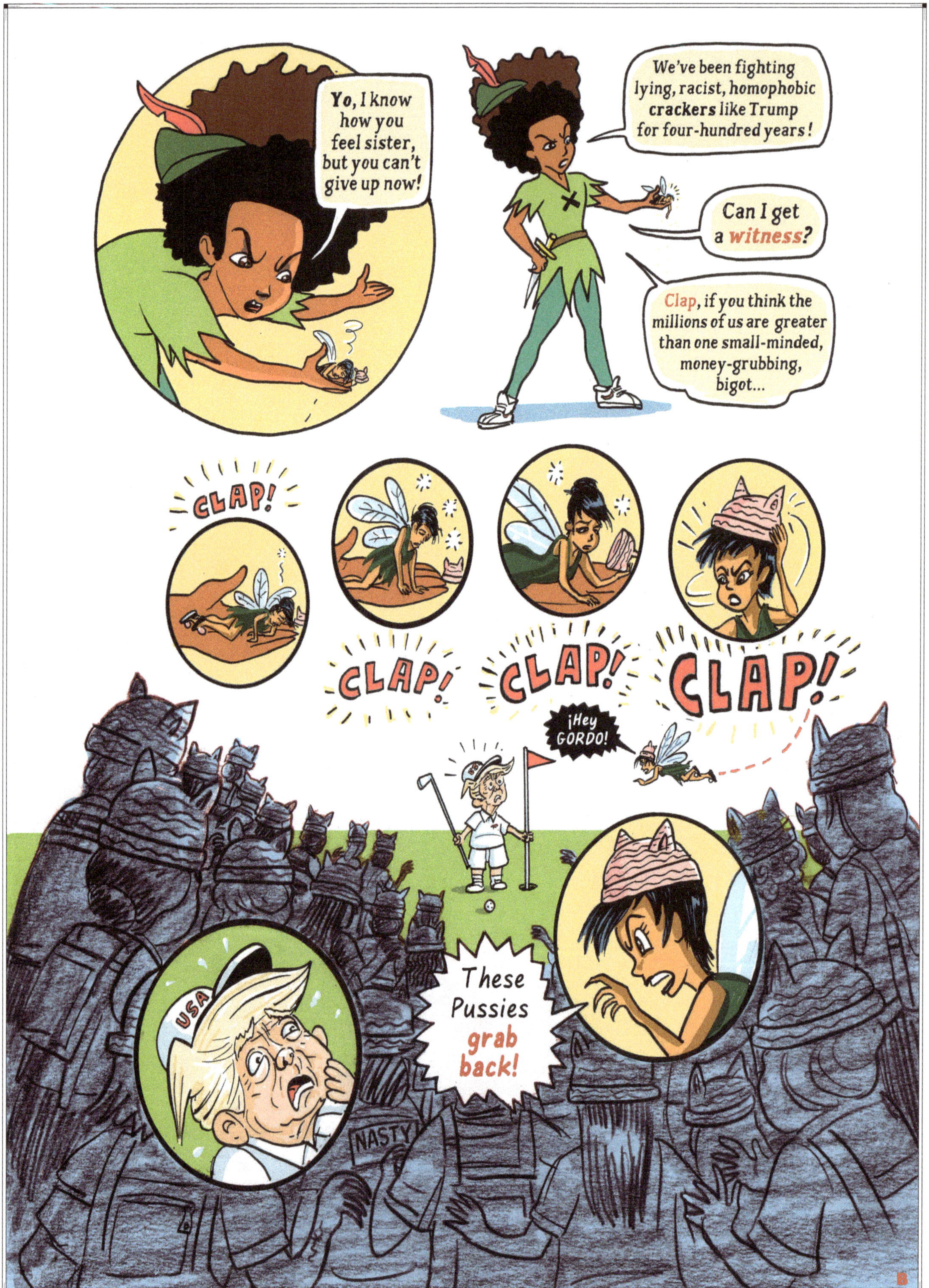

Yo, I know how you feel sister, but you can't give up now!
We've been fighting lying, racist, homophobic crackers like Trump for four-hundred years!
Can I get a witness?
Clap, if you think the millions of us are greater than one small-minded, money-grubbing, bigot...
CLAP!
CLAP!
CLAP!
CLAP!
¡Hey GORDO!
USA
These Pussies grab back!
NASTY

No Coffee

*Coffee wasn't invented until the 15th century.
This explains a lot of famous things people said.*

by Simon Rich
Illustrations by Farley Katz

Athens, 399 BC

What is the nature of death?
It is the greatest of all human blessings.
Whoa, Socrates, that's pretty harsh.
I'm sorry, I haven't had my coffee yet.
What's coffee?
It won't be invented for thousands of years.
Life is a nightmare and I'm going to kill myself.

Rome, 50 AD

Sometimes even to live is an act of courage.
Whoa, Seneca, that's nuts. Are you okay?
No, I'm really hungover, and I need some fucking coffee.
What is coffee?
Just please don't talk to me right now. I have that thing where everything is spinning around. Just don't talk. Nobody say anything. I just need to be totally still and not talk for hours.

China, 8th Century AD

Life slips away, a dream of little joy and mean content.
Yikes, Li Bai, that's bleak. What's with you?
Sorry. I just need coffee.
I don't know what coffee is.
No one does, it's not around yet. We have like tea and shit but it sucks. Now, if you'll excuse me, I'm going to go write more sad poems and then blow my goddamn fucking brains out. I'm serious, I'm going kill myself.

London, 16th Century

Life is a tale told by an idiot full of sound and fury, signifying nothing.
Whoa.
Sorry, I haven't had my coffee yet. I don't even know what coffee is because it's 15 hundred and something.
But wait, coffee was invested in the last century. You should know about coffee by now. It's around.
Yeah, but I haven't tried it.
Here's some.
(takes a sip) So long as men can breathe or eyes can see, so long lives this and this gives life to thee!
Nice line! You should put that in a sonnet.
Indeed I shall! But right now, all of a sudden, I have to take a shit.

Pricks Up Front

Words and music by **Andy Prieboy**
Transcribed by **Brian Moore**

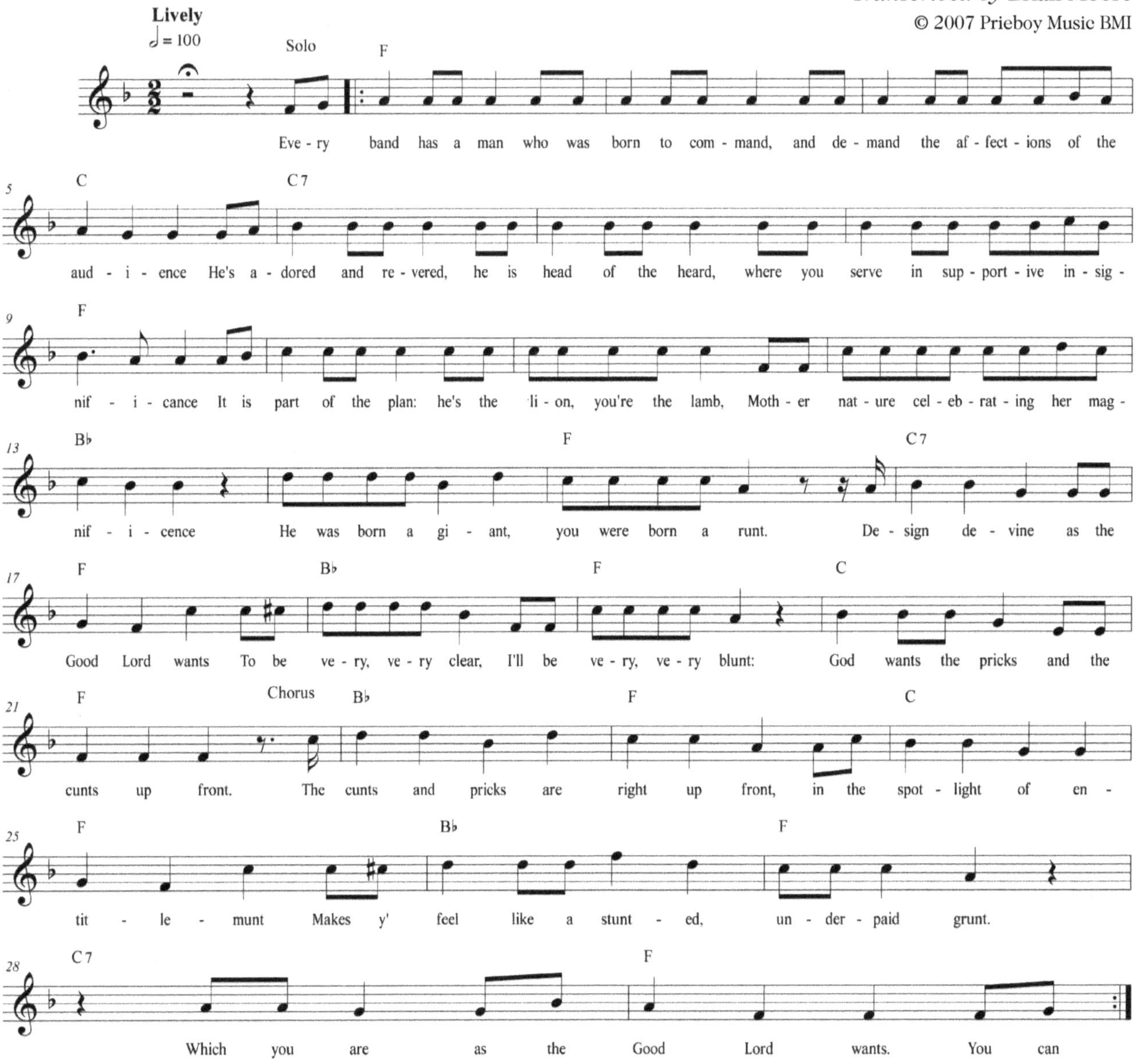
Lively
𝅗𝅥 = 100
Solo
F
Eve - ry band has a man who was born to com - mand, and de - mand the af - fect - ions of the
C C7
aud - i - ence He's a - dored and re - vered, he is head of the heard, where you serve in sup - port - ive in - sig -
F
nif - i - cance It is part of the plan: he's the li - on, you're the lamb, Moth - er nat - ure cel - eb - rat - ing her mag -
B♭ F C7
nif - i - cence He was born a gi - ant, you were born a runt. De - sign de - vine as the
F B♭ F C
Good Lord wants To be ve - ry, ve - ry clear, I'll be ve - ry, ve - ry blunt: God wants the pricks and the
F Chorus B♭ F C
cunts up front. The cunts and pricks are right up front, in the spot - light of en -
F B♭ F
tit - le - munt Makes y' feel like a stunt - ed, un - der - paid grunt.
C7 F
Which you are as the Good Lord wants. You can

Verse 2

You can cry in despair and declare 'unfair!"
And demand reparations or democracy.
You can equalize with the aim to revise
The unsporting distribution of ability.
You may level the field
But the playing will reveal
In spite of all your efforts to homogenize
He remains a giant.
You remain a runt
Suck it up if success you want.
It's bums to rear, to be so blunt

God wants the pricks and the cunts up front.
It's an unfair world and it ain't no fun't
The ones who kowtow subservi-unt.
But our Merciful Lord omnipo-tunt,
Wants the pricks and the cunts up front.

Verse 3

Every Rock Star, Movie Star, President
Or Pope or Czar in essence are pubescents
Shouting "Granpa: lookit me!"
And must be overcompensated
For an ego once deflated
In a narcissistic injury
'Tween ages one and three.
As they go grabbing up The Grammy
Or The Emmys or The Obie
And go blabbing their baloney
To a dazzled peasantry-
Don't ya 'feel like a stunted underpaid grunt?
Which you are as the Good Lord wants!
To be very, very clear I must be very blunt
Towards you metaphysical befuddle-munt
It's asses to the rear with the excre-munt
God wants the pricks and the cunts up front.

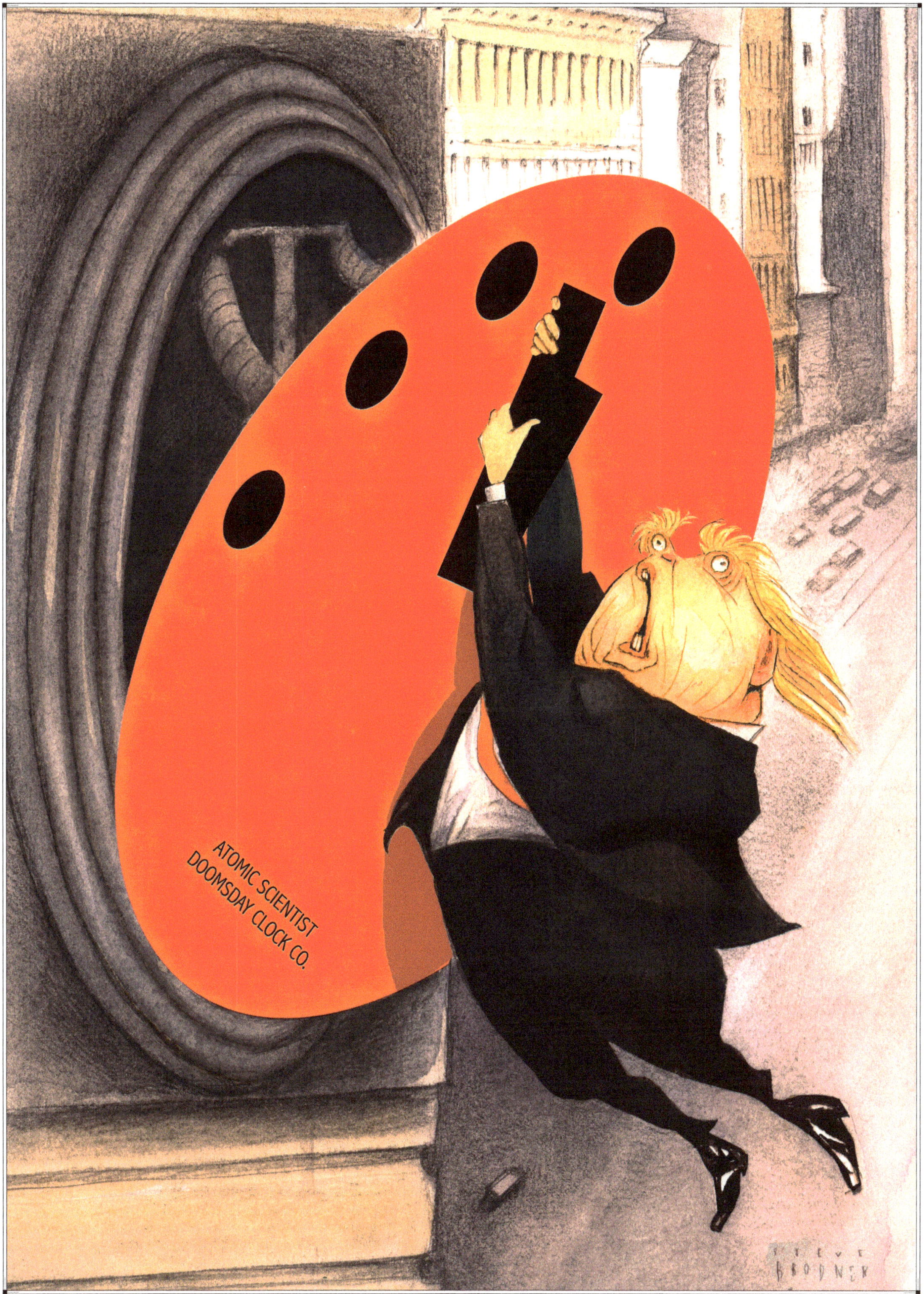
ATOMIC SCIENTIST
DOOMSDAY CLOCK CO.
STEVE
BRODNER

STEVE BRODNER

Find it **FREE** at 166 distribution points in over 42 states, or **ORDER NOW** at

www.resistsubmission.com

RESIST! is a new magazine of political comics by mostly female artists. This summer issue features some of the biggest names in comics —
Roz Chast, Kristin Radtke, Lauren Weinstein, Cathy Malkasian, Dan Clowes, Art Spiegelman, and many more
— alongside exciting new names, some never-before-published.

The 96-page magazine is edited and produced by **Françoise Mouly**, art editor of The New Yorker, and her daughter, writer **Nadja Spiegelman**.

LIMITED AVAILABILITY

A Man Called "Grumpy"

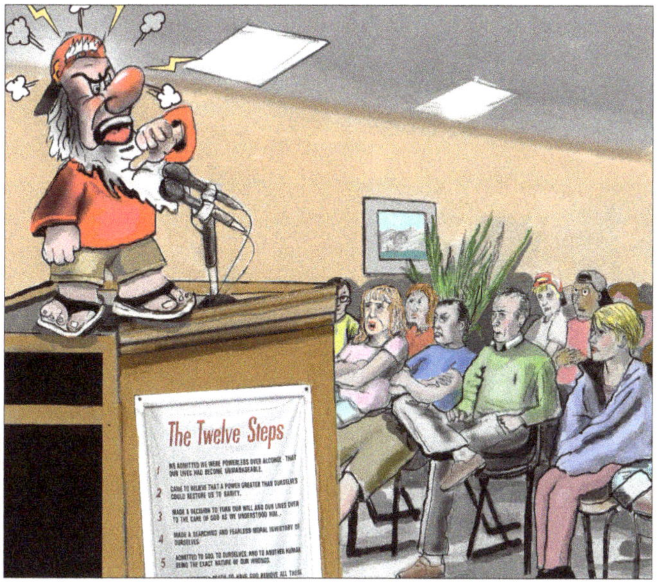
The Twelve Steps

EDWIN VACEK

In a church basement, filled with folding chairs arranged in a large circle, a designated meeting leader makes the announcement he always makes before the meeting ends.

"We reserve the last 10 minutes for any newcomers who care to share," he says. "Anybody?"

An extremely short bald man wearing a knit cap and sporting a long white beard raises his hand. "Hi. I'm Wilhelm."

"Hi, Wilhelm."

He pauses for a moment, then: "I've never been to a meeting before. You probably know me as Grumpy. Is that all right to say who I am? Oh! Sorry.

"To be honest with you, the only reason I'm here is the family counselor told me I better get to a meeting. I said, 'You're kidding! *Me*? Why should *I* go to a meeting? It's the rest of my family that's effed up!'

"You all know what I'm talking about: drinking, drugs, you name it. My wife's been in and out of treatment. My son's in rehab right now for the third time. My daughter — who knows what's going on there? She's not talking to me.

"But they're saying the problem is *me*? 'Too critical, too controlling, gives too much advice.' Maybe I cared too much, okay? Maybe I gave too much of a shit. Can I say 'shit' here?

"According to them, I'm ruining everyone's self-esteem by giving them all nicknames. Come on! It's just part of my culture — if you're a mountain dwarf in the diamond mining business, you get a nickname. Period. *Everybody* gets a nickname. So I called my wife 'Shlubby.' I called my daughter 'Porky' and I called my son 'Puny.' Friendly and affectionate. As nicknames go, completely harmless — a lot nicer than most.

"But now: 'You're body-shaming me.' 'You're being culturally insensitive.'

"I'll tell you this: Dopey never complained. Not a peep. Yes, he was kind of an idiot. Truth be told, all six of them had their issues. The way they would all laugh every time Sneezy sneezed — seriously, why is that so funny? I mean, sure, maybe the first time…but after that?

"I admit I'm not perfect. I get moody sometimes. But how chipper and upbeat would you be if you'd lived to 120 years old and all that people wanted to talk to you about was those few ridiculous months when you shared a nontraditional group home in the woods with a bunch of isolated asexual short-statured diamond miners and a wink-wink 'runaway princess wannabe'? What about all the great stuff I've done since? I sold garbage disposals, I was a racecar driver, I played 'Old Man Hasler' in *Pajama Game*. Life goes on!

"Talk about a situation where a bunch of deluded sick people are enabling each other to live out their worst fantasies. Seven grown men in one house, vying for one woman's attention. And everyone dressing alike. How nuts was that?

"And we're not talking about kids here. Someday do a little Googling and have a look at those photos of us that are everywhere online. Check out the level of male pattern baldness. We were all in our 40s and 50s. Doc was damn near 60.

"I mean, I get that the girl was a knockout. What girl her age isn't?

Merrill Markoe *has published eight books and written for a long list of television shows and publications, including the one you are holding.*

"Tell you the truth, none of us actually knew how old she was. It was weird. It was hard to tell. Was she 18? 25? Jesus, she could have been a mature 15 for all we knew. Porno is full of this kind of shit, right?

"It wasn't all negative. We had good times, too. I played keyboards in our band. We were pretty good before Snow started doing vocals. That high screechy voice of hers... The other guys seemed to love it, but I was the one classically trained musician in the group. Doc only knew that one trick on guitar. I guess Dopey was decent on drums when he wasn't being a showoff.

"Speaking of Dopey, did I mention that my daughter just moved out and isn't speaking to me, except through my wife? According to those two, I'm a little too 'old school' when it comes to women. Really? Fine. I'll play along if it keeps them out of rehab. I'm sure even that will probably turn out to be wrong...

"I'll admit, all those years of living with Snow White may have given me some unrealistic expectations. The family counselor claims we let her infantilize us — and maybe we did. She picked up after us, she cooked for us, she treated us like we were little children. That wasn't really healthy. To say nothing of that way she had of making it seem like she had a special relationship with each one of us. The forehead-kissing. It was weirdly seductive.

"But it was a two-way street. In return we allowed her to see herself as some wholesome flawless creature who could communicate with forest bunnies and what have you. Maybe she had some kind of daddy complex or a Danny DeVito fetish or something. Who the F knows?

"I suppose it's wrong to expect that kind of behavior from my wife and my daughter. At least, that's what they tell me anyway. But Snow was the first woman I ever lived with, so for a long time I compared every woman to her. She always looked great, always with the long skirt and the velvet whatevers and the high heels. Hair always perfect, even when she was doing our laundry or sweeping up. I mean, she had a lot of help from birds and the chipmunks and so forth... Do you know: We lived there for 25 years before she ever showed up. You think all those animals ever lifted a finger to help us?

"And then one day a tall, good-looking guy on a horse shows up and Snow leaves with him! Goodbye. Gone. 'I'm a "Princess" now. I'm leaving to "rule" in my "kingdom." Oh, and by the way, thanks for all the diamonds.'

"Then the shit hit the fan: Each of us accusing the other guy of being the reason she left.

"You see what she did there? Playing each one of us against the other? How messed up was that? Come to find out, years later, this was not the first time she pulled this.

"Finally I had enough. I had to get out of there. I said, "I'll see you guys later."

"And you know what they did? They got another Grumpy!

"In the beginning, I thought, 'Okay. Whatever. Good luck with that.'

"But when I heard they were still doing 'Heigh Ho'? That's when I lost it. I immediately called up Doc and said, 'You know I had something to do with that song.'

"I never even mentioned the belted waistcoats, which they're all still wearing. Totally my idea.

"I thought about getting a lawyer, but decided it wasn't worth it. But all that effed me up for years. I'm still trying to deal with it.

"At first I was angry. Really angry. But over time I just became Grumpy again.

"Now my family is on my case, saying that the whole 'Grumpy thing' has got to end.

"Really? Who am I supposed to be now? 'Empty?'

"That's why I'm here.

"I don't know if any of this makes any sense. But thanks for listening."

As the short man finishes, murmurs of approval and understanding rumble throughout the room.

"Thanks, Grumpy," they seem to say as one. "Keep coming back. You're in the right place."

PALINDROME PALACE

TEXT BY BEN CELSI ART BY DAVID CHELSEA

I AM SO MAD, YO! LLAMAS USE MANY NAMES: USAMA, LLOYD, AMOS, MAI...
TARA! NOT A RAT, A RAT ON A RAT!
EVIL TONY! AMY MAY NOT LIVE!
BOOBS IS TITS!
TITS IS BOOB!
UM, EMINEM SEES MEN? I'M EMU!
ROADIES WANTED
EMU
POOP, SAM! ALL LLAMAS POOP!

I Saw Your Mother's Ass

A husband gets into bed. His wife speaks first.

Wife: You okay?
Husband: Not really.
Wife: Want to talk about it?
Husband: No.
Wife: Why?
Husband: It's too weird.
Wife: What's too weird?
Husband: I'd rather not say.
Wife: Now you're scaring me.
Husband: Why?
Wife: Because we've been married a long time, and I've never seen you this color before.
Husband: Can't help it.
Wife: Please tell me.
Husband: Fine.
Wife: ...Well?
Husband: *(after a deep breath)* I saw your mother's ass.
Wife: What are you saying?
Husband: That I saw your 87-year-old mother's 87-year-old ass.
Wife: How?
Husband: I was on my way to the bathroom, a door was open, and there it was in all its horrifying glory.
Wife: God, she must've been embarrassed.
Husband: No.
Wife: No?
Husband: Not at all.
Wife: Why not?
Husband: Because she didn't see me.
Wife: How's it possible that you walk in on someone in the bathroom and they not see you?
Husband: Because she wasn't in the bathroom.
Wife: But you just said...
Husband: I said that I was on my way to the bathroom.
Wife: Yeah...
Husband: And I passed the gym, innocently looked in, and saw your mother on my stationary bike.
Wife: Naked?
Husband: Like an 87-year-old jaybird.
Wife: From behind?
Husband: Yes. That's where your mother's ass is located. In the back.
Wife: I think you'll get over it.
Husband: I'm not so sure about that. In fact, I'm wondering how I can ever look at her again. In fact, I'm wondering if you and I should separate and get back together after she dies.
Wife: You wouldn't be overreacting, would you?
Husband: Trust me, any normal man would be mortified.
Wife: Come on, you've seen her in a bathing suit. I'm sure there were no surprises.
Husband: Not so.
Wife: What do you mean 'not so'?
Husband: I can't talk about it.
Wife: What can't you talk about?
Husband: The surprise. Now let me go to sleep, okay?
Wife: Fine.

He turns off the light for about six seconds, then turns on the light.

Husband: Did you know your mother has a tattoo?
Wife: She what?
Husband: Yep.
Wife: Where?
Husband: On her four-score-and-seven-year-old ass.
Wife: Oh, please...
Husband: Why would I make this up? Why would I possibly want this conversation to go any longer that it already has?
Wife: May I ask what it's a tattoo of?
Husband: You sure you want to know?
Wife: No. But tell me anyway.
Husband: Ready?
Wife: Yeah.
Husband: Hitler.
Wife: Hitler?
Husband: Yep...
Wife: *The* Hitler?
Husband: That's the Hitler.
Wife: My 87-year-old mother has a tattoo of Adolf Hitler on her ass.
Husband: That's right. And I must say that the Fuhrer looks less than thrilled to be there.
Wife: You sure you're that you're not making this up?
Husband: Nope...
Wife: Or mistook, let's say, a mole, for Hitler?
Husband: A mole for Hitler? No. And I didn't mistake cellulite for Goebbels, either. This is a tattoo, and it's Hitler and if you don't believe me, go down and take a look for yourself.
Wife: I think I will.
Husband: Fine.

She gets out of bed, leaves the bedroom and returns about a minute later.

Wife: You're right. It's Hitler.
Husband: Told you.
Wife: Yes, but what you didn't tell me was that every time my mother pedals

---

Alan Zweibel's *latest book, a parody of the Haggadah titled* **For This We Left Egypt?**, *was co-written with Dave Barry and Adam Mansbach, who are less Jewish than Alan.*

Hitler's arm comes up in one of those Third Reich salutes.
Husband: I thought I'd spare you.
Wife: Thanks.
Husband: So, what do we do now?
Wife: What do you mean?
Husband: Well, we've solved the mystery of 'who' the tattoo is. Aren't you at all curious as to why it's there? As to why your 87-year-old, Jewish mother who's been a registered Democrat since Truman was president has a picture of the man who thought of the Final Solution on her butt?
Wife: Yes, but I'm scared…
Husband: Did she ever date Hitler?
Wife: What?
Husband: You know, they were young, impulsive, had too much to drink one night, took a cab downtown and got tattoos of each other before she realized he wasn't a guy to be trusted?
Wife: Lovely, so according to that scenario, Hitler, who was arguably the worst human being who ever lived, had a tattoo of my mother on his butt.
Husband: It's possible…
Wife: You're saying that in all those newsreels when he was giving those speeches and goose-stepping in those parades and invading Poland he may have had a picture of my mother on his ass.
Husband: Very, very possible…
Wife: Jesus, could we please end this conversation?
Husband: I'd love to.
Wife: Fine.

They turn off their lights. About a minute later, he speaks first.

Husband: I can't sleep.
Wife: Neither can I.
Husband: I keep thinking about your mother's ass.
Wife: I keep thinking about Hitler's ass.
Husband: And I keep thinking I'll need a new seat for my stationary bike. **B**

JOHN CUNEO

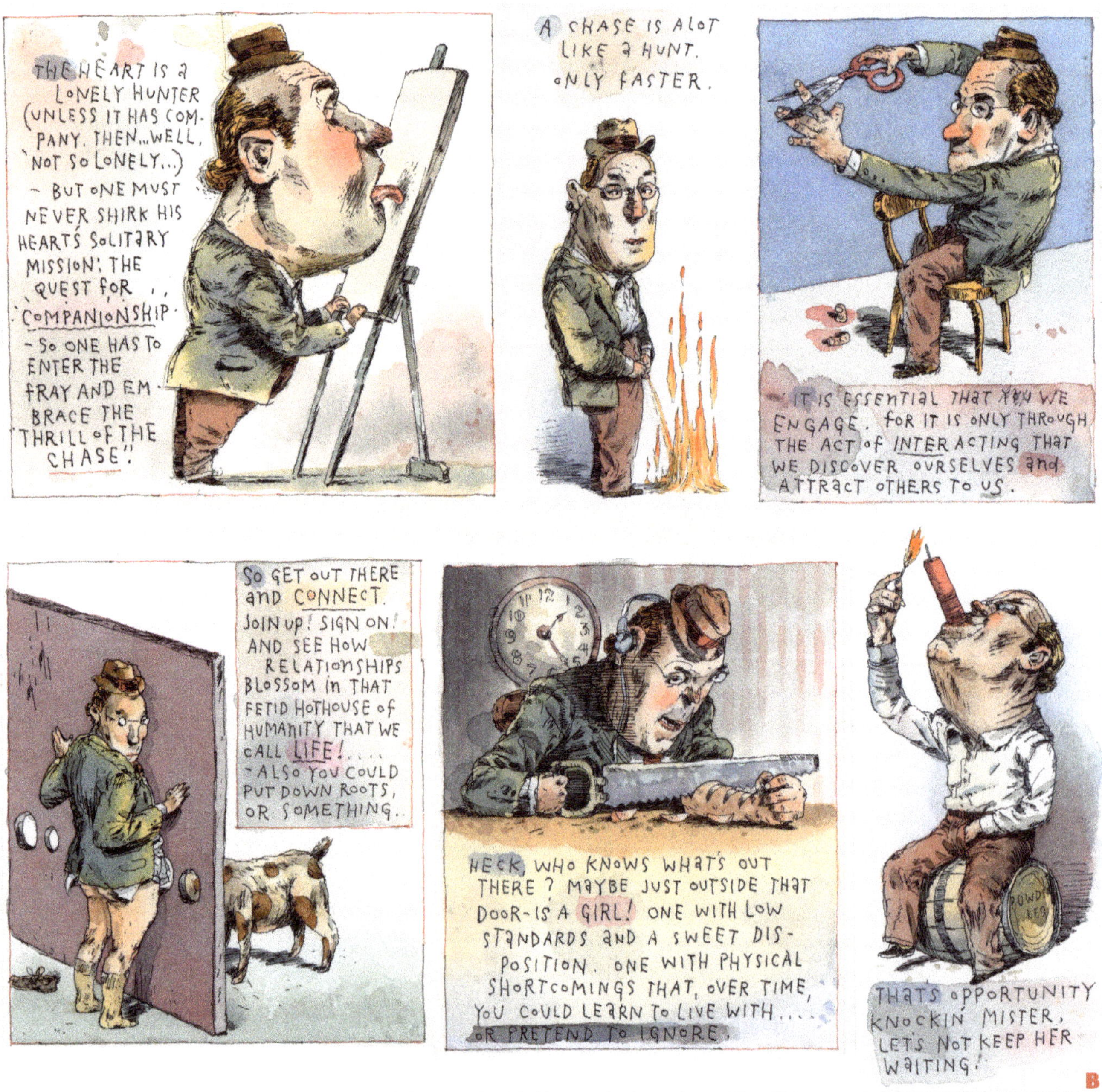
THE HEART IS A LONELY HUNTER (UNLESS IT HAS COMPANY. THEN...WELL, NOT SO LONELY...) – BUT ONE MUST NEVER SHIRK HIS HEART'S SOLITARY MISSION: THE QUEST FOR "COMPANIONSHIP" – SO ONE HAS TO ENTER THE FRAY AND EMBRACE THE "THRILL OF THE CHASE".
A CHASE IS ALOT LIKE A HUNT. ONLY FASTER.
IT IS ESSENTIAL THAT WE ENGAGE. FOR IT IS ONLY THROUGH THE ACT OF INTERACTING THAT WE DISCOVER OURSELVES AND ATTRACT OTHERS TO US.
SO GET OUT THERE AND CONNECT. JOIN UP! SIGN ON! AND SEE HOW RELATIONSHIPS BLOSSOM IN THAT FETID HOTHOUSE OF HUMANITY THAT WE CALL LIFE!.... – ALSO YOU COULD PUT DOWN ROOTS, OR SOMETHING..
HECK, WHO KNOWS WHAT'S OUT THERE? MAYBE JUST OUTSIDE THAT DOOR – IS A GIRL! ONE WITH LOW STANDARDS AND A SWEET DISPOSITION. ONE WITH PHYSICAL SHORTCOMINGS THAT, OVER TIME, YOU COULD LEARN TO LIVE WITH.... OR PRETEND TO IGNORE.
THAT'S OPPORTUNITY KNOCKIN' MISTER, LET'S NOT KEEP HER WAITING!

B

THE COMICS SUPPLEMENT TO THE AMERICAN BYSTANDER!

LOUCHE & SEEDY PRESTIDIGITATOR APPROVED!

VOL. 2, NO. 2 • FALL 2017

Marvy

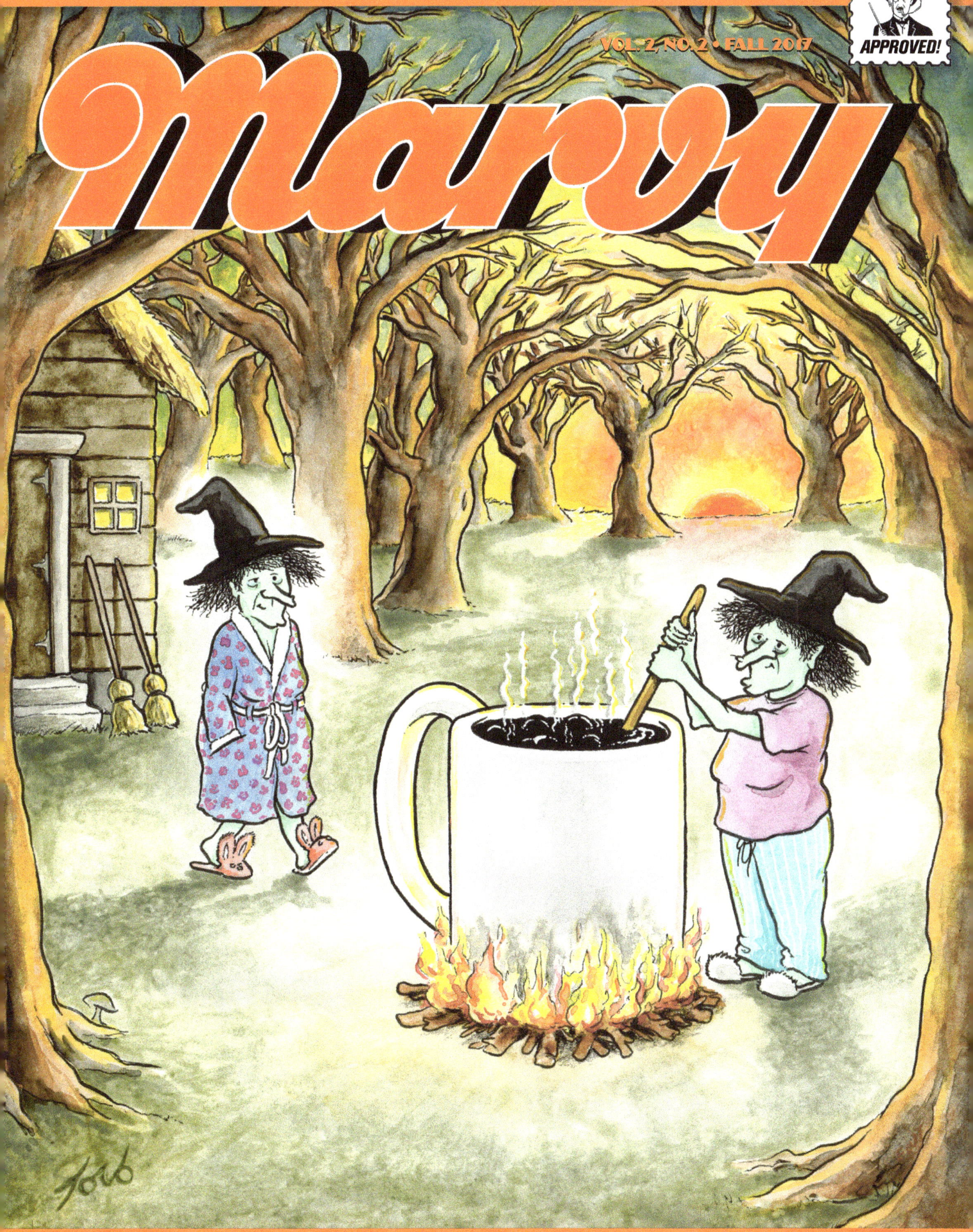
Toro

TORO • KOFORD • MOTLEY • POND • SIERGEY • ADAMS
BLECHMAN • BARRETT • ENOS • GAMMILL • GROSS & HACHTMAN

"Extraterrestrials live among us."

LEARN HOW TO IDENTIFY AND BEFRIEND THEM.

THE KEY TO MAKING FRIENDS WITH AN ALIEN FROM OUTER SPACE IS TO LEARN THEIR LANGUAGE. THAT'S WHERE WE COME IN. OUR 17 VOLUME SET OF DICTIONARIES AND INSTRUCTIONS WILL HAVE YOU SPEAKING ALIEN IN NEXT TO NO TIME. HERE'S AN EXAMPLE OF THE ALIEN LANGUAGE YOU'LL BE MASTERING:

A TYPICAL ALIEN — FUN, RIGHT?

ALIEN DICTIONARIES & INSTRUCTIONAL MATERIALS.
DEPT ᴜᴍᴏɪʟᴏᴜ=ᴜ=ɪ
BOX ɴ=ᴡ=ɴ=ɴ=ᴏ=ʀᴀɪɪ
BROOKLYN NY

☐ PLEASE SEND ME AS MUCH INFORMATION AS YOU ARE ALLOWED, AS SOON AS IS HUMANLY POSSIBLE.
☐ PLEASE DO NOTHING, AND FORGET WE EVER MET. GOOD BYE.

PRINT NAME_____ AGE____
ADDRESS_____
CITADEL_____ PLANET_____

TURN YOUR HANDS INTO CLAWS!!

OUR TIME-HONORED METHOD GETS INSTANT RESULTS

OUR PATENTED CURSE IS VERY EFFECTIVE & ALMOST INSTANT. THRILL YOUR FRIENDS WITH WITHERED HANDS!

BEFORE — AFTER

RUSH YOUR ORDER NOW TO:
WITCHES KNOLL
THE CLEARING BEYOND THE DAWN
HUT 7. c/o KOBLINKA THE ANGRY
BROOKLYN NY. NO ZIP REQ'D.
• ACT NOW OR ELSE •

INCLUDE:
☐ 1 CURSE   ☐ CURSE, POTION AND
☐ 1 CURSE + 1 POTION   ANTIDOTE

NAME_____
ADDRESS_____
CITY_____ STATE____ ZIP____
FINAL PRICE FORTHCOMING

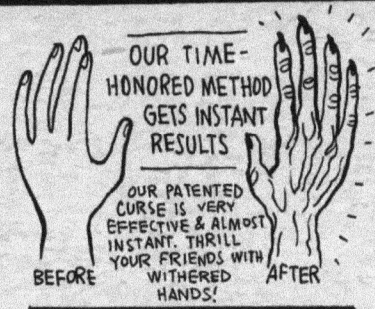

BIKE DECALS
RUIN THE PRISTINE FINISH OF YOUR BRAND NEW BICYCLE!!

PUT THEM ON YOUR DAD'S CAR — $1.00 — IMPOSSIBLE TO REMOVE WITHOUT THE ASSISTANCE OF HARSH CHEMICALS.

350 PERMANENT STICKERS — THE CRAZIEST DESIGNS YOU EVER DID SEE! ONCE A MONTH FOR LIFE.

HI! — YOUR DAD

COMIC BOOKS FOR SALE
FOR THE EMOTIONALLY STUNTED

10s of thousands of titles to choose from. Captain Ennui? Got it. Therapy Boy? Yep. Tommy's Revenge? Sure. Tales of Closure? Yes! (Except for issue 17.)

• CALL FOR COMPLETE LIST •
NO DEALERS OR THERAPISTS PLEASE
Brooklyn NY

YOU CAN HAVE A HE-MAN VOICE

Send today for FREE booklet. We will help you get those vocal chords in shape to defend Eternia against the forces of this guy called SKELETOR.
• BOX 312 • ETERNIA NJ •

FREE COMIC BOOK FREE
READ THE CRAZY ADVENTURES OF A GUY TRYING TO SELL AD SPACE IN COMIC BOOKS!

1001 THINGS YOU CAN GET FREE
COMPLETE LIST For Only 50¢

WE WILL TEACH YOU HOW TO STEAL VARIOUS ITEMS OF INCONSEQUENTIAL VALUE. KETCHUP PACKETS. NAPKINS. STUFF LIKE THAT.
Brooklyn, NY

FREE — A MIND-BENDING PSYCHEDELIC POSTER

WORDS JUST CAN'T DESCRIBE THE REALITY-ALTERING BEAUTY OF THIS POSTER WE ARE TRYING TO SELL YOU. BUT WE BOUGHT THIS WHOLE AD SPACE SO WE MAY AS WELL TRY. HERE GOES: IMAGINE A BEAUTIFUL WATERFALL IN OUTER SPACE AND SURROUNDED BY THE MOST COLORFUL JELLYFISH KNOWN TO MAN. THERE. THAT DESCRIBES IT PERFECTLY. SO HOW ABOUT YOU BUY ONE FROM US? WE WERE KIDDING ABOUT THE "FREE" PART. BOX 7. BKLN

HOME BUSINESS — BIG $ —

HERE'S HOW IT WORKS: WE DROP-SHIP STOLEN ITEMS TO YOUR HOUSE & IT IS UP TO YOU TO SELL THEM — BY ANY MEANS NECESSARY!!!
PERFECTLY LEGAL • BROOKLYN, NY

WE WERE UNABLE TO SELL THIS ADVERTISING SPACE

AND SO IT SITS EMPTY, FOR ALL THE WORLD TO SEE. SHAME ON US!

If this keeps up much longer, we will surely have to fire our advertising team and just include blank pages in our comic books where the ads belong.

OUR SINCEREST APOLOGIES — the management

Fox on a Bike

HE HAS A MIND OF HIS OWN

FROM **$79.50** REWARD — BORN TO RIDE

JUST TRY TO CATCH HIM!

My daughter Myrtle made the mistake of bringing home a feral fox. We brought it into our garage and the dang thing stole my miniature motorcycle!

THAT'S WHERE YOU COME IN — We are forming a search party to find the little scamp. Will you join us? Call for details.
BROOKLYN 7-452 • NIGHTS ONLY

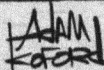

HECTOR

BY T MOTLEY

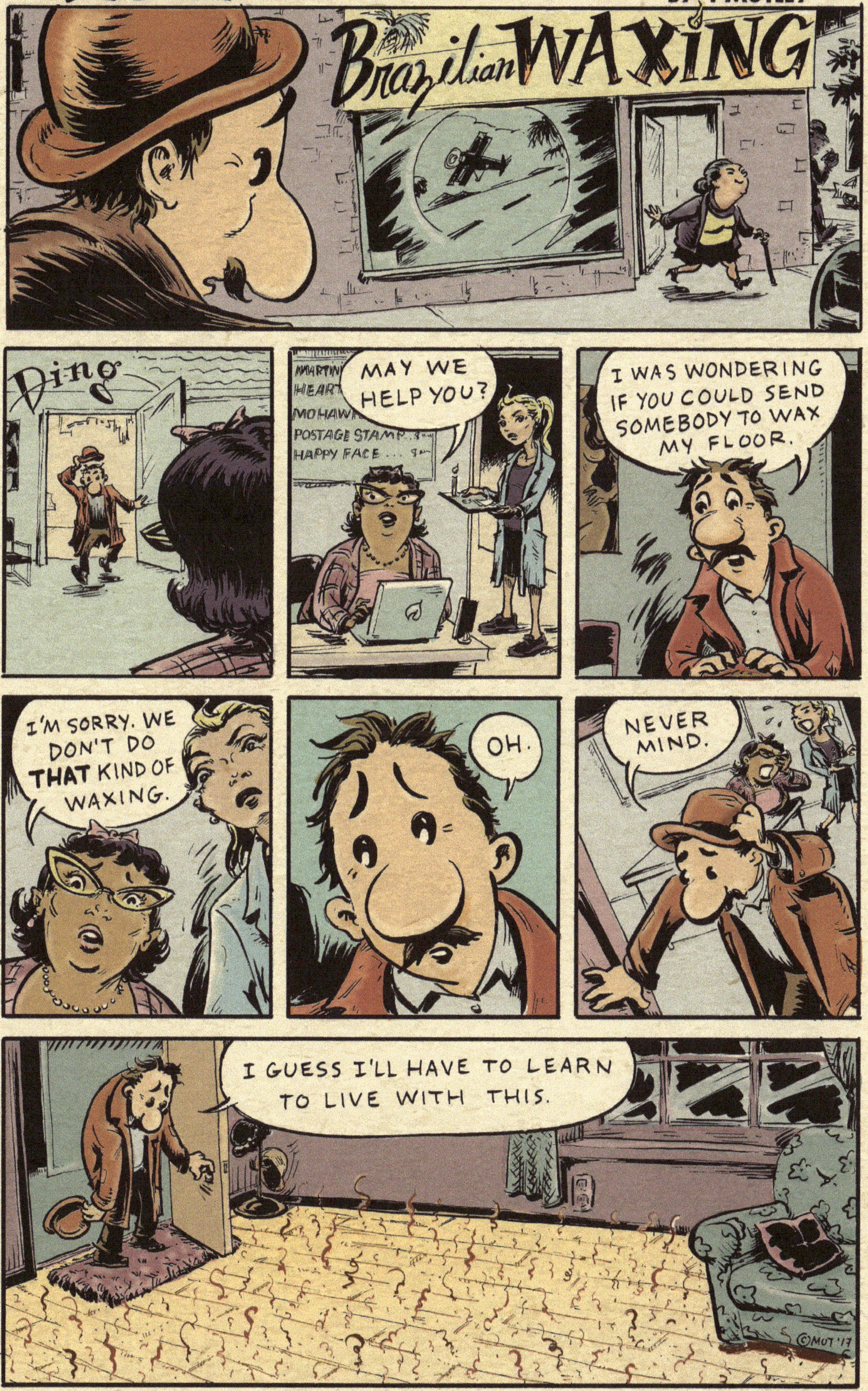
Brazilian WAXING
Ding
POSTAGE STAMP
HAPPY FACE
MAY WE HELP YOU?
I WAS WONDERING IF YOU COULD SEND SOMEBODY TO WAX MY FLOOR.
I'M SORRY. WE DON'T DO **THAT** KIND OF WAXING.
OH.
NEVER MIND.
I GUESS I'LL HAVE TO LEARN TO LIVE WITH THIS.
©MOT '17

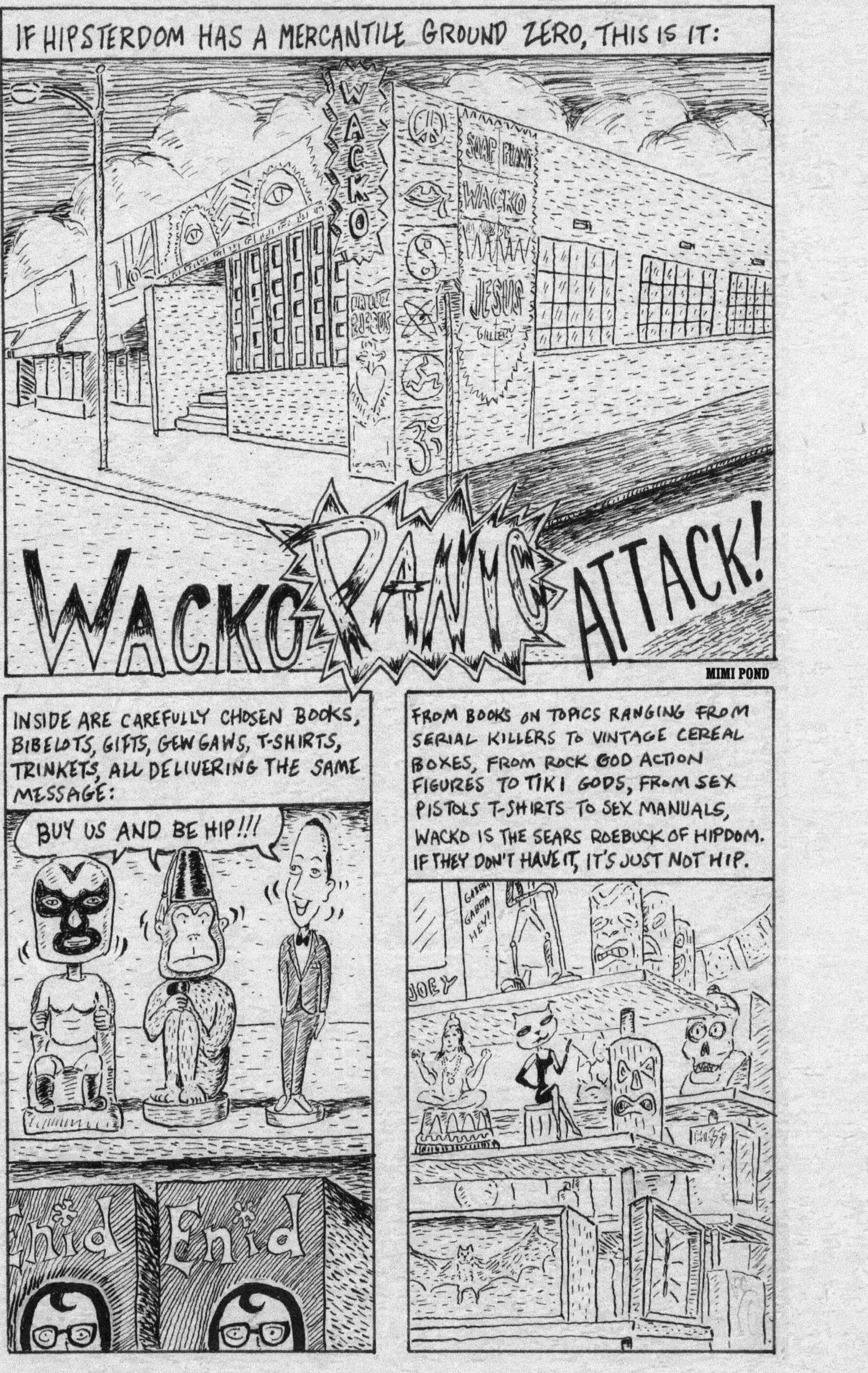
IF HIPSTERDOM HAS A MERCANTILE GROUND ZERO, THIS IS IT:
WACKO
SOAP PLANT
WACKO
JESUS
GALLERY
WACKO PANIC ATTACK!
MIMI POND
INSIDE ARE CAREFULLY CHOSEN BOOKS, BIBELOTS, GIFTS, GEWGAWS, T-SHIRTS, TRINKETS, ALL DELIVERING THE SAME MESSAGE:
BUY US AND BE HIP!!!
Enid
Enid
FROM BOOKS ON TOPICS RANGING FROM SERIAL KILLERS TO VINTAGE CEREAL BOXES, FROM ROCK GOD ACTION FIGURES TO TIKI GODS, FROM SEX PISTOLS T-SHIRTS TO SEX MANUALS, WACKO IS THE SEARS ROEBUCK OF HIPDOM. IF THEY DON'T HAVE IT, IT'S JUST NOT HIP.
GABBA GABBA HEY!
JOEY

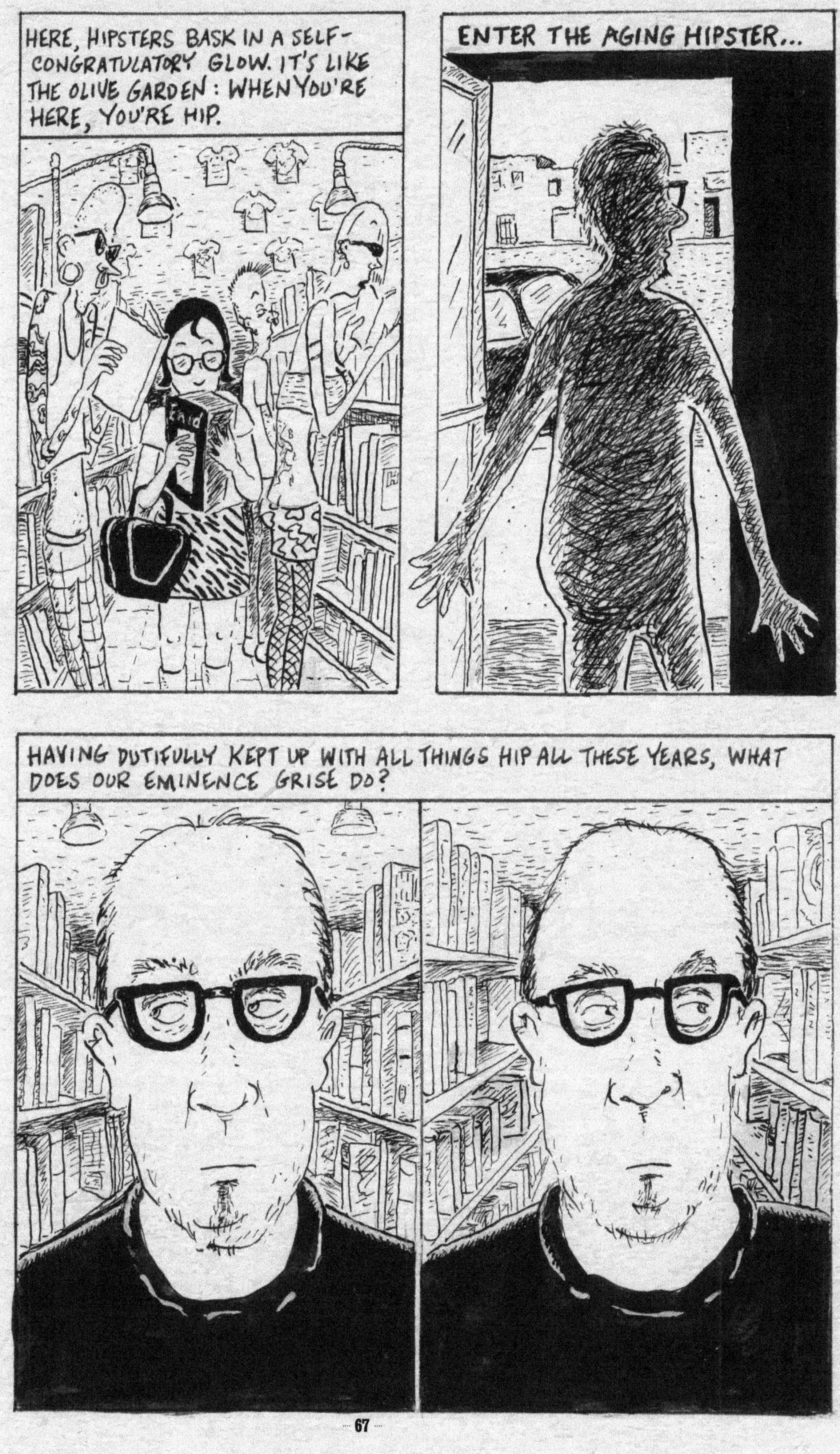
HERE, HIPSTERS BASK IN A SELF-CONGRATULATORY GLOW. IT'S LIKE THE OLIVE GARDEN: WHEN YOU'RE HERE, YOU'RE HIP.
Enid
ENTER THE AGING HIPSTER...
HAVING DUTIFULLY KEPT UP WITH ALL THINGS HIP ALL THESE YEARS, WHAT DOES OUR EMINENCE GRISE DO?

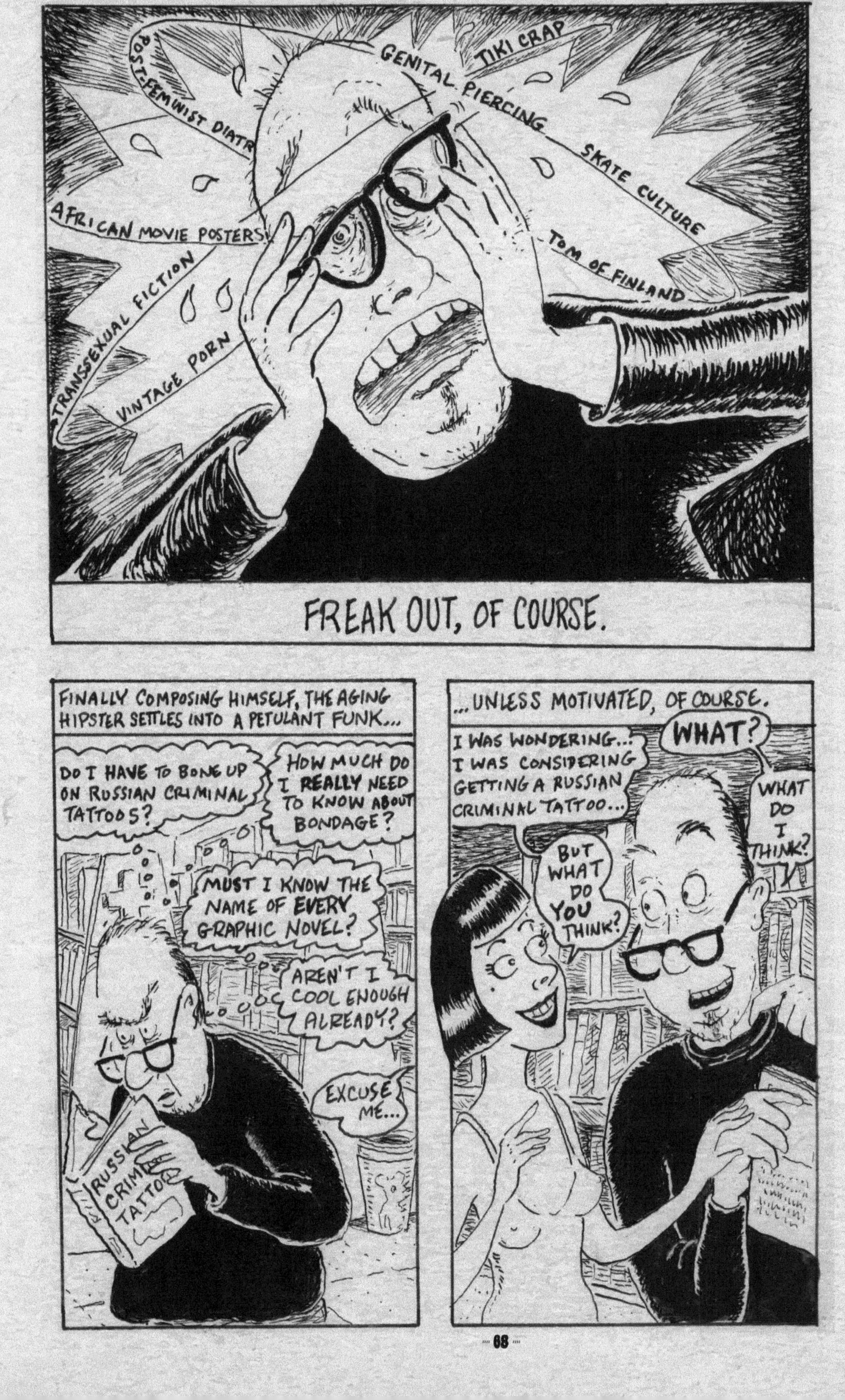
POST-FEMINIST DIATR
GENITAL PIERCING
TIKI CRAP
SKATE CULTURE
AFRICAN MOVIE POSTERS
TOM OF FINLAND
TRANSSEXUAL FICTION
VINTAGE PORN
FREAK OUT, OF COURSE.
FINALLY COMPOSING HIMSELF, THE AGING HIPSTER SETTLES INTO A PETULANT FUNK...
DO I HAVE TO BONE UP ON RUSSIAN CRIMINAL TATTOOS?
HOW MUCH DO I REALLY NEED TO KNOW ABOUT BONDAGE?
MUST I KNOW THE NAME OF EVERY GRAPHIC NOVEL?
AREN'T I COOL ENOUGH ALREADY?
EXCUSE ME...
...UNLESS MOTIVATED, OF COURSE.
I WAS WONDERING... I WAS CONSIDERING GETTING A RUSSIAN CRIMINAL TATTOO...
WHAT?
WHAT DO I THINK?
BUT WHAT DO YOU THINK?

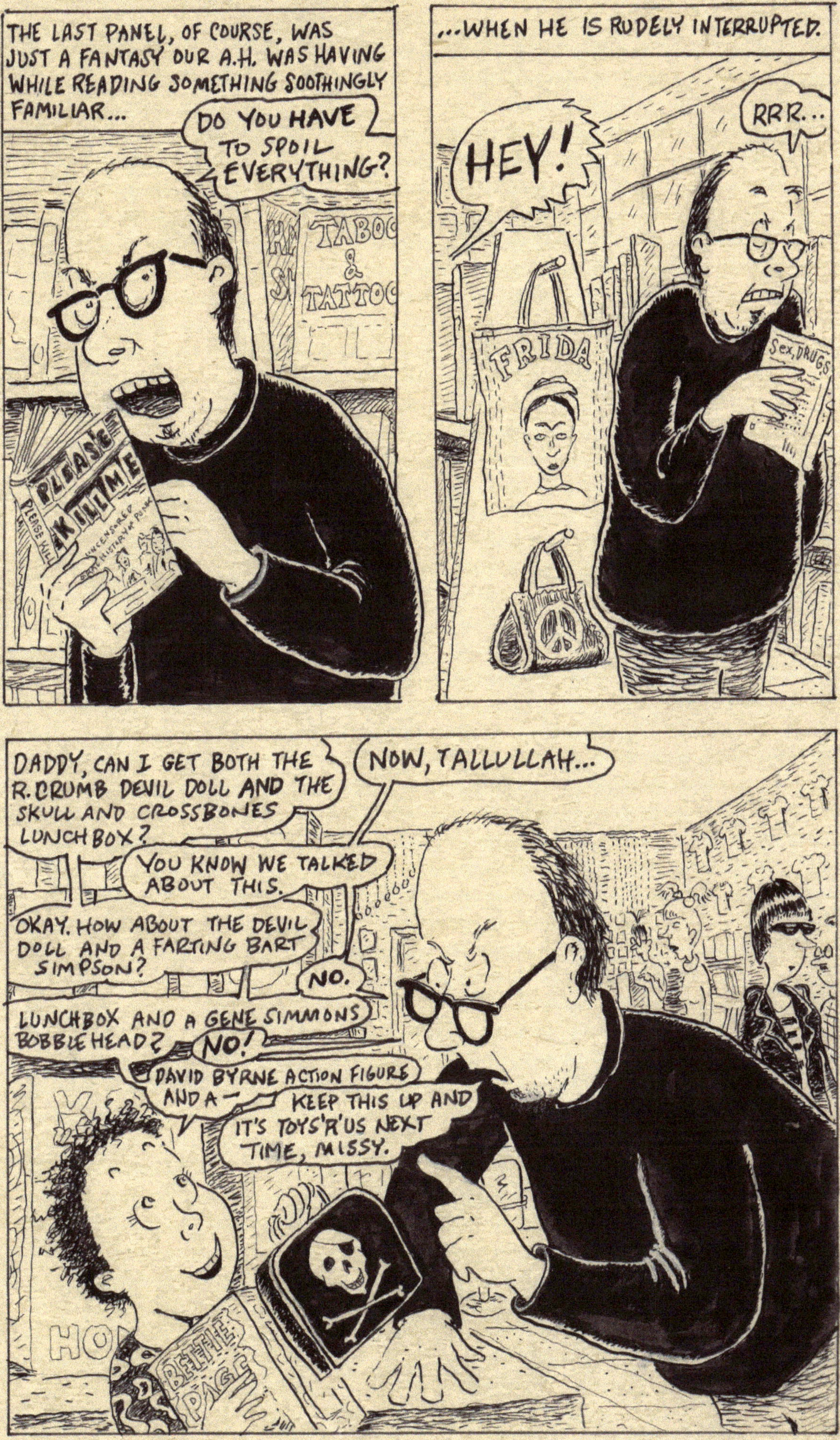
THE LAST PANEL, OF COURSE, WAS JUST A FANTASY OUR A.H. WAS HAVING WHILE READING SOMETHING SOOTHINGLY FAMILIAR...
DO YOU HAVE TO SPOIL EVERYTHING?
TABOO & TATTOO
PLEASE KILL ME
...WHEN HE IS RUDELY INTERRUPTED.
HEY!
RRR...
FRIDA
SEX, DRUGS
DADDY, CAN I GET BOTH THE R. CRUMB DEVIL DOLL AND THE SKULL AND CROSSBONES LUNCHBOX?
NOW, TALLULLAH...
YOU KNOW WE TALKED ABOUT THIS.
OKAY. HOW ABOUT THE DEVIL DOLL AND A FARTING BART SIMPSON?
NO.
LUNCHBOX AND A GENE SIMMONS BOBBLEHEAD?
NO!
DAVID BYRNE ACTION FIGURE AND A—
KEEP THIS UP AND IT'S TOYS'R'US NEXT TIME, MISSY.
BETTIE PAGE

GORILLA, YOU'RE A DESPERADO!

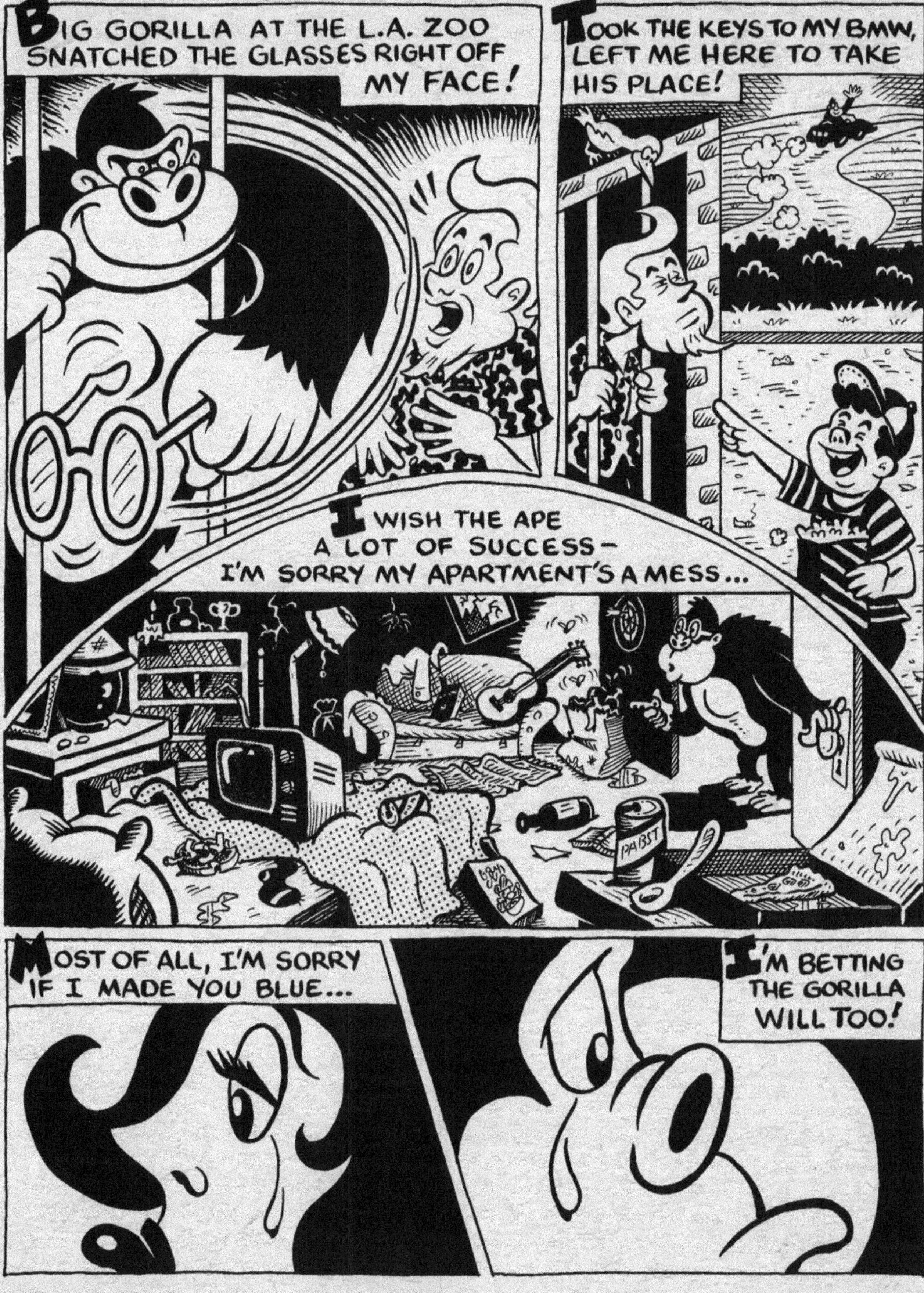
BIG GORILLA AT THE L.A. ZOO SNATCHED THE GLASSES RIGHT OFF MY FACE!
TOOK THE KEYS TO MY BMW, LEFT ME HERE TO TAKE HIS PLACE!
I WISH THE APE A LOT OF SUCCESS— I'M SORRY MY APARTMENT'S A MESS...
PABST
MOST OF ALL, I'M SORRY IF I MADE YOU BLUE...
I'M BETTING THE GORILLA WILL TOO!

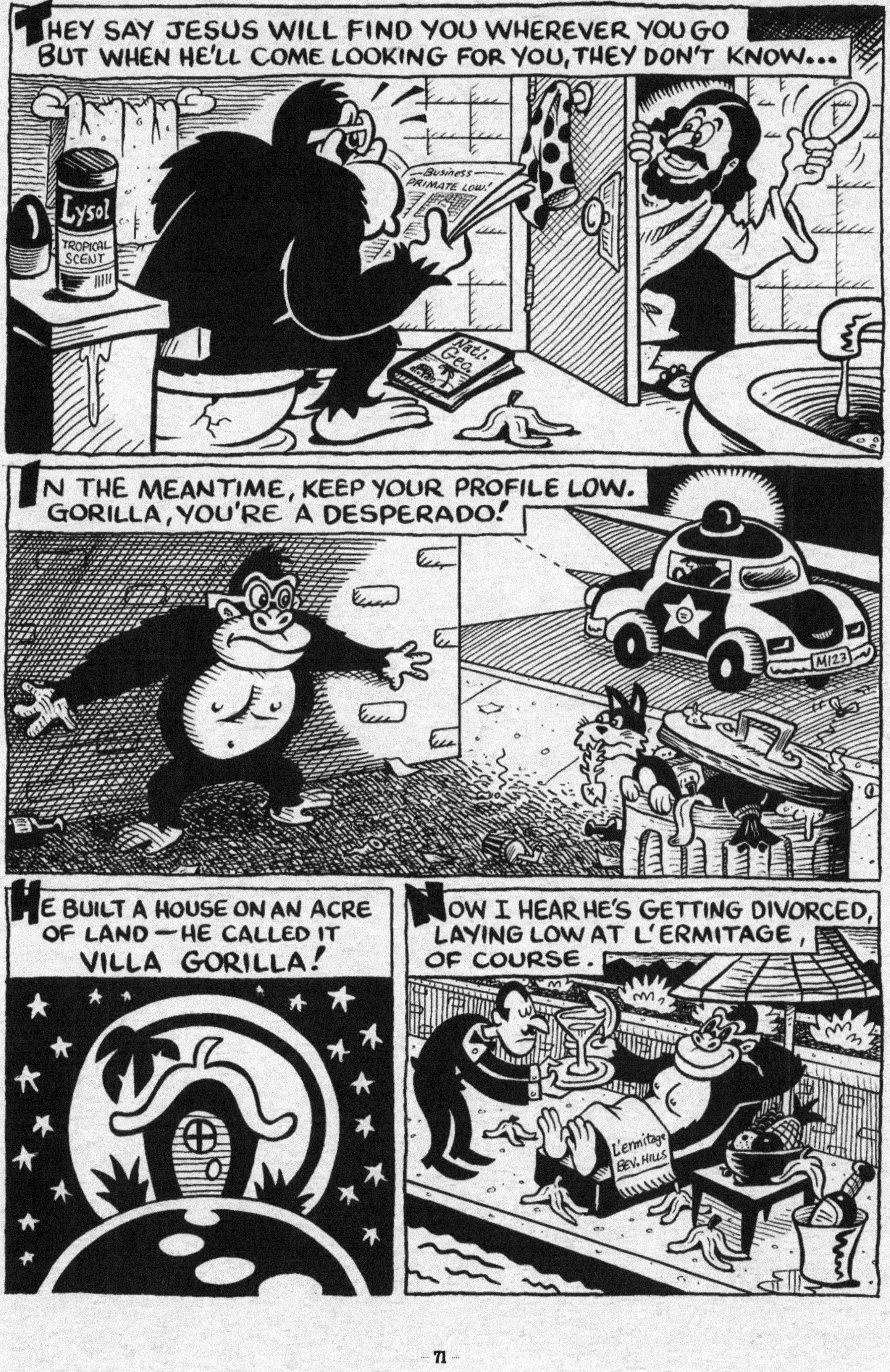
THEY SAY JESUS WILL FIND YOU WHEREVER YOU GO
BUT WHEN HE'LL COME LOOKING FOR YOU, THEY DON'T KNOW...
Lysol
TROPICAL SCENT
Business
PRIMATE LOW!
Natl. Geo.
IN THE MEANTIME, KEEP YOUR PROFILE LOW.
GORILLA, YOU'RE A DESPERADO!
M123
HE BUILT A HOUSE ON AN ACRE OF LAND — HE CALLED IT
VILLA GORILLA!
NOW I HEAR HE'S GETTING DIVORCED, LAYING LOW AT L'ERMITAGE, OF COURSE.
L'ermitage
BEV. HILLS

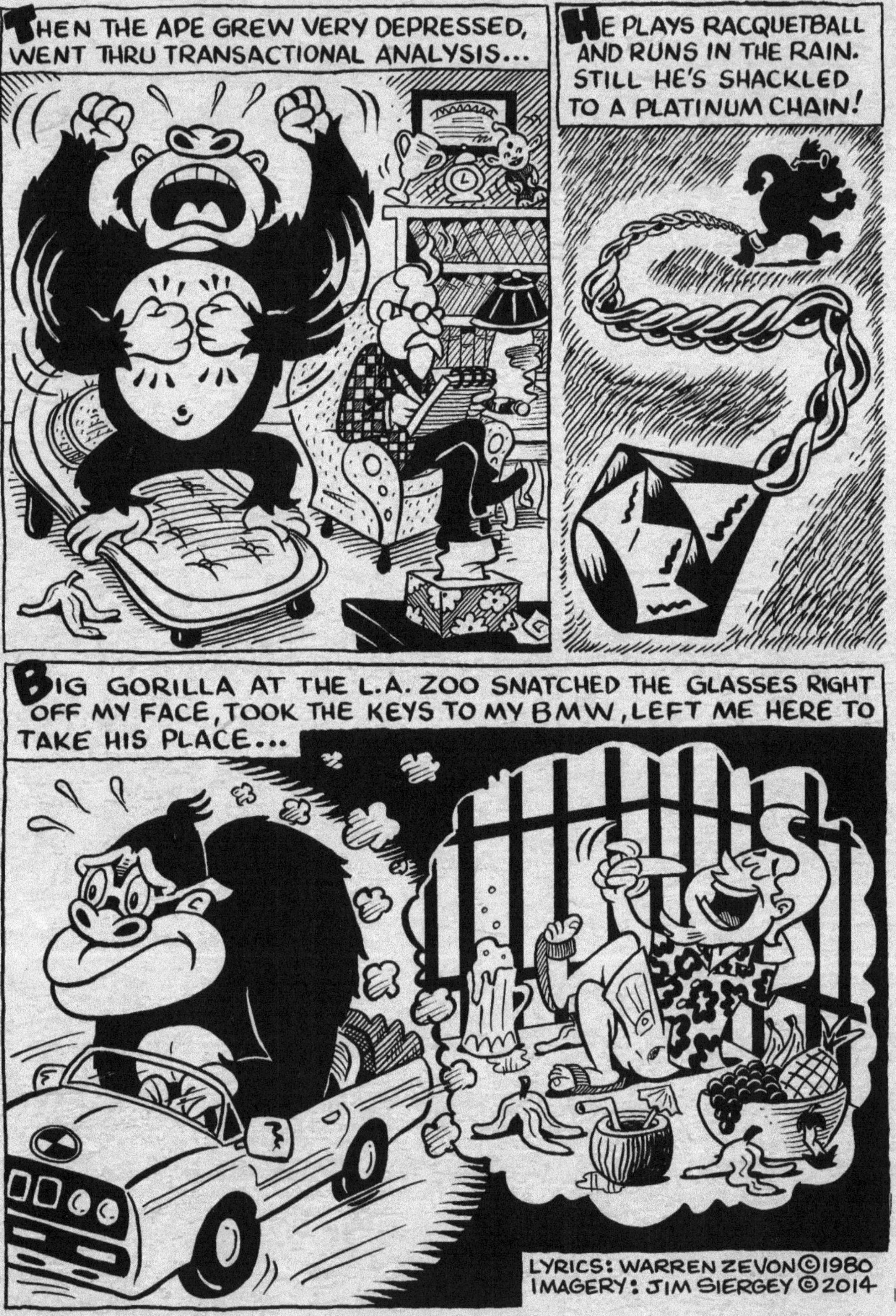
THEN THE APE GREW VERY DEPRESSED, WENT THRU TRANSACTIONAL ANALYSIS...
HE PLAYS RACQUETBALL AND RUNS IN THE RAIN. STILL HE'S SHACKLED TO A PLATINUM CHAIN!
BIG GORILLA AT THE L.A. ZOO SNATCHED THE GLASSES RIGHT OFF MY FACE, TOOK THE KEYS TO MY BMW, LEFT ME HERE TO TAKE HIS PLACE...
LYRICS: WARREN ZEVON ©1980
IMAGERY: JIM SIERGEY ©2014

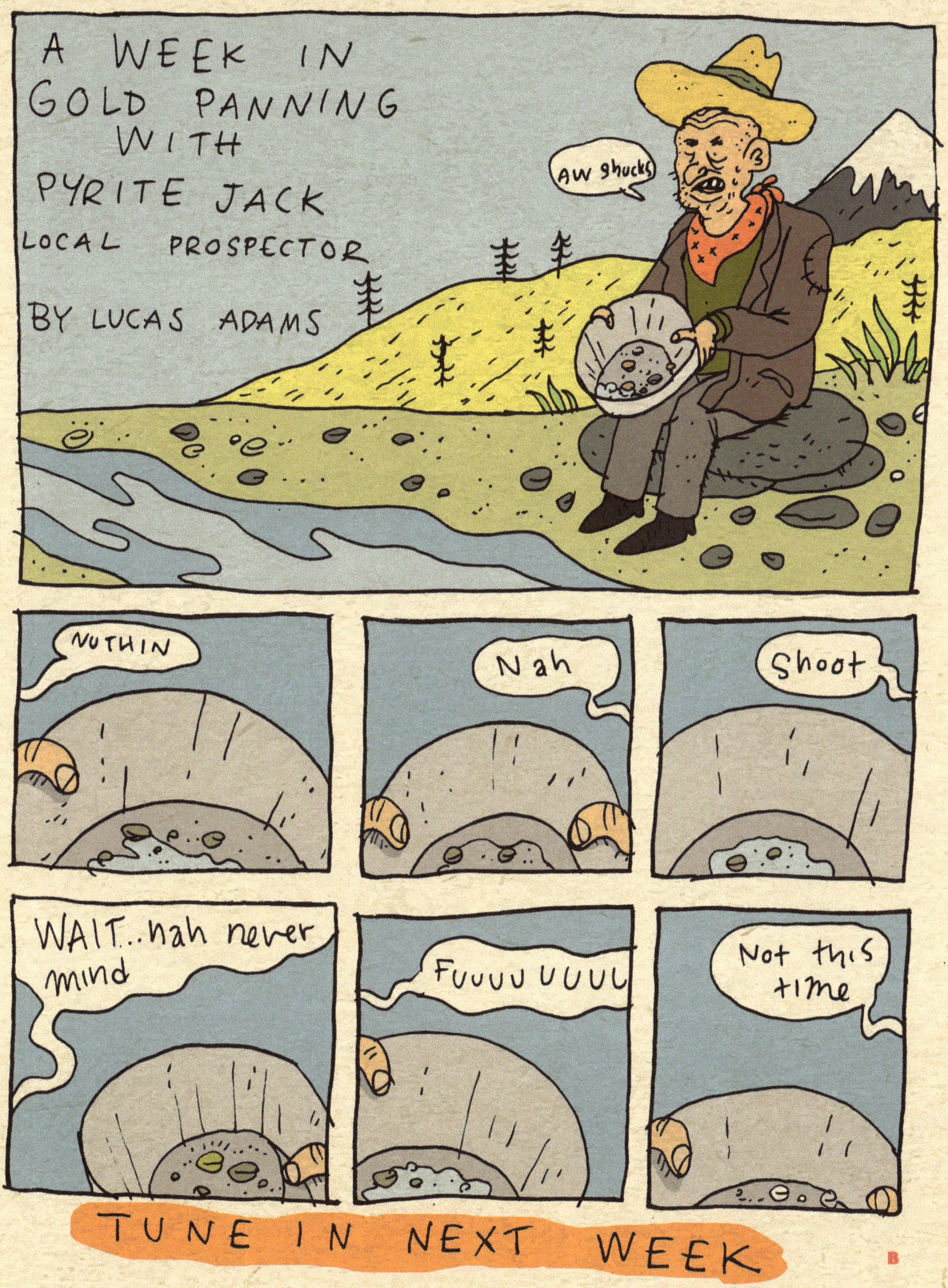

A WEEK IN GOLD PANNING WITH PYRITE JACK
LOCAL PROSPECTOR
BY LUCAS ADAMS
AW shucks
NUTHIN
Nah
Shoot
WAIT..nah never mind
FUUUUUUUL
Not this time
TUNE IN NEXT WEEK

AN OLD STORY

R. O. Blechman

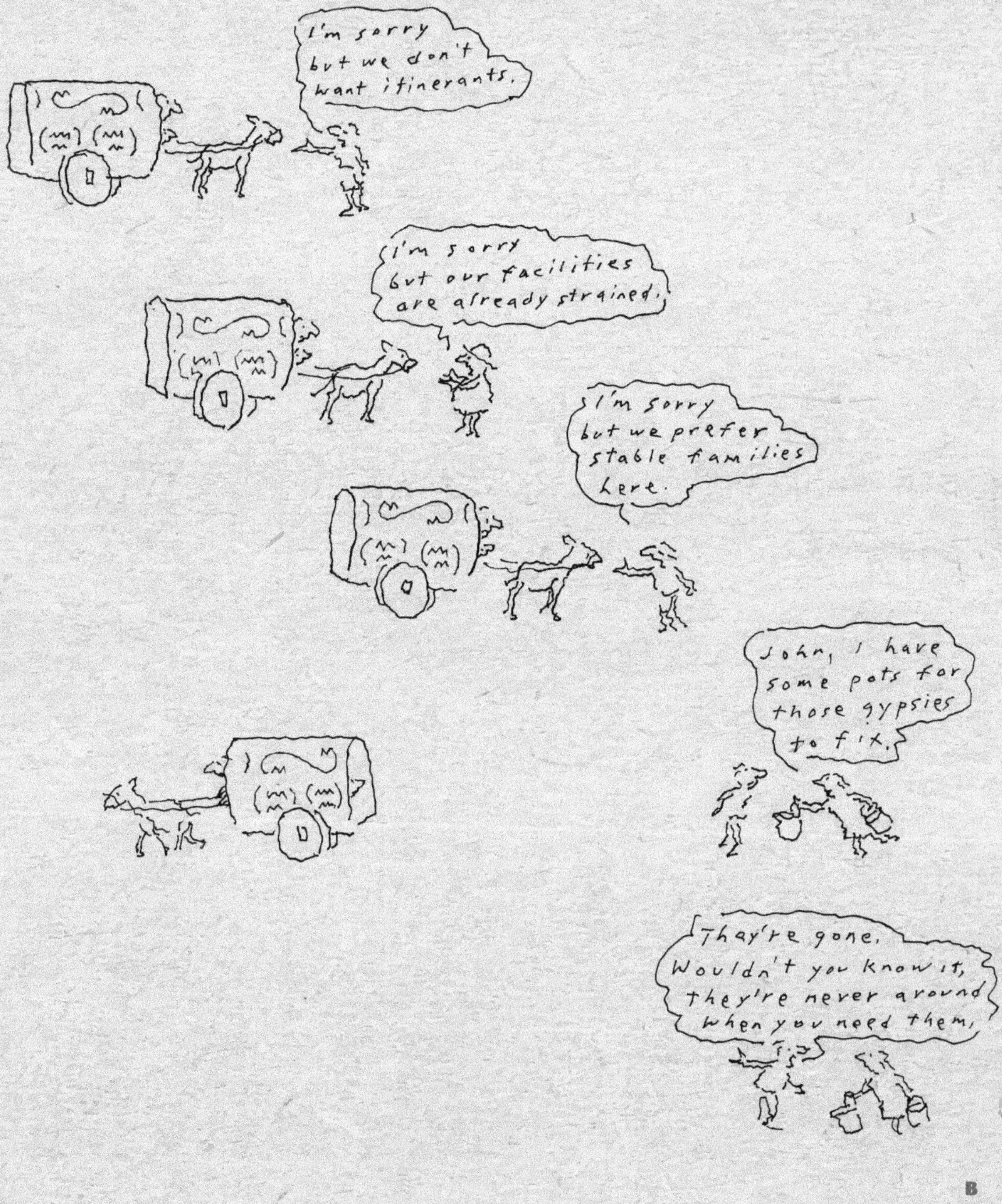
I'm sorry but we don't want itinerants.
I'm sorry but our facilities are already strained.
I'm sorry but we prefer stable families here.
John, I have some pots for those gypsies to fix.
Thay're gone. Wouldn't you know it, they're never around when you need them.

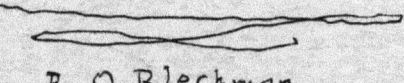

MANY UNHAPPY RETURNS

BY RON BARRETT | MADE IN CHINA | QUALITY CONTROL: GARY JACOBS

PLEASE INDICATE REASON FOR DISSATISFACTION

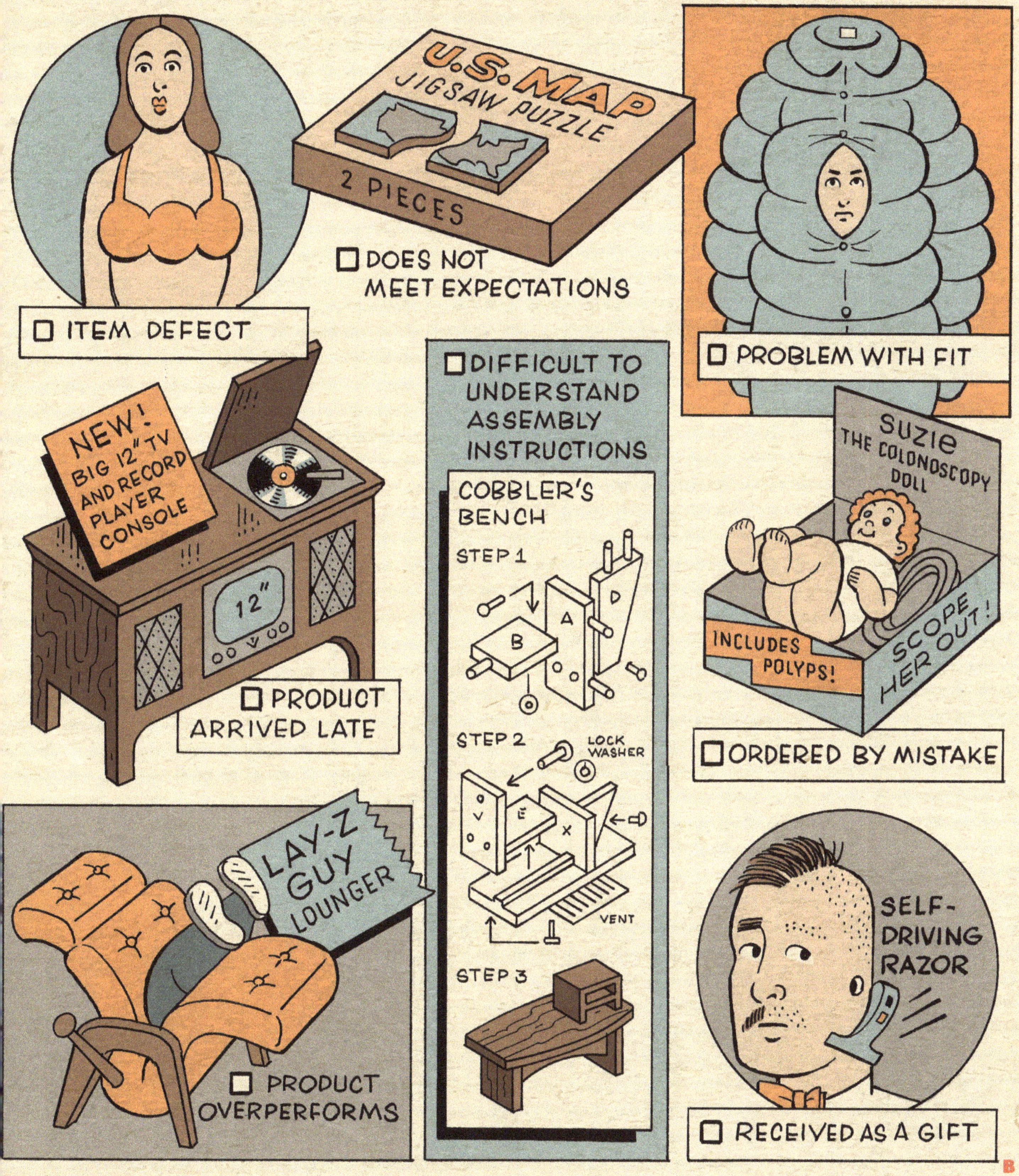
☐ ITEM DEFECT
U.S. MAP
JIGSAW PUZZLE
2 PIECES
☐ DOES NOT MEET EXPECTATIONS
☐ PROBLEM WITH FIT
NEW! BIG 12" TV AND RECORD PLAYER CONSOLE
12"
☐ PRODUCT ARRIVED LATE
☐ DIFFICULT TO UNDERSTAND ASSEMBLY INSTRUCTIONS
COBBLER'S BENCH
STEP 1
A
B
D
STEP 2
LOCK WASHER
E
X
VENT
STEP 3
SUZIE
THE COLONOSCOPY DOLL
INCLUDES POLYPS!
SCOPE HER OUT!
☐ ORDERED BY MISTAKE
LAY-Z GUY LOUNGER
☐ PRODUCT OVERPERFORMS
SELF-DRIVING RAZOR
☐ RECEIVED AS A GIFT

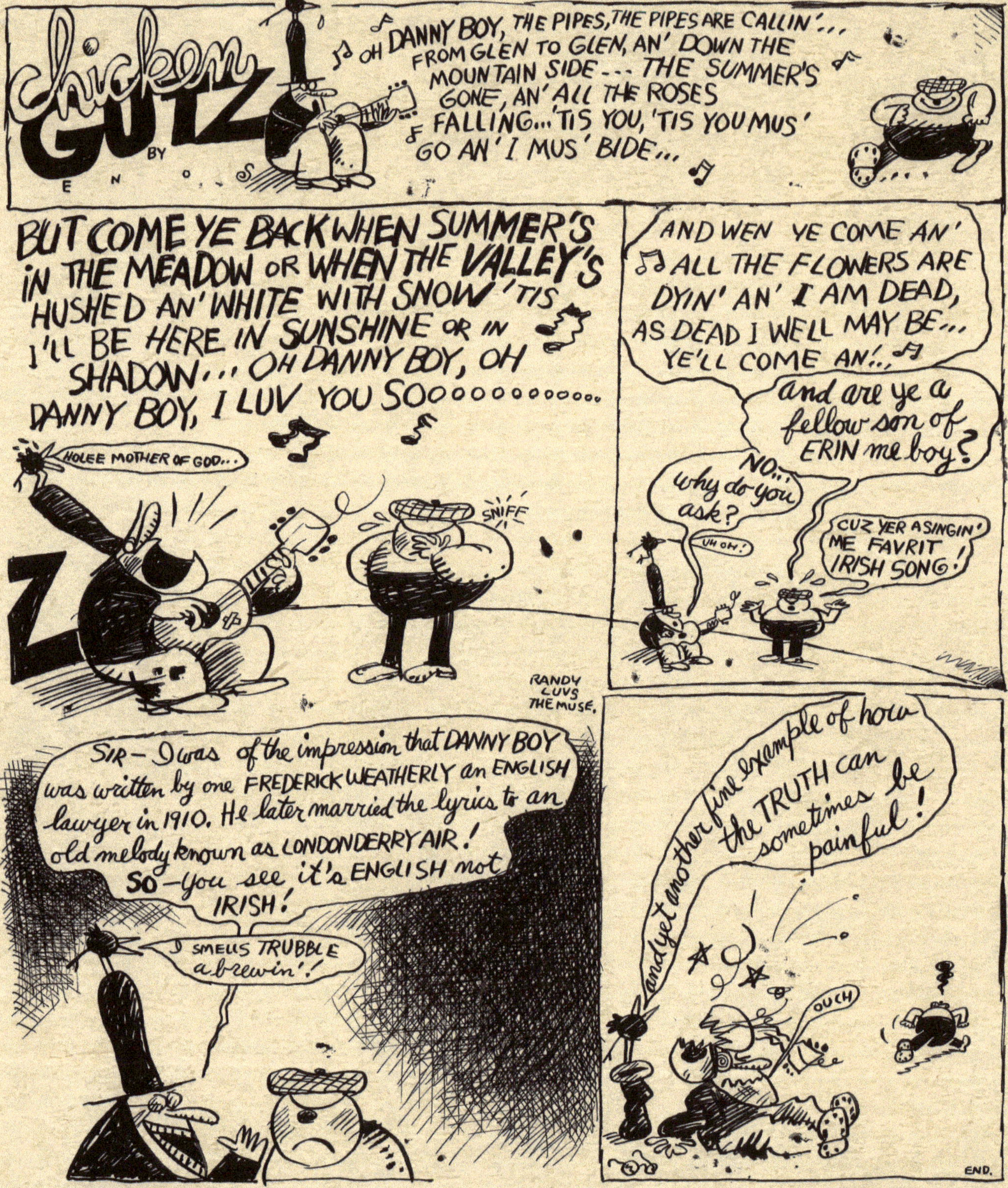
chicken GUTZ
BY E N O S
OH DANNY BOY, THE PIPES, THE PIPES ARE CALLIN'... FROM GLEN TO GLEN, AN' DOWN THE MOUNTAIN SIDE--- THE SUMMER'S GONE, AN' ALL THE ROSES FALLING... 'TIS YOU, 'TIS YOU MUS' GO AN' I MUS' BIDE...
BUT COME YE BACK WHEN SUMMER'S IN THE MEADOW OR WHEN THE VALLEY'S HUSHED AN' WHITE WITH SNOW 'TIS I'LL BE HERE IN SUNSHINE OR IN SHADOW... OH DANNY BOY, OH DANNY BOY, I LUV YOU SOooooooooooo
HOLEE MOTHER OF GOD...
SNIFF
RANDY LUVS THE MUSE.
AND WEN YE COME AN' ALL THE FLOWERS ARE DYIN' AN' I AM DEAD, AS DEAD I WELL MAY BE... YE'LL COME AN'...
and are ye a fellow son of ERIN me boy?
NO... why do you ask?
UH OH!
CUZ YER A SINGIN' ME FAVRIT IRISH SONG!
SIR - I was of the impression that DANNY BOY was written by one FREDERICK WEATHERLY an ENGLISH lawyer in 1910. He later married the lyrics to an old melody known as LONDONDERRY AIR! SO - you see it's ENGLISH not IRISH!
I SMELLS TRUBBLE a brewin'!
and yet another fine example of how the TRUTH can sometimes be painful!
OUCH
END.

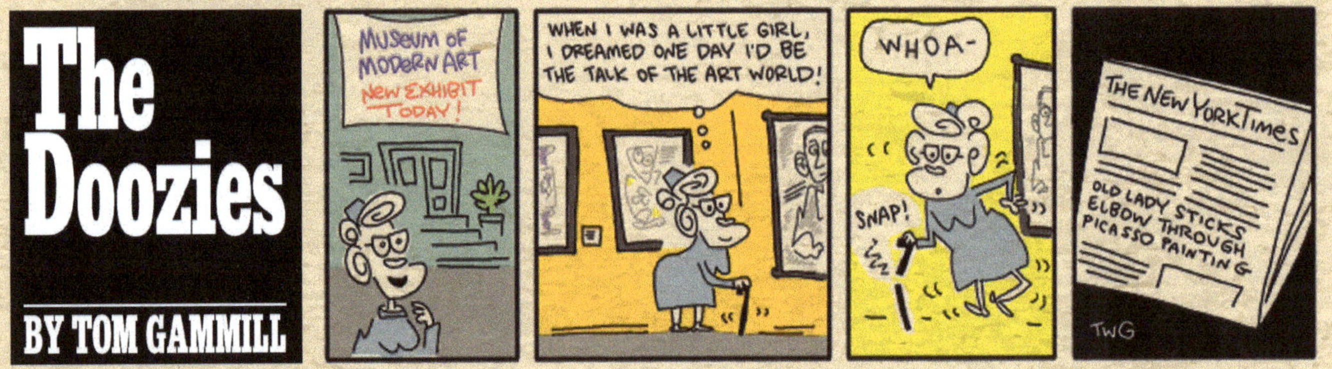
The Doozies
BY TOM GAMMILL
MUSEUM OF MODERN ART
NEW EXHIBIT TODAY!
WHEN I WAS A LITTLE GIRL, I DREAMED ONE DAY I'D BE THE TALK OF THE ART WORLD!
WHOA-
SNAP!
THE NEW YORK TIMES
OLD LADY STICKS ELBOW THROUGH PICASSO PAINTING
TWG

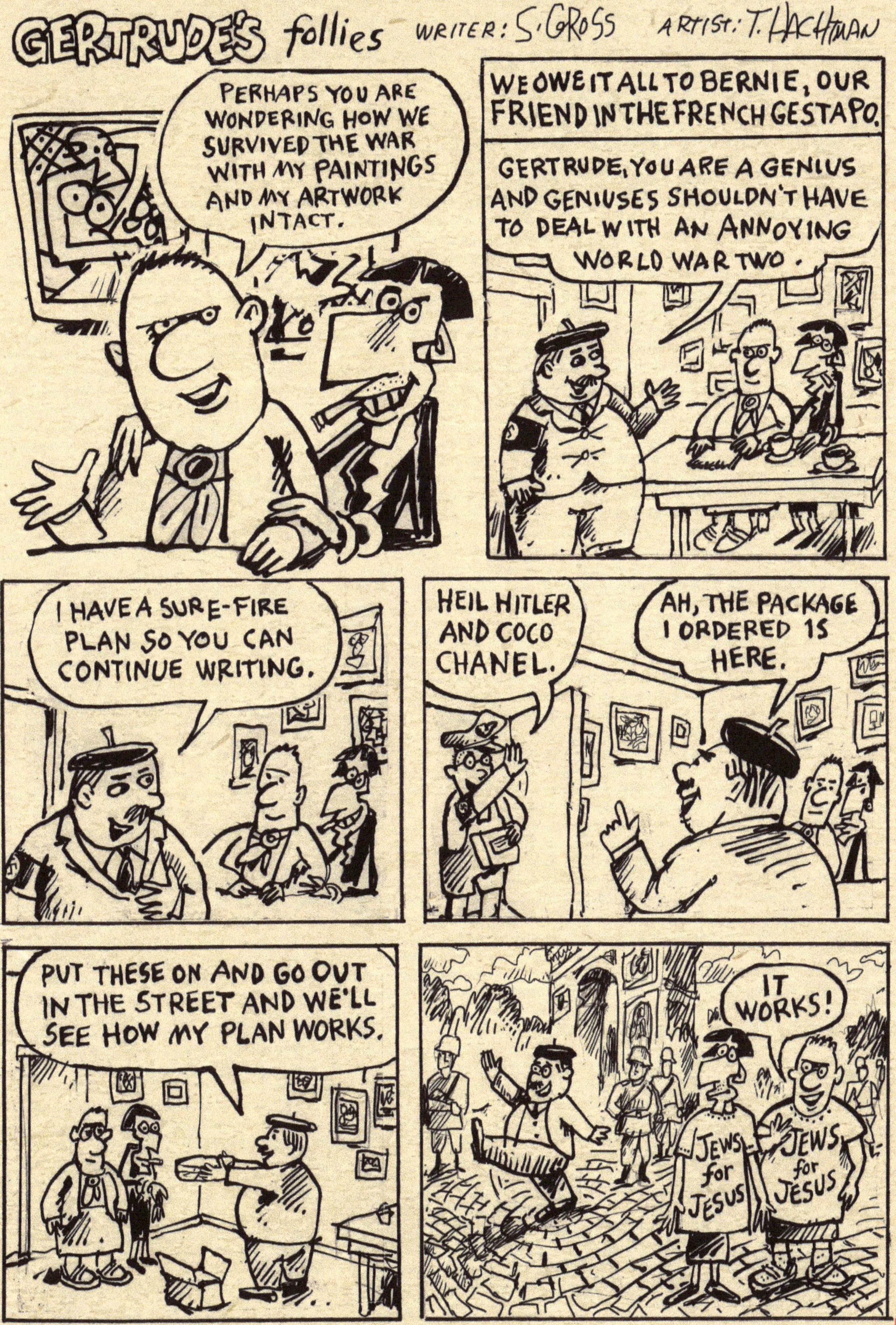
GERTRUDE'S follies WRITER: S. GROSS ARTIST: T. HACHTMAN
PERHAPS YOU ARE WONDERING HOW WE SURVIVED THE WAR WITH MY PAINTINGS AND MY ARTWORK INTACT.
WE OWE IT ALL TO BERNIE, OUR FRIEND IN THE FRENCH GESTAPO.
GERTRUDE, YOU ARE A GENIUS AND GENIUSES SHOULDN'T HAVE TO DEAL WITH AN ANNOYING WORLD WAR TWO.
I HAVE A SURE-FIRE PLAN SO YOU CAN CONTINUE WRITING.
HEIL HITLER AND COCO CHANEL.
AH, THE PACKAGE I ORDERED IS HERE.
PUT THESE ON AND GO OUT IN THE STREET AND WE'LL SEE HOW MY PLAN WORKS.
IT WORKS!
JEWS for JESUS
JEWS for JESUS

Drew Friedman's
CHOSEN PEOPLE

FOREWORD BY MERRILL MARKOE

THE GREATS, THE NEAR-GREATS, AND THE NOT-SO-GREATS, BY THE MAN BOING BOING CALLS "THE GREATEST LIVING PORTRAIT ARTIST."

"Drew Friedman's portraits capture his subjects' best and worst qualities at once. His work is both beautiful and grotesque, brilliant and cruel." — Jimmy Kimmel

"Drew Friedman is a genius illustrator, a genius comics artist." — Marc Maron

"Drew Friedman isn't just a brilliant artist. He takes you to a place. He takes you back in time." — Sarah Silverman

"Drew Friedman is my favorite artist." — Howard Stern

"Drew Friedman is the unchallenged living master of the art of caricature." — Chris Ware

Coming in November from Fantagraphics Books: Publisher of the World's Greatest Cartoonists

FANTAGRAPHICS BOOKS

OUR BACK PAGES

JOAN'S OTHER KITCHEN

Deep in the Rwandan jungle, Pepper Jones is on the hunt • By Brian McConnachie

The Gorilla Lady's Jungle Diary

My name is Pepper Jones, and I've been dedicated to studying and protecting the endangered silverback mountain gorillas here in the jungles of Rwanda for almost three years now.

No one asked me to do this. In fact, some people from the wildlife preserve have tried to stop me. Some have even hired lawyers to get a restraining order against me. Legally, I can't get within 25 feet of a gorilla. But I don't care; this is a passion I was born with; it's a mission that has chosen me, and I cannot abandon it. My work is too important.

My only contact with other humans comes every two months or so, when a team from the Shop Africa Shop makes the trip up here to bring supplies, medicine and scientific equipment. My diaries and my gorillas are all the company I have or need. Poachers used to come around occasionally, but they don't do that anymore. (I'm a pretty good shot.) Every now and then, a camera safari will come poking around. But they don't stay very long either.

Though I am here studying the gorillas' way of life, you could say they're also studying mine. They are truly beautiful creatures: sensitive, gentle, smart, faithful — well not so much Tongo, Jo Jo, Elvis, Fletcher or Paulie… Today can be all "snuggles," and tomorrow they'll knuckle-walk right on by! That's males for you, am I right, ladies?

Still, they're a lot more reliable than Shop Africa Shop, who've once again screwed up the order I put in. I specifically told them: Beefeater's gin. I even wrote it down for them and drew a little picture of a Beefeater, for God's sake. But what did they bring? Sir Walter Cooper's Sparkling Dry London Gin! Christ! I could barely get the gorillas to drink it. They got used to it, eventually, but that's not an excuse to bring the cheap stuff. Part of my mission is to instill good taste.

MONDAY

I decided to have a party to celebrate my third anniversary here and invite all of the gorillas except Kiki and she knows why. But then I thought: Why bother? Kiki'll probably crash the party anyway and make it *all about her*.

I can't help thinking that Kiki is getting deeply jealous of the way her mate Tongo has started bringing me things, like bananas. And then he takes one and holds it in front of himself, you know. "You're so naughty," I tell him, but I can't help giggling. He's soooo bad. I tell him: "You are! You're such a *bad* monkey! Who's my bad monkey? Where's my Mr. Naughty Pants, Prince of the bad Monkey Men? There you are. Yes you are." They really are so playful, despite their immense bulk.

TUESDAY

I'm having real issues with Kiki. She gave me this look the other day, you know the one: *"You think you're better than I am, but you're so not."* And then she slowly turned her back, like *she's* better! What a bitch! I snuck up behind her and I swear, I came this close to braining her with the steel omelet pan. The real heavy one.

Her mate Tongo likes to sneak into my cot at night and snuggle. I must have taught him the sign for snuggle, ha ha! I know I had to teach him the sign for "NO! *That's* not snuggle. Quit it, you dumb baboon." But I really can't stay mad at him — he's so sweet with those big sad eyes of his. I don't think he's happy at home.

WEDNESDAY

Jo Jo suddenly thinks it's simply hilarious to hide my clothes. Then he makes a big show of putting his hands over his eyes — but I know he's peeking. He's such a bad boy. I tell him: "You're a Peeping Tom. Who's my big hairy Peeping Tom? That's right, point to yourself. No, not at that. Higher."

I tell him to stop it, I mean it, but it's all a big game to him. Then after all that, I'll spend half the morning looking for something to put on.

He's doing this every day; it's infuriating! I wonder why I even bother to wear clothes.

THURSDAY

I'm not sure, but I think Pixie was getting upset that Jo Jo seems to be losing interest in her. So I initiated "a girl's afternoon" together; I broke out my stash of lipstick and eyeliner, then topped it off with a healthy splash of Taboo.

(I practically had to use up half the bottle. Gorillas are a pretty stinky bunch, truth be told.)

My heart was in the right place, but in the future, I won't waste eyeliner on the gorillas. It doesn't show, and they don't appreciate it. Also, I must order more Taboo. And send back the hoop earrings I ordered; I just noticed apes really don't have earlobes.

BRIAN McCONNACHIE is Founder and Head Writer of *The American Bystander*.

Who writes features on guilty *Bystander*-s like Drew Friedman, Robert Grossman, Kate Beaton, Peter Kuper, Paul Krassner, and Rick Geary? Me, that's who …and maybe Steve Heller.

printmag.com/author/michaeldooley

The Digest Enthusiast
Explore the world of digest magazines, past and present, through interviews, articles, and reviews; along with genre fiction.
larquepress.com   amazon.com

THE H. P. LOVECRAFT HISTORICAL SOCIETY
AN ALTERNATIVE UNIVERSE SINCE 1986
Are you a member? Join us at WWW.CTHULHULIVES.ORG

CHARLTON COMICS MOVIE
charltonmovie.com
@charltonmovie

Please Stop the Deep Thoughts
Jack Handey
Order now at JACKHANDEY.COM

WHISPERINGTUBE (on Facebook)

AN EXCESSIVE ALPHABET
Avalanches of As to Zillions of Zs
from the *Cloudy With a Chance of Meatballs* team
A fine book now available at fine booksellers

FRIDAY

One thing about gorillas is, they all look pretty much alike after a while. I've tried tying different colored kerchiefs around their necks to tell them apart, but only the females will wear them. Kiki's is red, and Pixie's is pink. The guys keep blowing their noses (?) into them and then losing them. Do they think I'm just around here to do the wash?

I've ordered a box of those stickers that say, "Hello, My Name Is." That might work if those dweebs from the supply preserve can remember to bring them. Along with the right gin, that won't make the gorillas so hungover that they sleep most of the next day. A gorilla with a gin hangover is some sorry sight, believe me. It's shameful. You just try to get them to keep the ice bags on their heads!

Until tomorrow…

SATURDAY

Some of the males dropped by my tent tonight as I was setting up for the party. I put on some CDs. They like Lady Gaga/Tony Bennett okay, but they're nuts about Dean Martin. They really seem to dislike Frank Sinatra. They're split on *The Lion King* but they're crazy about, *Into The Woods*. I believe I am the first ever researcher to discover this.

We opened a few bottles of that Stinky McGin. I had to keep screaming at them to use their bloody coasters. What is it with gorillas never wanting to use their coasters? What were they, raised in a barn? There was some dancing if you could call it that. It was more "get your zombie-robot on."

I wound up putting on a fashion show. Some of the males helped pick out what dress I should wear. It was between my black cocktail dress with the spaghetti straps and the red Oscar de la Renta. They voted for the classic black. I think.

SUNDAY

I just had a disturbing thought: Maybe the gorillas don't understand sign language at all. Outside of a few phrases about "snuggling" and "not snuggling," I certainly haven't taught it to them. I don't know why, I just kind of thought they knew it. Like dogs are born knowing how to turn around three times before lying down. But the more I think of it, the gorillas do give me a lot of vacant looks when I'm explaining things.

Truth be told, I'm hardly an expert on signing myself. What I know comes from my brother, who was a third-base coach for a minor-league baseball team. Touch your hat, two fingers on your forearm, clap a few times. The players got it.

Maybe the gorillas understand, too. Or do they? It seems like I have to throw rocks at them to get them to do anything. I must look into this, for real this time.

MONDAY

I'm getting annoyed at the camera safari that's been sneaking around taking pictures when some people around here might not be quite ready to receive company. Some people are professional researchers and do not want their pictures taken without their makeup on. What goes on here is none of their business.

A few warning shots should do it. I need to order more ammo. Yesterday, I saw Kiki and Pixie taking a few bullets. Those two love anything shiny.

TUESDAY

Now, apparently, I may have accidentally and unintentionally shot one of the camera safari people by mistake. If I did, I must have thought he/she was a poacher, and I can't believe we finished all that awful gin. The gorillas got real sad about the dead guy. They took off his red kerchief very tenderly, and covered up the body with leaves. It was sweet. They'll totally surprise me with things like that. I think what noble, gentle creatures they are, and feel terrible that I spent half the morning yelling and throwing rocks at them.

WEDNESDAY

I've done some thinking, and it's clear that my work here with the gorillas is far too important and complicated to risk any setbacks like me entering the logjam that is the Rwandan legal system. I see two choices: Blame the shooting on Kiki, who in fact, could have done it, or I can methodically shoot the rest of the safari before they get back to the preserve. If I could only find that rifle.

What's that? Someone's at the door, probably the monthly supplies. I better go and see how wrong they got it this time.

Until tomorrow!

P.S. MUELLER THINKS LIKE THIS

The cartoonist/broadcaster/writer is always walking around, looking at stuff • ***By P.S. Mueller***

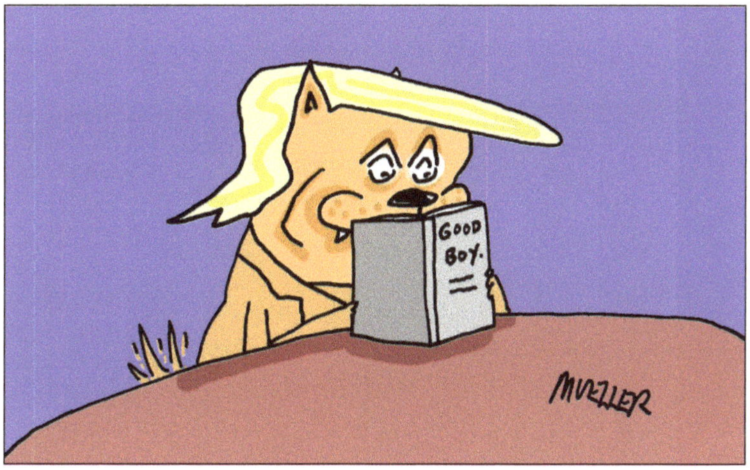
GOOD BOY.
MUELLER

Why There Is No White House Dog

There's no Fido or Rover proudly strutting at the end of the presidential leash, leading our commander in chief to Helicopter No. 1 and a quick ride to Camp David for a tinkle and a romp. Not in this White House. Truth be known, Donald Trump has never owned a pet.

George Washington rescued a Northeastern mudhound and brought him home. The dog was fitted with not one, but two little whalebone legs, and the pair would go out walking together every morning. Eyewitnesses of the day, aware of Washington's wooden dentures, reported the two playfully clacking at each other during a rowdy game of Rotten Shoe.

Lincoln taught his Labradoodle Secesh to walk backwards on its hind legs, while peeing on Edward Stanton's shiny boots; Harry Truman owned a miniature chihuahua that would crawl up his master's sleeve for hidden bits of kibble; Ronald Reagan utterly believed his Robot Pup to be a real miracle pooch. Pup's tail wags on to this day, in the restaurant of the Gipper's presidential library.

But Donald J. Trump has never had a dog or pet of any kind because he keeps his own counsel and serves as his own pet. His inner circle has long been rumored to play its proper role in the privacy of the Oval Office — papers are spread as the president cheerfully emerges from behind his desk to accept hearty belly rubs and "Who's a good boy?"

Sad.

◆

It's time for real cowboys to do their job and change that cow litter.

◆

The first and last taser tag emporium has closed its doors in Duluth, Minn. The short-lived sport required at least two participants armed with police tasers, but due to frequent involuntary urination, the game never really caught on and will be replaced with a promising new diversion called Glue-Ball.

Seacrest World

In 2030, SeaWorld declared bankruptcy and was ordered to be drained. By then the organization's last remaining theme park consisted of about 200 acres along a piece of Texas coastline, depending on the time and tide. Seaworld's last captive orca whale, Jimmy, had won its freedom in a park-sponsored gin rummy tournament and headed off to Key West to dine on wet revelers.

Aging television presenter Ryan Seacrest soon acquired the property with the idea of creating a palatial theme home, with each room constructed to precisely duplicate a set from each of his wildly successful programs. Youthful and robotic Seacrest facsimiles were placed beneath warm spolights and programmed to cheerfully smile and chat with millions of anticipated visitors. The show business mogul, however, remained secluded in an off-site control room and was sustained by liquids and tubes, not to mention the unwitting companionship of his 40-year-old spaniel, Chop.

Seacrest World thrived for many years. The park, fortified to survive the rising sea, remained solid and true, and something of a monument to the engineering miracle of riprap. But no one knows what became of Seacrest. He simply disappeared during the great "Logo Shift" of 2070 and his foundation carried on, taking orders from the lead Seacrest automaton, Seacrest the Nice. The superstorms of the 2080s eventually messed with Texas, and the legendary Seacrest riprap. Seacrest World began to sink into the Gulf of Mexico, which had by then acquired the color and texture of an oily milkshake.

But as was noted earlier, Seacrest world had been constructed to survive any insult. Yes, the vast building flooded, but the water within was highly filtered and crystal clear, allowing the fleet ☛

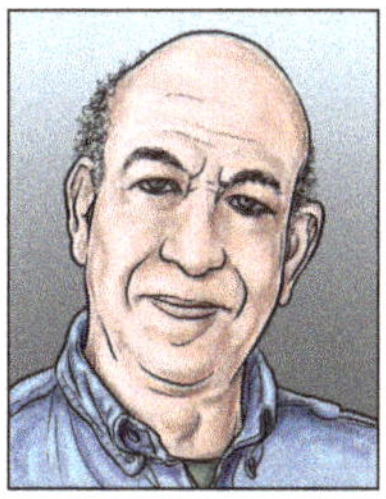

P.S. MUELLER is Staff Liar of *The American Bystander*.

of "Iron Ryans," as they came to be known, to continue grinning and chatting as before. Diving tours allowed aging millennials to experience Total Seacrest Re-enactments daily from noon to 4, super-hurricanes permitting.

Sadly, by 2090 the maintenance costs provided an opportunity for the heirs to the SeaWorld name to purchase Seacrest World lock, stock and animatron. With the millennials mostly gone, Ryan Sea-World Under America opened its air locks to the curiously mutated descendents of Jimmy the orca, who return year in and year out to this very day to play gin rummy with smiling, chatty algae-covered robots.

.... ◆ ....

A bill to extend Medicare benefits to cover experimental monkey people created by drunk MIT bioengineers has been voted down. Observers say it will only be a matter of time before those whiz kids figure out how to make something from a pile of lips that can add, subtract and argue before the Supreme Court.

The Road Not Taken

As a young actor weighing in at 325 pounds, Alternate Universe Mickey Rourke sadly endured nearly 500 performances of Alternate Universe Samuel Beckett's little-known play *The Silent Couch*. The production toured breakfast theaters across the Midwest and featured a rotating cast of elderly game show hosts. Rourke came to know each of them by the shape and texture of their ass, especially the retired host of *Password* Allen Ludden, who became kind of pillowy late in life. Rourke did not go unnoticed in his role and often found himself patted down for keys and loose change after the show — by audience members of a certain age.

This Mickey Rourke — who might well have gone on to star in his dimension's *9 1/2 Weeks* and *The Wrestler*, had he quit the pizza and beer — lives on to this day in a large chair outside of Neptune, N.J.

.... ◆ ....

There was sad news from the Morton Salt Company today, which was shuttered by the EPA due to excessive salinity. Former union salt miners with the company for over 100 years are believed to be striking out for Sugartown.

The Great Late Change

We knew something was up near the end of the year, when dogs started walking backwards and tattoos began to liquify and whirl beneath a million crepey skins. A total eclipse had recently come and gone, confusing wildlife and people who deliver Amazon orders. Walnuts cracked open to reveal smaller walnuts and so on. Indeed, the people of the earth began to dimly wonder, "What the fuck?"

I stepped out the front door of my surburban ranch home and looked up at a trademarked moon. Migrating birds were headed north toward frosty oblivion. Spontaneously occurring bran flakes fell lightly around me, adding a special nutty crunch to my perfectly manicured yard. The religious guy across the street had Krazy Glued himself into a tarp, leaving eyeholes and a gap for his AR-15. He walked circles inside his garage.

The stock market hit 50,000 that afternoon, and Wall Street, by then completely socked in with celebratory cotton candy, had become a sugary mire of immobile billionaires who couldn't make the trains to Westbester, Hemcluster or the Framptons. I, too, had become a billionaire, though I didn't know it yet. Somehow, during the course of what I call the Great Late Change, our cat Puddum figured out English, at least enough to tell me I was rich. We celebrated together with a game of backgammon in the basement.

Media of all kinds remained serviceable and steady, even as the news grew from peculiar to downright weird and alarming. In fact, as the late summer cicadas altered their chorus to harmonize with a famous soup jingle, most of us billionaires remained inside, usually surrounded with prepper supplies. We stared at flat screens emitting billionaires from other places, billionaires calmed by precious meds and certain of the obvious benificence coming with the Great Late Change.

By Christmas, the bran flakes had turned to gold and gold had bottomed out on the Heavy Metal Exchanges. I sat and combed gold flakes from Puddum's coat as a cold winds pushed in from the gray Atlantic, and Puddum turned to me and said: "Great News! We're all having dead fish tomorrow!"

CHUNK-STYLE NUGGETS

...to briefly distract you from the inevitable • ***By Steve Young***

Congratulations on purchasing Slacker Grove Memorial Park's Perpetual Sort-of-Care Package for your loved one's grave. Your package includes:

- Occasional mowing, depending on availability of a functional mower/employee who feels up to it;
- If mowing isn't happening for some reason, stomping down of tall grass once in a while;
- Reproachful looks directed at anyone spotted on the cemetery grounds carrying grave-robbing tools;
- "Loaner" gravestone if actual gravestone is lost, stolen or vandalized (name/date details may vary);
- Shooing away of teens discovered partying/making out on top of your loved one's grave during normal business hours;
- In the event the cemetery moves, we will try to remember to send you a "change of address" card.

Anyway, thanks for signing up or whatever.

Latest U.S. State Department Travel Warnings

U.S. citizens are warned to avoid the Spanish resort destination of Ibiza, because it is so over.

U.S. citizens are cautioned to be on high alert when traveling in Canada, because while Canadians seem nice, what if they're secretly up to something?

U.S. citizens traveling to Paraguay are warned to double check that they didn't intend to go to Uruguay, and vice versa.

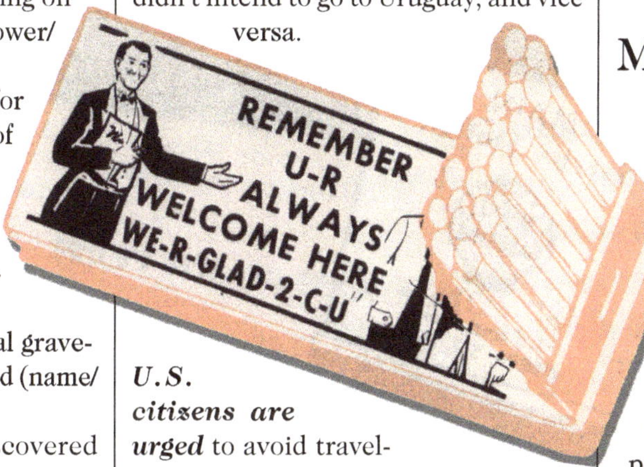
REMEMBER
U-R
ALWAYS
WELCOME HERE
WE-R-GLAD-2-C-U

U.S. citizens are urged to avoid traveling to Iran unless accompanied by Ben Affleck, because in that *Argo* movie he's very clever about escaping from Iran.

Until the political situation improves, U.S. citizens are cautioned to avoid the U.S.

Things: A New Perspective

Pants — leg shirts

Lawnmower — badly designed helicopter

Fish — bookmark

Book — storage for fish

Reasons You Failed Your Driver's Test

- While changing lanes, licked windshield.
- Signaled for turns by shouting "left!" or "right!"
- Steered with chin.
- Exceeded posted speed limit while operating vehicle in reverse.
- During stop at red light, forced examiner into trunk.

I Would Like To Clear Up Some Misconceptions About My Store, The Sundries Shop

- I do not sell sundaes. I do not sell sun-dried tomatoes or anything else sun-dried. I sell sundries, which are small, miscellaneous dry goods.
- My store is not The Sundries Superstore, which is across the street.
- The fact that The Sundries Superstore also sells sundaes and sun-dried tomatoes is, in my opinion, a bad long-term strategy, despite its current success.
- I am the sole proprietor of The Sundries Shop. My former business partner, Jeff, now owns and operates The Sundries Superstore, which has no connection to The Sundries Shop.
- To further elaborate on the nature of sundries, they may be, for example, small toiletry articles or hardware items.
- I do not agree that my store should be named The Small Toiletry Articles & Hardware Items Shop, as that would mislead people into thinking that I did not also carry other items such as bows, notepads or gum.
- At this time I do not carry bows, notepads or gum. The Sundries Superstore has undercut my prices so severely that it is no longer practical for me to stock them.
- I have not threatened to attack Jeff with a hardware item. While words may

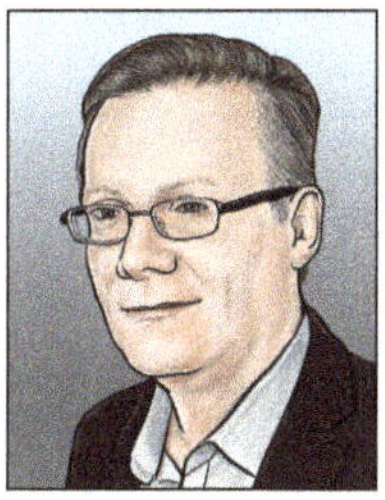

STEVE YOUNG (@pantssteve) is Oracle for *The American Bystander*.

have been spoken in anger, there was no threat of physical violence.

• The Sundries Shop is not going out of business next month. It will close permanently at the end of this month. ◼

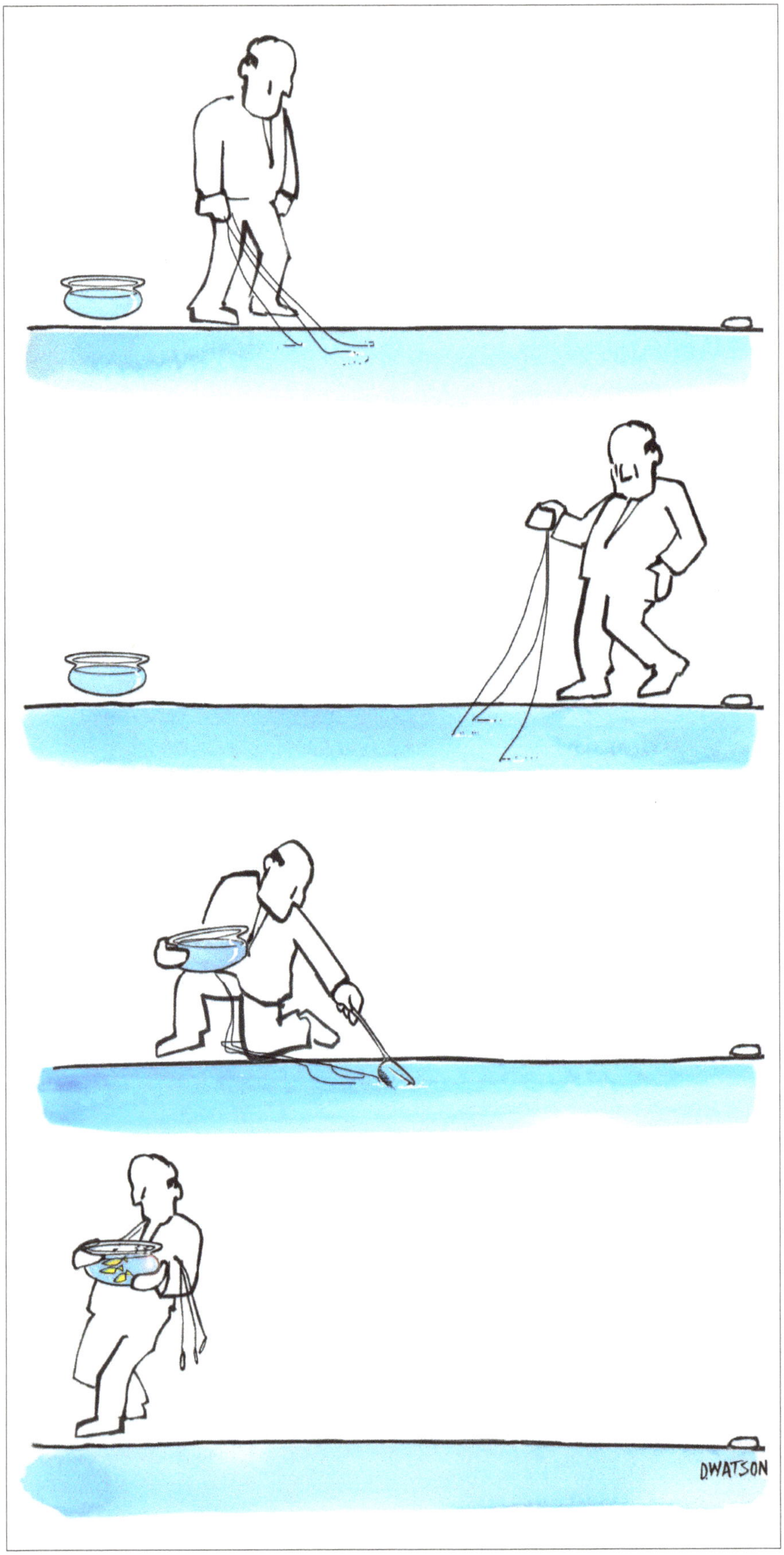

OUR BACK PAGES

KNOW YOUR BYSTANDERS

*We asked. **Hana Michels** answered.*

REBECCA ARANDA

One of the unforeseen benefits of editing this magazine has been discovering Hana Michels's Facebook feed. Her daily cascade of mordant observations on life, love and finding oneself — or, more accurately, the seeming impossibility of any of these while living as a female stand-up in Los Angeles — is delightful for two reasons. One, Hana is very honest, and very funny. Two, in our youth-worshipping culture, it's always a good idea to remember that unless you were a Beatle or something, your 20s sucked.

When I thought of this department (which, God willing, will be a regular thing), Hana was a natural choice to kick us off. I gave her a list of 60 questions, and she answered the ones that struck a spark. — Ed.

NAME: *Hana Michaels*
PROFESSION: *Writer & Stand-Up*
LIVES IN: *Los Angeles*
PIECES: *"Pick Up Artistry, Volume IV"* (#3); *"Mom, You Can Stop Hiding Behind All My Mirrors Now"* (#5).

Do you have a nickname? How did you get it? Han Solo, Honda, Hannukkah, Hana Bah-nah-nah. None of these are consensual nicknames. They come from people realizing my name is not pronounced like "Hannah" and needing to say something about it. Also, because there's a city named Hana, two separate people have asked if I was "conceived on Maui."

I have the only name that forces me to think about my parents fucking.

Where were you born, and did that have any bearing on the person you've become? I was born in Santa Monica, which had no bearing on who I became because I have 0 rich friends and 0 composting worms.

Is there anything interesting about your family? They are all therapists. ALL OF THEM. I swore I would never go into the family business, but then I became a woman so I have to do it for free.

If you had unlimited funds to build a house that you would live in for the rest of your life, what would the house be like? It would have a bunch of twists, turns and dead ends, just like my career.

What was your most notable pet? Jessica the toad because she brought a plague of crickets to our home. Also my rats because that's where I learned about testicles that drag on the floor.

What subject(s) do you wish you knew more about? Taking basic care of myself; blacksmithing.

What's your first question after waking up after being frozen for 100 years? "Do we still hate Guy Fieri?"

What is something that a ton of people are obsessed with but you just don't get the point of? Men.

What are you most looking forward to? Success, followed by finding out success didn't make me happy.

Where is the most interesting place you've been? Either Costa Rica or the bedroom of a popular ska frontman. Both had stray animals!

What amazing thing did you do that no one was around to see?
I spotted a California condor back when we were down to like 60 of them in the wild. I swear I saw it, but I was 7 so no one believed me. It was eating our first-grade class's trash. I hope it didn't choke on a Pog.

What's the best way to start the day? Waking up in your own bed without questioning all your life choices.

What job do you think you'd be great at? Is there a job that requires leaving my desk to cry in the bathroom? Because I'm really, really good at that.

What fad or trend do you hope comes back? Children viciously beating each other with yo-yos. Also moon boots.

What's the title of your autobiography? "WHY?"

What's worth spending more on to get the best? Anti-aging skincare, therapy for your aging dysmorphia.

What's your perfect day? My perfect day is spent surrounded by models, actors and other hot people, but instead of hooking up with them they just wear baby boomer clothes and say, "We love you daughter, and we approve of your lifestyle."

What's something you like to do the old-fashioned way? Date people I meet in life instead of on Tinder. In July, *The Daily Mail* put my Tinder profile in an article called "Are These The World's Worst Tinder Profiles?" So I probably made the right call.

What one thing do you really want but can't afford? My medication, not from Canada. Also a donkey. And someone to follow the donkey around and pick up

America's LIVE Japanese Gameshow

BATSU!

Now Playing: New York City & Chicago
Tickets: www.batsulive.com

"Hilarious, strange and kind of sick" — Thrillist

International Waters
A comedy quiz show where land laws don't apply.
a podcast from maximumfun.org

Cultural analysis. Drama. Feats of strength. Spandex.
A weekly podcast about professional wrestling.
From maximumfun.org

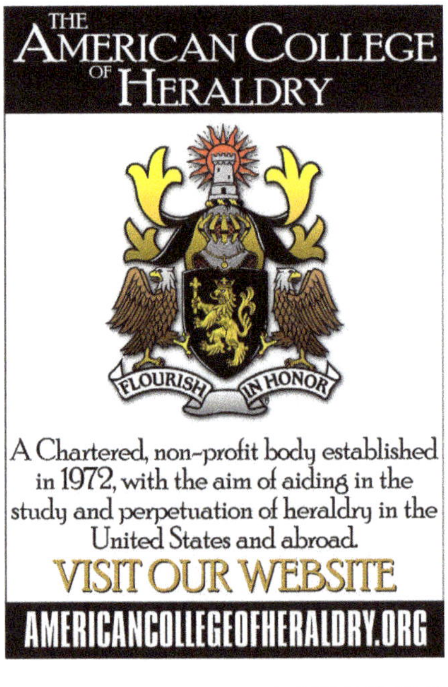

THE AMERICAN COLLEGE OF HERALDRY

A Chartered, non-profit body established in 1972, with the aim of aiding in the study and perpetuation of heraldry in the United States and abroad.

VISIT OUR WEBSITE
AMERICANCOLLEGEOFHERALDRY.ORG

the poop. Ehh, I can probably just tie a bag to its butt. A good old butt bag!
What are you absolutely determined to do? Write for actual TV and never use the phrase "YouTube Channel" again. I'm also determined to never stop eating cheese, no matter what it does to my body or loved ones.
What was the best compliment you've received? "Your comedy transcends your hair."
Which of your scars has the most interesting story behind it? I have a scar on my chin because one day when I was 16 I got really bored, so I dumped a bunch of shampoo on the floor and slid around on my butt. When I tried to get up, I slipped and banged my chin. Are you a psychiatric professional? What is this?
If you could make one rule that everyone had to follow, what would it be? If you don't know a female comic in person and you tag her joke on social media, Venmo her five bucks.
I owe you some money. What are you addicted to? Personal validation.
What is one of your favorite smells? Sunscreen & condom rubber. It reminds me of the beach where I grew up.
What quirks do you have? I know this is a written interview so just imagine I handed you a copy of the DSM-V.
What's the best piece of advice you've ever gotten? Or, the worst? "Wear a shorter skirt onstage" was both.
If you could make a 30-second phone call to yourself at any age, past, present or future, when would you call, and what would you tell yourself? I would call myself 5, 10 or 20 years in the future to say, "STOP WHAT YOU'RE DOING RIGHT NOW!" I don't know what I'll be doing, but I know the call applies.
When do you feel truly alive? When my doctor takes my pulse, then says, "Whoa, too fast!"
What's the worst thing about getting older? Watching my value in a sexist society slowly dwindle until I become invisible. I mean uh, "kids and their music" or something. Snapchat. Yeah.
What's your favorite holiday? Yom Kippur, because I get to hear my mom say "I'm sorry."
Who or where would you haunt, if you were a ghost? I'd haunt the men I've casually dated, with my emotions. Actually it wouldn't be that different from now. I'd be see-through, I guess.
What do you hope your last words will be? I'd like to pull an Oscar Wilde, say something witty and lie around silently for weeks waiting to die.
What's your last meal? My last meal will consist of the hearts and minds of the people who dared condemn me to death. If those people are God, so be it. **B**

NY/NJ COMEDIC ACTOR (40s-50s) available for auditions, readings, runs of any length. Resume and pictures: **DavidCNeal.com.**

IT CAME FROM THE BOTTOM SHELF!
Bottomshelfmovies.com is a film recommendation website focusing on forgotten classics, lesser-known gems, and oddball discoveries. It's the video collector's resource for movie reviews, weekly new release video picks, upcoming Blu-ray/DVD announcements, sales alerts, and other cinematic news. **Bottomshelfmovies.com**

JANE AUSTEN MUSIC Live music from the English Regency era for dancing or ambience in the San Francisco area. **jameslangdell@gmail.com**

DOPEY PODCAST
On the dark comedy of drug addiction.
www.dopeypodcast.com

FREAK CHIC STUDIOS
Jewelry, Art & Accoutrements for the Eclectic Heart.
www.freakchicstudios.com
that's Dubyah Dubyah Dubyah dot FreakChicStudios dot See Oh Em. Twitter: @FreakChicStudio / Instagram: Freak Chic Studios / CB Callsign: Freak 2 The Chic. Be a good human and buy my stuff! Ten-four good buddy. Keep the bugs off your glass, and the bears off your... TAIL. Over and out.

THE MISADVENTURES OF LI'L DONNIE
Making Comics Great Again - Since 2017!
donniecrys.blogspot.com or follow "Donald Littles" (w/the asterisk pic) on the facebooks!

MYXPROJEKT
Free long-form Ambient Drone music. Great for relaxation, meditation, sleep. Nod off in style! Money back guarantee.
soundcloud.com/myxprojekt

COMEDIANS DEFYING GRAVITY
Comedians Defying Gravity highlights Chicago comedy: interviews, weekly events calendar and more. CDG is part of ChicagoNow, the Chicago Tribune Media Group's blogging network.**http://www.chicagonow.com/comedians-defying-gravity**

FULL OF WIT Funny poems and more. The Killing Tree by J.D. Smith can be found at most online sellers and at the link. **www.finishinglinepress.com/product/the-killing-tree-by-j-d-smith/**

PATSY O'BRIEN
Alt-Celtic Songwriter
Award-winning
NPR - featured.
www.patsyobrienswebsite.com

¿GOT TSUNAMIS?
Or some other annoyingly inconvenient problem at your local beach, port or 5-star resort? Give a shout, we'll sort you out!
http://eCoast.co.nz
jose@ecoast.co.nz
coastal dynamics • tsunamis • erosion • wave pools • surfing reefs • resorts • marinas • marine ecology
Solutions offered worldwide!
No beach out of reach!
The absurdity of advertising coastal engineering services to a bunch of writers and English majors isn't lost on me, but hey, I like the *Bystander*, so why not?

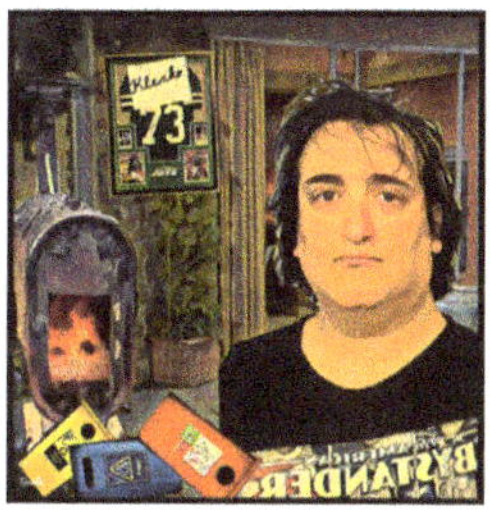

IN MEMORIAM:
Johnson Dunst, Jr., the deaf-mute imbecile who would bring our pre-separated trash and recyclables from the *Bystander* main offices to his religiously-excepted home incinerator just over the border in West Los Angeles, has died. Cause of death is believed to have been his correct knowledge that the life expectancy of a deaf-mute imbecile in AD 1732 was nine combined with his apparent, yet woefully misguided, belief that it is now AD 1732. Mr. Dunst, Jr., leaves no known next of kin, though he was known to smile for days whenever he successfully spelled the word "Klecko" in cursive. We wish him well.

TONY ISABELLA'S NEW BOOK
July 1963: A Pivotal Month in the Comic-Book Life of Tony Isabella Volume One. Obsessive nostalgic fun that inspired the career of the creator of Black Lightning, Misty Knight, Tigra and more. Available in print and digital formats from Amazon. Superman competes in the Interplanetary Olympics. The coming of the Avengers. Baby Huey's criminally negligent parents. Batman's super-powered dog. All this and so much more.

A (VERY GOOD) LITERARY AGENCY
Why, you must have stellar taste to be here. Are you also an extremely talented writer with a book idea? Let's talk. I'm Scott at **sgould@rlrassociates.net.**

www.kingcormack.com

DRUNK MONKEYS
America's finest "two women drinking odd liquors and talking about it" web series may be found at drunkmonkeyshow.com – only one 's', so it's Drunk Monkeys how?

CLASSIFIEDS

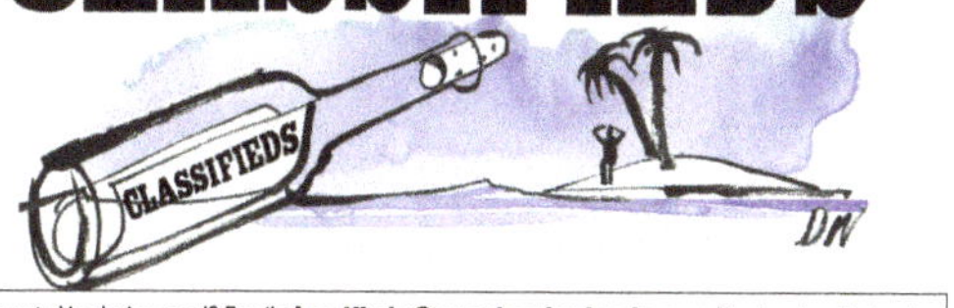

CLASSIFIEDS
DH

Interested in placing an ad? Email **classifieds@americanbystander.org**. The American Bystander reserves the right to reject any ad for any reason. We do not guarantee the quality of the items being sold, or the accuracy of the information provided. Ads are provided directly by sellers and are not verified.

CARTOON COMPANION
Cartooncompanion.com is a new website that discusses and rates the cartoons in *The New Yorker*. Co-hosts Max and Simon trade amusing observations and barbs with each new issue. *TNY* cartoonists have contributed to the site and praised it. Future posts will include interviews of the cartoonists and cartoons that *The New Yorker* rejected.
cartooncompanion.com

DO YOU READ THE OTHER A.B.?
Attempted Bloggery – An art blog about cartoons and other high culture. Published more or less daily since 2011.
attemptedbloggery.blogspot.com

CURRENCY CONVERSION BY MAIL
Convert unwieldy US folding money into small denominations! Send $10 bill get back $5 bill. Send *one* $20 bill receive a completely different bill. Never ask for change again! Do not delay!
Contact **@Specky4Eyes**
Serious inquiries only. No fatties.

YOU LIKE COMICS?
Sure you do! Who doesn't? (well, ignore those dweebs). For the finest in graphic storytelling, look ahead to 2018 for the premiere of BERGER BOOKS, created by the legendary Karen Berger, founding editor of VERTIGO! And the Art Director? The also legendary - except not so much - Richard Bruning! Top notch talent too. Watch for this revolutionary new imprint from indy pioneer Dark Horse.

THE COMIC TORAH
Stand-up comic Aaron Freeman and artist Sharon Rosenzweig reimagine the Torah with provocative humor and irreverent reverence. Each weekly portion gets a two-page spread. Like the original, the Comic Torah is not always suitable for children. "Hyperactive, colorful art brings the story to life." – Publisher's Weekly "If God was a comic artist, this is what She would have drawn." –Harold Ramis "Awesome!" – Alison Bechdel "Sacred & profane at the same time." – Paul Krassner
benyehudapress.com/ct or amzn.to/2npmv4V

STUDY CARTOONING and Illustration at the School of Visual Arts. We offer courses by Tom Motley, Steve Brodner, Carl Potts, and more! Fall courses are enrolling now.
www.sva.edu/continuing-education/illustration-and-cartooning

VISUAL REALIA
Photography, food and everything visual:
www.visualrealia.com.

CONFEDERACY OF DRONES POLITICAL SATIRE
Using humor to shoot down the political hypocrisy of mindless drones.
confederacyofdrones.com

LOTS OF NATIONAL LAMPOON
Lots of Nat Lamps for sale. Various monthly issues and Best Ofs. Mostly in pretty good condition. $4 each or more per issue plus postage. Email me with any particular issue you need at **bardinerman@aol.com.**
Thank you and Godspeed.

COMIC STUDIES at the University of Wisconsin-Madison http://humanities.wisc.edu/research/borghesi-mellon-workshops/past-workshops/comics2

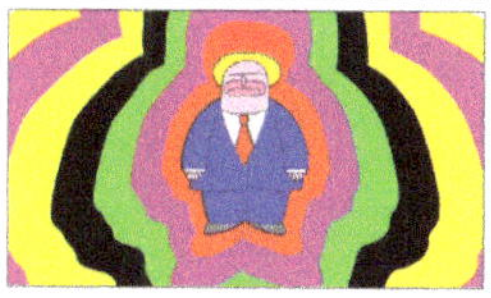

THE MAN WHO KILLED REALITY
The Prefab Messiahs explain all! Observe their hit animated musical video on the Youtubes: **youtube.com/prefabmessiahs**

Actor Natalie's Castles?

C	C	S		S	C	I	S		T	S	H	I	R	T
A	H	A		T	O	N	E		S	O	O	N	E	R
T	E	L		A	M	E	N		A	S	S	I	S	I
F	L	U	M	M	O	X	E	S				T	O	P
I	S	T	O	O		I	C	H		N	E	I	L	L
S	E	E	D	S		L	A	O		A	G	A	V	E
H	A	D	I		B	E	S	P	A	N	G	L	E	S
			F	I	T				B	U	S			
H	A	B	I	T	U	A	T	E	S		A	F	R	O
A	R	R	E	T		L	A	P		G	L	U	E	D
S	C	A	R	Y		E	G	O		R	A	L	L	Y
A	H	I				C	A	N	O	O	D	L	E	S
C	I	N	E	M	A		L	I	P	S		O	A	S
O	V	E	R	L	Y		O	N	E	S		U	S	E
W	E	D	G	I	E		G	E	N	E		T	E	Y

2017

TABLETOP TALK - a YouTube channel for gamers by gamers. We create raw tabletop gaming content by filming our games. No scripts, just gaming. www.youtube.com/user/TabletopTalk

TOONS BY STEV-O (by Steve McGinn). some cartoons I hope'll make ya laff! drawn fresh in ink & then posted every day - 7 days a week! look for us on Facebook and The Comx Box Syndicate.

THE AMERICAN VALUES CLUB Crossword (formerly the Onion AV Club Crossword): It's rude, it's clued, and you'll get used to it. Subscribe at avxword.com.

Buy **THE LAFAYETTE CAMPAIGN** mybook.to/lafayettecampaign "Andrew Updegrove brings a rare combination of drama, satire and technical accuracy to his writing. The result is a book you can't put down that tells you things you might wish you didn't know." - Admiral James G. Stavridis, former NATO Supreme Allied Commander Europe

UNICORN BOOTY WANTS YOU ...to read some of the most outrageously fun news, pop culture, and opinions on the web! Unicorn Booty serves up original news, film, TV, art, sports, fashion, travel and other weird wonders from around the world. Check us out at http://unicornbooty.com.

THE NEW YORK REVIEW OF SCIENCE FICTION Reading Science Fiction Like It Matters for 28 Years. The first one's free! http://www.nyrsf.com

AN ILLUSTRATED ZARATHUSTRA Hilarity ensues as excerpts and epigrams from Nietzsche's timeless classic comes to life in this madcap comic-strip-style dub version. Embrace your Fate and read it online at: ScottMarshall.org

BOOKS, POSTCARDS, ORIGINAL art by Rick Geary, available exclusively at www.rickgeary.com. I also take commissions.

FREE LUNCH!! NO BALONEY! Attention all hungry cartoonists passing through Chicago: Contact Jonathan Plotkin Editorial Cartoonist & Illustrator Minister of Ways and Means NCIS Chicago Chapter Spontoonist@gmail.com spontoonist.com

COMICS WITH PROBLEMS All problems solved. The Internet's BEST archive of the world's WEIRDEST comic books. http://www.ep.tc/problems

HACKER HUMOR You need tech humor, I've got it. Jokes, pitches, consulting, articles, posts. 35+ years experience (in parents' basement). rob.warmowski@gmail.com

WANTED: MURDERER I'm looking for someone to kill me please, inquiries: @ZackBornstein on Twitter & Instagram

STRANGER THAN LIFE 250-page collection of single panel cartoons and strips from National Lampoon, The New Yorker, Playboy, Mother Jones and Arcade Comics by MK Brown. Available from Fantagraphics and Amazon. MK happy to inscribe. Contact at mkbrown88@hotmail.com

You can't make a website worth a damn. *But we can.* Contact us posthaste. MerchantAndBlack.com

DELICIOUSLY SATISFYING CONTEMPORARY NOIR a persuasive Hollywood thriller, taut and gutsy debut novel with clean, brilliant writing. COLDWATER by Diana Gould. In all formats, wherever books are sold. (Support your local independent bookstore.) Or, http://amzn.to/2dJh1Kk

THE KILLING TREE Part funny. Part serious. Part cynical. All intelligent. J.D. Smith's fourth collection of poetry, from Finishing Line Press. Advance praise and ordering information available at: http://bit.ly/2ebGJuw

WRITING A BOOK? GETTING NOWHERE? Don't give up – get help (from me!). I'm a ghostwriter/writing coach who partners with you one-on-one to get your book done. Packages range from 45-minute "Copy Therapy" sessions to twelve-week intensive book coaching programs. For more info, go to copycoachlisa.com.

CLOWN NOIR James Finn Garner (PC Bedtime Stories) has a new mystery series for fans of noir, sideshow freaks and Americana. The "Rex Koko, Private Clown" thrillers have won Chicago Writers Association's Book of the Year TWICE! It's *Freaks* meets *The Maltese Falcon*. For info and samples, go to rexkoko.com, pally.

THE VIRTUAL MEMORIES SHOW What's the best books-art-comics-culture interview podcast you've never listened to? Discover The Virtual Memories Show at www.chimeraobscura.com/vm/podcast-archive

I LOVE MAKING BEET CHIPS I love it so much that if you come to my apartment I will make some for you. I am not, to my knowledge, a serial killer. @tinyrevolution

GEORGE BOOTH: cartoons, illustrations. Other services: grass fires stomped out and despots deterred. 929-210-0707

HAVE WHAT IT TAKES TO BE A GOOBER DRIVER? Avoid World's Largest Peanuts envy. Navigate to offbeat tourist sights with the leaders for thirty years– RoadsideAmerica.com. Free e-subscription to Sightings. Easy sign-up. RoadsideAmerica.com/newsletter

SNOW ANGEL IS HERE! In the tradition of The Tick and Venture Brothers comes this all-new hilarious full-color graphic novel about **SNOW ANGEL**, the newest tween superhero! From American Bystander contributor and Eisner nominee **DAVID CHELSEA**, this massive Dark Horse comic is fun for all ages (except, oddly, 37)! Available at your local bookstore, or email dchelsea@comcast.com to learn how you can receive a signed copy! GUARANTEED MERMAID FREE!

YOUR ANDREW JACKSON $20s will soon be worthless! Use one to buy our non-award-winning, non-best-selling comedy anthology, **The Lowbrow Reader Reader**, available from Drag City Books. Or check out the The Lowbrow Reader zine itself, eminently purchasable at lowbrowreader.com.

VEGETARIANS EATING HAGGIS PIZZA *Cosmic quarks!* It's the Zen of Nimbus comic created by Michael Sloan. Nimbus, the celebrated immobile astronomer, is visited by a variety of repulsive creatures and events. Will they ever disturb his meditations? View the comic and blog, shop for Zen of Nimbus t-shirts and artwork: www.zenofnimbus.com

EULOGIES WRITTEN ON DEMAND Need a touching tribute...*stat*? Semi-professional eulogist offers her services. Quick turnaround guaranteed; encomium completed while the body's still warm or it's free. Little knowledge of the deceased in question necessary. Email megan.koester@gmail.com for rates.

WELCOME TO DISTRACTIONLAND Too much time on your hands? Watch RANSACK RABBIT and other engaging animated entertainments. **Xeth Feinberg**, proprietor. As seen on the internet! www.youtube.com/distractionland

UTILITY RIGHT FIELDER Available Also draws, writes. For more information contact Deerfield (Illinois) Little League. Or visit kenkrimstein.com.

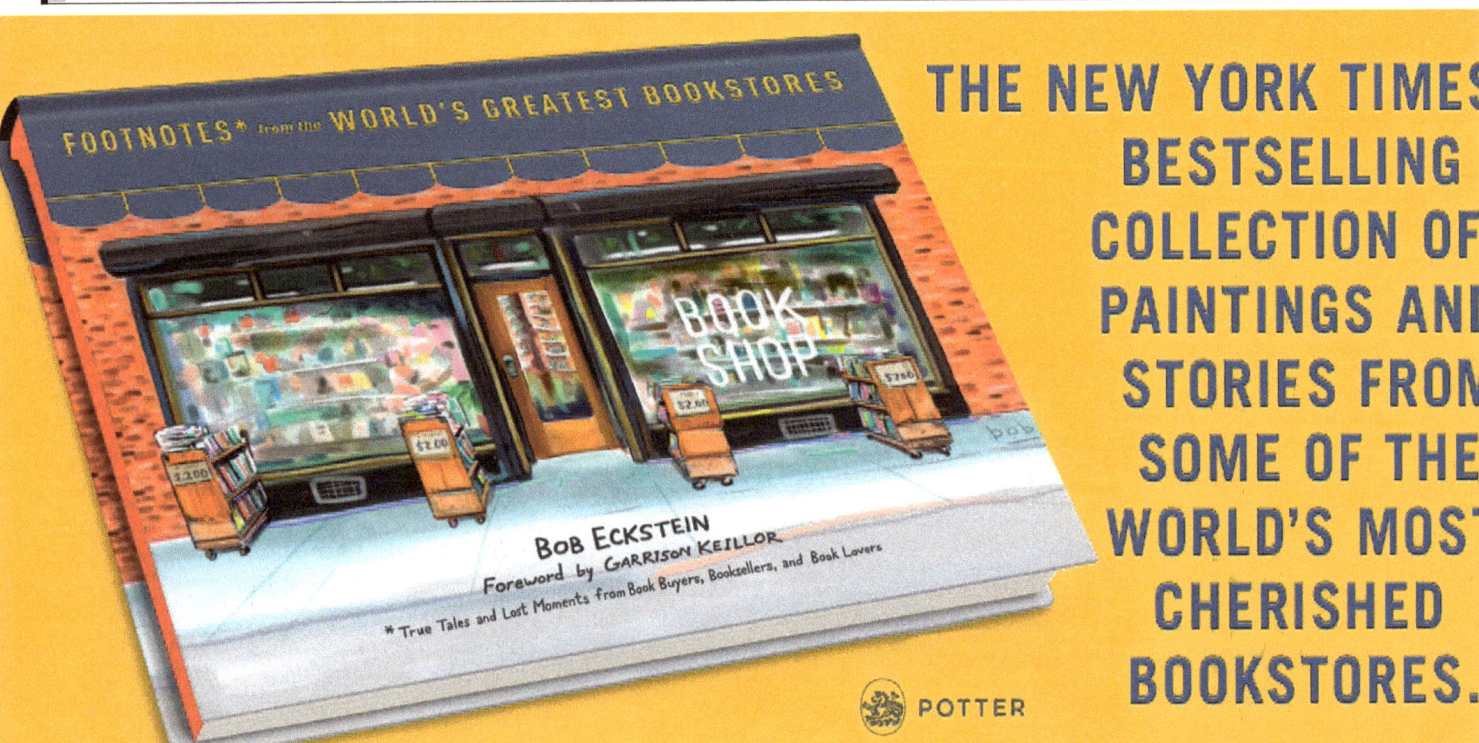

THE NEW YORK TIMES BESTSELLING COLLECTION OF PAINTINGS AND STORIES FROM SOME OF THE WORLD'S MOST CHERISHED BOOKSTORES.

AVAILABLE EVERYWHERE BOOKS ARE SOLD | BOBECKSTEIN.COM

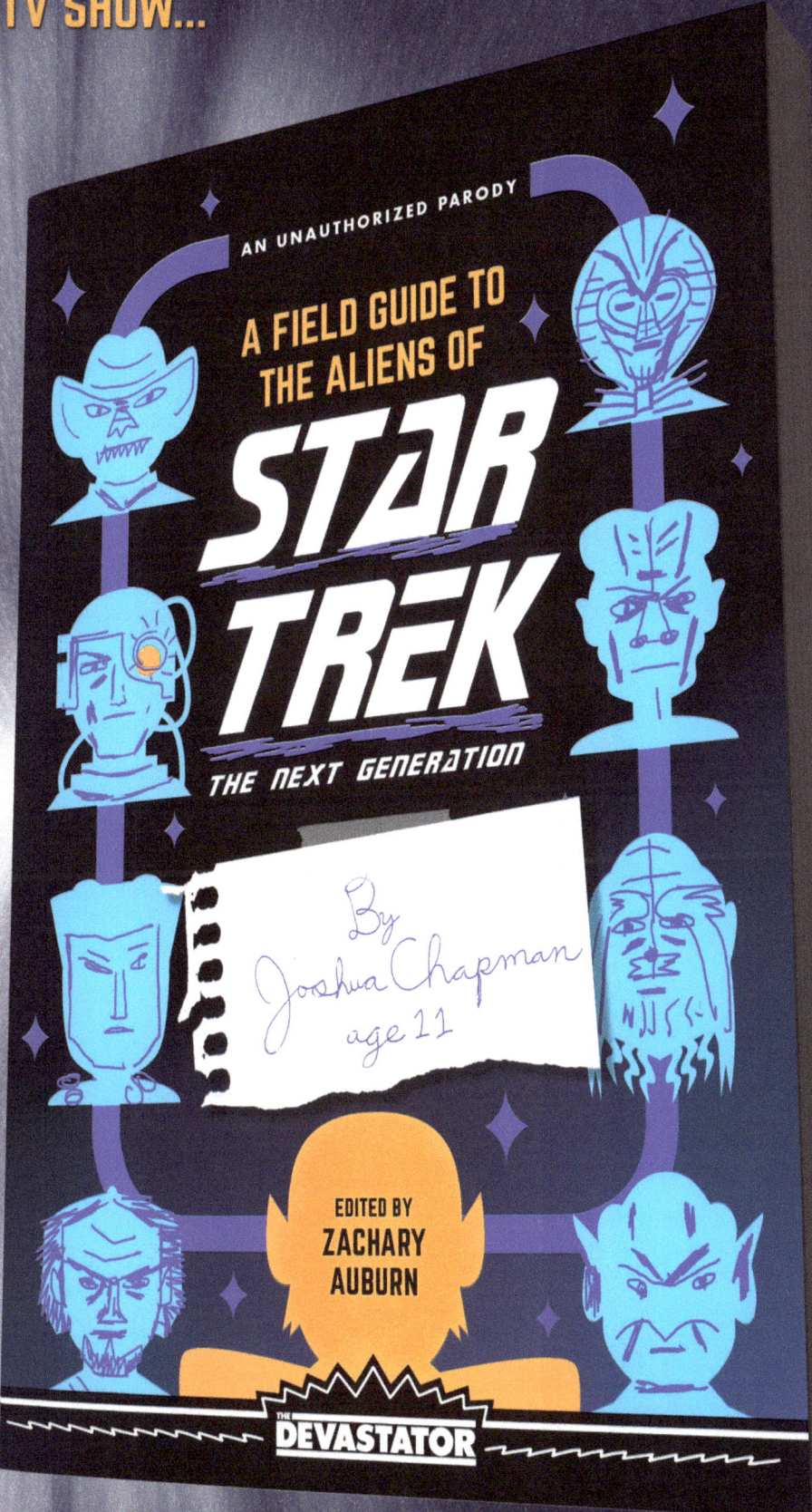

AVAILABLE NOW from Dock Street Press

"How do you make a joke out of a joke? Not easy, but Tom Toro crushes it."—*Garry Trudeau*

"*Tiny Hands* is very, very funny. And if you have any interest in keeping your sanity during the reign of the Orange Gasbag, it's also necessary."—*Roz Chast*

"Scathing work, from an expert at wielding a big-boy-sized pen."—*Emma Allen*

ORDER ONLINE: dockstreetpress.com/our-books

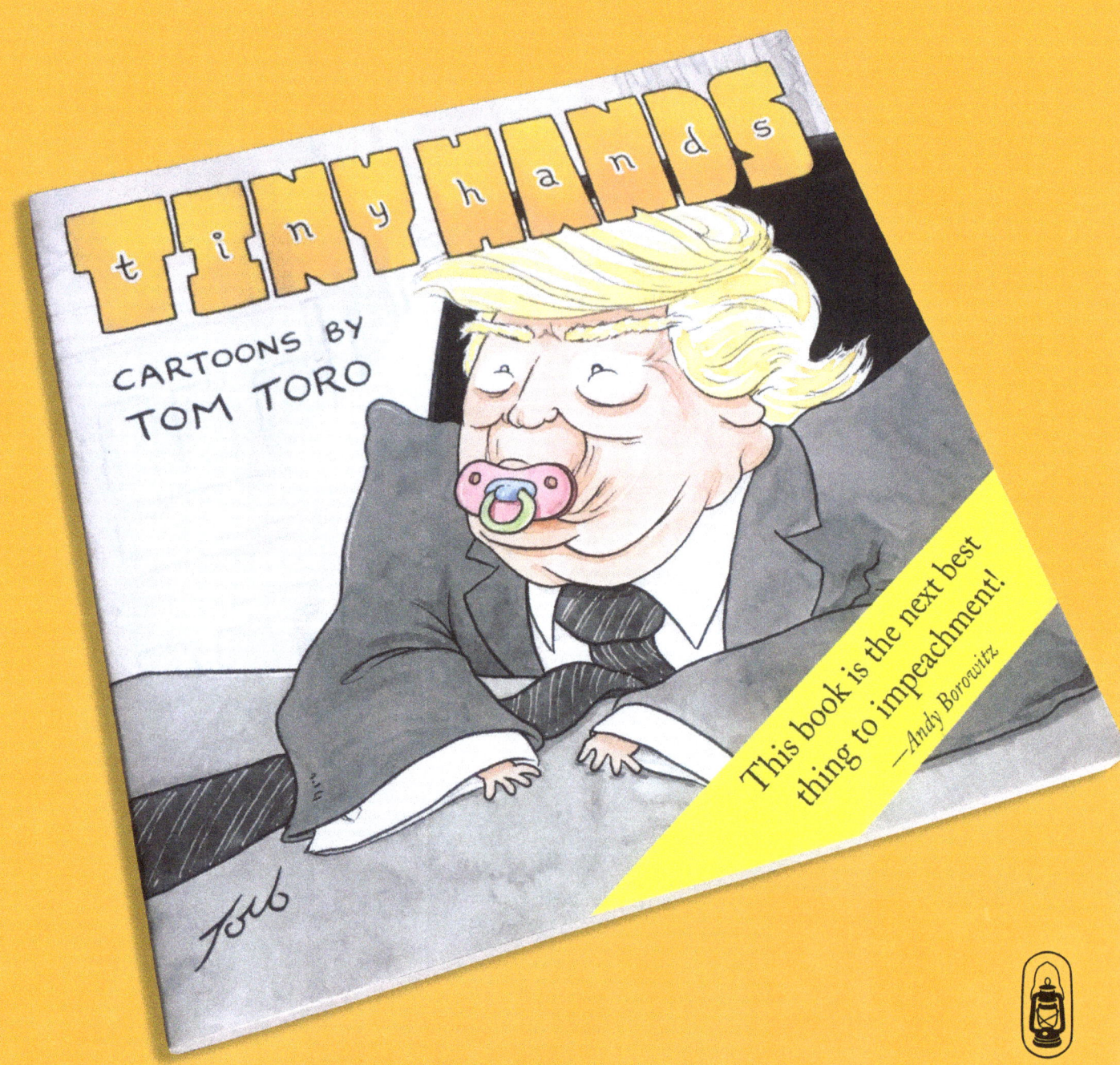

dockstreetpress.com

INDEX TO THIS ISSUE
Stuff you might not have noticed • By Dirk Voetberg

Aardvarks, 43
   Aare assholes, 43
al-Assad, Bashar, as victim of evil-shaming, 19
Ants, dismissed as "try-hards," 82
Artisanal small-batch heroin, 124-125
Averroes, Pomeranian named, 101
Baby shower registry, 77
   on Dark Web, 77
Birth control, homemade, 16
Blood diamonds, 9-11
   "He went to Blood Jared," 10
   Spotting blood cubic zirconium, 11
Celebrating the You That's Inside of You, 93
   Organ by organ, 93
   Throwing self surprise party, 93
   Sending invitations, 93
   Do I need to RSVP?, 93
Christmas, 4
   back thrown out in attempt to shove the "Christ" back into, 4
Clapper, The, one-hand clap recognition, 95
"Coolness," Confucian ideas regarding, 99
Cuban, Mark, misplacing of Dallas Mavericks, 6
Deathbed, death couch that folds out into, 23
Degenerate Art, 108
   Degenerate Home Ec, 109
Deep State, rise of, 111
   Deep DMV, surprising efficiency of, 111
Deodorant, "Spicy Marinara" scent, 18
Dictionary, new audio book of, 30
Female sexual vocalization, 27-8
   As evolutionary strategy, 27
   As ringtone, 28
Frosty the Snowman, 54
   Promise to "be back again some day," 54
   Frostian prophet warning that "some day" nearly upon us, 54

Game of Thrones "Which Character Are You" app, Russian hacking of, 72
Handel, George Frederic, composer of "Grandma Got Run Over by a Reindeer," 81
Halloween costumes, most popular of 2017, 73
   Ai Weiwei, 73
   Bitcoin, 73
   "Our once-vibrant democracy," 73
Kids home metallurgy kits, 71
   Buyer's guide to, 71
   Funny stories involving, 71
   Horrific dangers of, 71
Jong-un, Kim, weird sense of humor of, 70-73
   Love of General Sung-Il's Woody Allen impression, 71
   Quest for ICBM that shoots out a flag reading "BOOM!", 73
Juggs magazine, onion dome on Manhattan skyrise headquarters, 17
Kipchoge, Eliud, Kenyan marathoner, 40
   Breaks world record, 40
   Receives coveted 26.2 sticker, 40
Librettist, finding the best one for you, 55
MacArthur Foundation, sarcastic "Total Friggin' Genius" Grant, 89
Macy's Thanksgiving Day Parade 2017, Breitbart float in, 40
Mascara for infants, 60
Mount Rushmore, 13-14
   Lincoln nostril, Hitchcock boxers found in, 14
   Unidentified one with glasses, 14
Nostradamus, 83
   Prediction of Ben & Jerry's Salted Caramel Core flavor, 83
   Suspicious reluctance to play the Lotto, 83
NRA bill to outlaw thoughts and prayers, 67
Piñatas, for adults, 93
   Divorce papers inside, 93
   Filled with single-malt, 93

   With cobras as murder weapon, 93
Pop-up books, sourcing in academic papers, 16
   Invention by Hitler to promote the Volkswagen, 16
Renaissance of 11th century, shitty regional theme park based on, 118
Should I Give My Dog a Brazilian?, 104
Sexual harassment, nemonic device for remembering not to, 81
Silent e, MIT detects sound emitting from, 17
Soylent Green, "Autumn blend," 8-9
   It's people (and pumpkin spice), 9
Tattoos, taint, 90
   "Taintoos" on Venice Boardwalk, 90
   Who would ever see that? 90
   Worn away by friction of walking, 90
"That's Incredible!" TV show (1980-84), 41-3
   not really incredible, 42
   actually, John Davidson's hair was pretty incredible, 43
Titanic, novelty "ah-OOO-gah!" horn of, 59
   Predicted by Jeanne Dixon, 59
"Titty twisters," use in martial arts, 93
Typefaces, proper use of, 103-7
   Sectarian violence related to, 104
Weather, as infallible signal of God's emotions, 34
   Partly-cloudy day after man puts ketchup on hot dog, 34
   Unseasonable warmth as pleasure over legal weed, 34
Weinstein's Guide to Gentlemanly Behavior, 39-40
   Always offer a drink or movie role before beginning to masturbate, 39
   Sure, "no means no," but what does that second "no" mean?, 40
Yankovic, "Weird Al," 31
   "34'46.719," spoof of John Cage's "34'46.776," 31

Dirk Voetberg *is a comedy writer best known for* The Fightin' Guy Lady Tigers of St. Barry High.

BY MATT MATERA & ALAN GOLDBERG

ACTOR NATALIE'S CASTLES

You'll put it together eventually — if not, there's always page 87

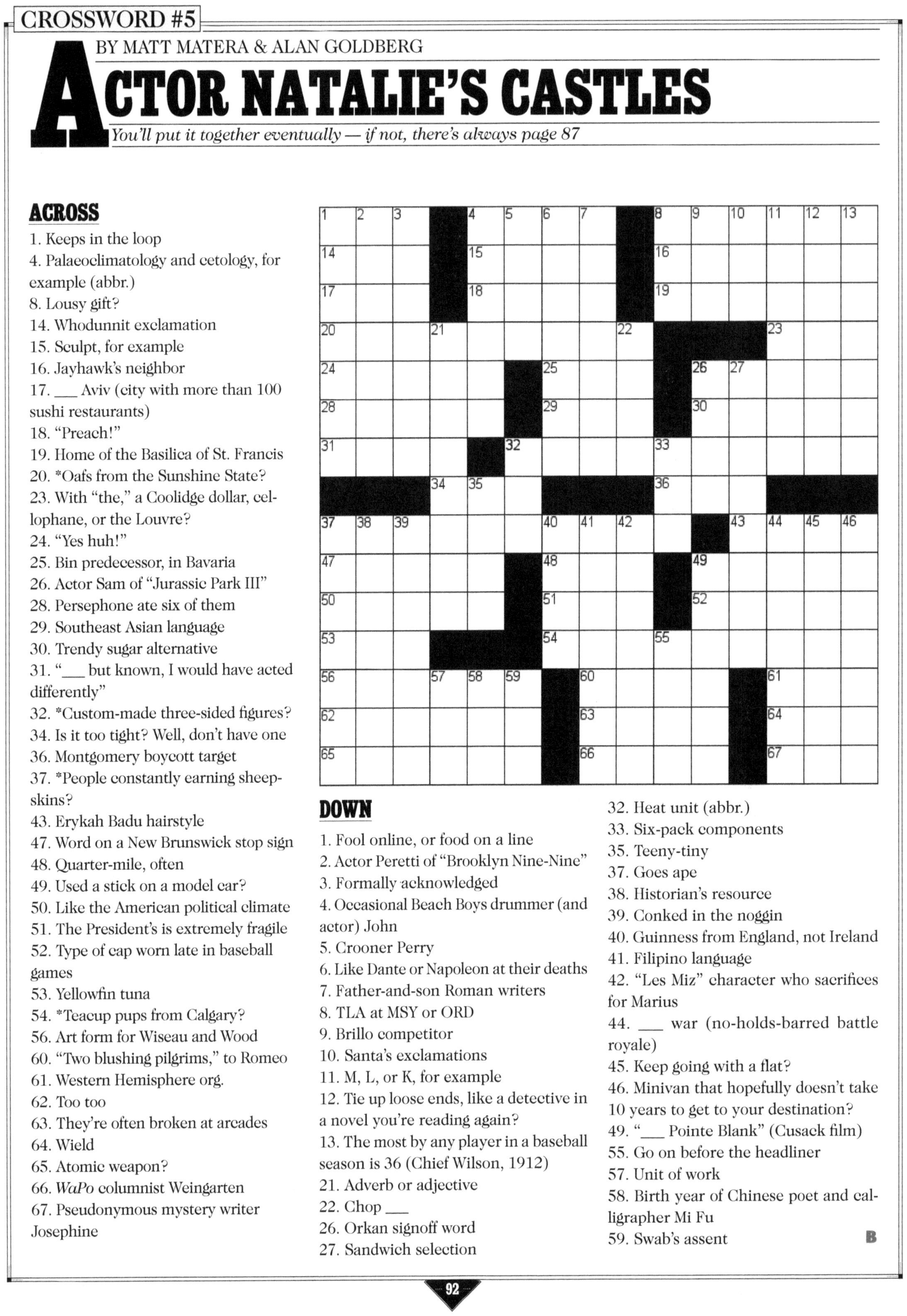

ACROSS

1. Keeps in the loop
4. Palaeoclimatology and cetology, for example (abbr.)
8. Lousy gift?
14. Whodunnit exclamation
15. Sculpt, for example
16. Jayhawk's neighbor
17. ___ Aviv (city with more than 100 sushi restaurants)
18. "Preach!"
19. Home of the Basilica of St. Francis
20. *Oafs from the Sunshine State?
23. With "the," a Coolidge dollar, cellophane, or the Louvre?
24. "Yes huh!"
25. Bin predecessor, in Bavaria
26. Actor Sam of "Jurassic Park III"
28. Persephone ate six of them
29. Southeast Asian language
30. Trendy sugar alternative
31. "___ but known, I would have acted differently"
32. *Custom-made three-sided figures?
34. Is it too tight? Well, don't have one
36. Montgomery boycott target
37. *People constantly earning sheepskins?
43. Erykah Badu hairstyle
47. Word on a New Brunswick stop sign
48. Quarter-mile, often
49. Used a stick on a model car?
50. Like the American political climate
51. The President's is extremely fragile
52. Type of cap worn late in baseball games
53. Yellowfin tuna
54. *Teacup pups from Calgary?
56. Art form for Wiseau and Wood
60. "Two blushing pilgrims," to Romeo
61. Western Hemisphere org.
62. Too too
63. They're often broken at arcades
64. Wield
65. Atomic weapon?
66. *WaPo* columnist Weingarten
67. Pseudonymous mystery writer Josephine

DOWN

1. Fool online, or food on a line
2. Actor Peretti of "Brooklyn Nine-Nine"
3. Formally acknowledged
4. Occasional Beach Boys drummer (and actor) John
5. Crooner Perry
6. Like Dante or Napoleon at their deaths
7. Father-and-son Roman writers
8. TLA at MSY or ORD
9. Brillo competitor
10. Santa's exclamations
11. M, L, or K, for example
12. Tie up loose ends, like a detective in a novel you're reading again?
13. The most by any player in a baseball season is 36 (Chief Wilson, 1912)
21. Adverb or adjective
22. Chop ___
26. Orkan signoff word
27. Sandwich selection
32. Heat unit (abbr.)
33. Six-pack components
35. Teeny-tiny
37. Goes ape
38. Historian's resource
39. Conked in the noggin
40. Guinness from England, not Ireland
41. Filipino language
42. "Les Miz" character who sacrifices for Marius
44. ___ war (no-holds-barred battle royale)
45. Keep going with a flat?
46. Minivan that hopefully doesn't take 10 years to get to your destination?
49. "___ Pointe Blank" (Cusack film)
55. Go on before the headliner
57. Unit of work
58. Birth year of Chinese poet and calligrapher Mi Fu
59. Swab's assent

B

www.ingramcontent.com/pod-product-compliance
Lightning Source LLC
Chambersburg PA
CBHW061823290426
44110CB00027B/2957